N[...]

Nat Segnit's inve[...]
to withdraw took him to India, Greece, [...]
States and the Arctic Circle, until unforeseen
circumstances forced his own retreat, along with
the rest of humanity.

He has written for the *New Yorker*, *Harper's*,
1843 magazine and the *TLS*, and regularly writes
and broadcasts for BBC Radio 4. *Retreat* is his
second book.

NAT SEGNIT

Retreat

Adventures in Search of Silence,
Solitude and Renewal

VINTAGE

1 3 5 7 9 10 8 6 4 2

Vintage is part of the Penguin Random House
group of companies whose addresses can be found at
global.penguinrandomhouse.com

Penguin
Random House
UK

First published in Vintage in 2022
First published in hardback by The Bodley Head in 2021

penguin.co.uk/vintage

A CIP catalogue record for this book is available from the British Library

ISBN 9781529111309

Extract taken from 'Poetry of Departures', by Philip Larkin, copyright The
Estate of Philip Larkin, first appeared in *The Less Deceived* (Marvell Press,
Yorkshire: 1955). Reproduced by permission of Faber & Faber Ltd.

Printed and bound in Great Britain by Clays Ltd, Elcograf S.p.A.

The authorised representative in the EEA is Penguin Random House Ireland,
Morrison Chambers, 32 Nassau Street, Dublin D02 YH68

Penguin Random House is committed to a sustainable future for
our business, our readers and our planet. This book is made from
Forest Stewardship Council® certified paper.

MIX
Paper from
responsible sources
FSC® C018179

To Niki, Edie and Raff

Sometimes you hear, fifth-hand,
As epitaph:
He chucked up everything
And just cleared off,
And always the voice will sound
Certain you approve
This audacious, purifying,
Elemental move.

Philip Larkin, 'Poetry of Departures'

CONTENTS

1.

Who, Me? or Sister Nectaria's Stillness

I was sitting on the floor with my legs loosely crossed and my hands resting on my knees. My spine was straight, my chin slightly tucked in so I could feel a pleasant stretching sensation at the back of my neck. My gaze was trained on a point four or five feet in front of my nose. I breathed in, lips pursed as if sucking through a straw, paused, then loosened my lips and breathed out, drawing in the muscles behind my belly button. One. Then repeat, two, three, counting at the end of each out-breath, noticing the thoughts that drifted like floaters across the vitreous humour of my consciousness, before letting them go, returning my attention to my breath in time for the next count, four, before, inevitably, a floater-thought snagged and I lost track of what number I was on. Back to the start: meditation as snakes and ladders.

I wondered if it was especially bad, especially unmindful, that the thoughts I'd been instructed to note and let pass were not really that random, but rather concerned what I was looking forward to doing when this session was over – chiefly, not having to note and let go of my thoughts. It was late August on the south coast of Devon. The sessions took place in a light, airy room near the waterfront, with exposed, whitewashed walls and a mandala-print wall hanging pinned loosely to the ceiling so it billowed in the breeze from the open windows. The sliver of sky I could see above the rooftops was a yearning, cloudless blue. The Indian flute track playing on the hi-fi in the corner was so relaxing that it was hard to object to its blandness: music from the world's mellowest elevator. Smoke rose from an incense burner like the ghost of a hypnotised cobra. In between sessions retreatants were free to mingle as they pleased, although the atmosphere of quiet reflection tended to discourage this. For the most part retreat meant retreat: a cordial but firm withdrawal into one's own ambit. Over lunch, I got talking to the one fellow retreatant who seemed less protective of her privacy – who had flipped the implied 'Do Not Disturb' sign the others had hung around their necks. Carla was originally from Louisville, Kentucky, with a peroxide crop and a laugh like the first few attempts at starting an outboard motor. What brought her here, I asked?

Carla thought for a bit. 'The chance to take a step back. It's like, you're stressed at work, at home, whatever, you *are* the stress. A couple of days here, and the stress doesn't exactly go. You can just look at it from the outside, see how small it is.'

'I can't help feeling it's a bit selfish, though,' I said. 'I mean, I've gone on holiday, haven't I? Without my family. Actually, it's worse than that. I've gone on a holiday dressed up as self-improvement.'

Carla laughed. 'I guess.'

'I'm selfish *and* sanctimonious.'

'But wouldn't you be a worse dad if you didn't give yourself a break now and then?'

We dads, I thought to myself, were generally pretty good at giving ourselves breaks. Still, I took Carla's point. The idea, it seemed, was to withdraw from the world, for a limited period, in order to return better able to deal with its trials. To inhabit it better. After lunch we returned to the mandala-print room for a body-scan meditation, lying on the floor with our feet slightly apart and a cushion under our heads. Our teacher that afternoon was Yvonne, a woman in her late thirties with a deep tan, a dancer's lithe economy of movement and an air of vaguely vegan congeniality that repeatedly took me back to my childhood, on the fringes of the hippie-ish self-sufficiency movement in Wales, when I was meant to be focusing my attention on my body. Yvonne's voice was pitched to the music: soft, rhythmic, soothing.

'Notice the sensations in your body as you breathe. Notice the feeling in your chest, your back, your legs, your feet. Don't worry if your mind wanders. This is not a competition. Simply notice that it *has* wandered, and bring your attention back to your body.'

I brought my mind back to my feet, and the weird hot-and-cold, tingling sensation I'd had in them since a back operation the previous year. And that was it: I was away again. Mindfulness might not be a competition, but if I couldn't focus for more than five seconds, I was surely losing at *something*. My mind was off on a meander through the streets of its own subjectivity, taking me via my tingly feet and my surgeon's unnerving habit of looking grave before delivering good news to the fact that I'd promised my wife, before leaving for Devon, that the main thing I was going on retreat to address was my tendency to worry too much, about my health especially. My tendency to ruminate, to catastrophise, to fail to live in the moment: to let my mind wander off in precisely the way it was doing right now, lying on the floor in a Devon yoga studio.

The idea of withdrawing from everyday life for a period of reflection, meditation or prayer has been fundamental to human existence since at least the Bronze Age. By the time of the Buddha, who lived in ancient India in the fifth to fourth century BC, the three-month 'Vassa' or 'rains retreat' was already long established, by holy men following traditions dating back up to a thousand years into the Vedic period. One of these traditions was to avoid travelling during the monsoon season, both because it was difficult and for fear of treading on animals that came out in wet weather. To retreat offered the twin benefits of intensified meditative practice and not squashing frogs. From Jesus' forty days in the wilderness, and the retirement, two and a half centuries later, of the earliest ascetics to the Egyptian desert, retreat has been central to the Christian experience. To renounce the world was to take a step closer to heaven. In the modern era, traditional religious retreat – the silence and solitude offered by monasticism, for instance – has lost ground to new forms, some purportedly spiritual, adapting Eastern mysticism to Western sensibilities, others shorn of the spiritual element in favour of the short-termist, goal-oriented priorities of wellness tourism. There could scarcely be more difference between the Benedictine Abbey of Solesmes and a high-vibrational raw-food retreat in New Mexico. And yet both promise something comparable – breathing space, a more or less temporary respite from the hectic, asphyxiating press of modern existence, alone or among like minds. Retreat is, and always has been, humanity's pressure valve.

And the need has never been greater. The world population is 7.8 billion and counting. For the first time in history, more than half of that population lives in urban settlements. By 2030, the UN projects that one in three people will live in cities with at least half a million inhabitants. It's no wonder that we are gasping for air. Research by the Global Wellness Institute shows that international wellness tourism – of which meditation and other forms of spiritual retreat form a major part – was worth $678.5 billion in 2017, up from $494 billion in 2013. Just over 14 per cent of adult Americans now report practising mindfulness. Vocations to Christian monasteries have been dwindling for decades, but short- and medium-term monastic retreats are increasingly popular. Demand for alternative, eastern-influenced and secular retreats has been soaring – even while the ticket price of these retreats, and the indirect costs of absence from work or of childcare, place them out of reach to all but the most privileged. Although problematic in many respects, the forms of digital retreat offered by meditation apps go some way to addressing these structural inequalities, one reason why the sector has seen exponential growth in recent years.

All of which speaks to an impulse to draw back from an overcrowded, stressful world beset by cultural, political and environmental problems. The Italian ethnobiologist Giorgio Samorini has speculated that periods of ecological crisis amount to 'depatterning factors', auguring such radical change that long-established survival strategies become rapidly obsolete. In the face of rising sea levels, thawing permafrost, cascading forest dieback, might we be evolutionarily programmed to step back and rethink? Or to cut our losses and head for the hills? We are frightened, fed up, burnt out, alienated by social media, bewildered by the assault on Western liberal democracy by plutocratic populists, or, for that matter, by the failures in liberal democracy that gave the populists their chance. Retreat is not limited to monasteries and New Age treatment centres. It applies just as much to any urge to withdraw, to step back from the thick of it, be that as a response to personal or political adversity, out of fear or an intention to change, out of a yearning for calm or an aversion to company. To disentangle yourself from the social fabric is an impulse as old as the fabric itself, an ancient idea that could scarcely be more contemporary.

This book is an exploration of that idea. You might say that retreat in its modern context describes a spectrum of engagement, from the most arduous, lifelong commitment to meditation and prayer to the faddier and more commodified extremes of first-world self-development. In the course of my research I have travelled all over the world – from rural France to India, suburban Manchester to San Francisco, the Aegean to the Arctic Circle – as well as deep into the history, literature and neuroscience of isolation and contemplative practice, to take in that spectrum, to determine, in as many of its diverse traditions and manifestations as I had the time and resources to analyse, *why* precisely people go on retreat, what rewards it offers, what dangers it poses, and whether there is, ultimately, any common ground between the hermit in the Himalayan cave and the fairweather meditator sipping a turmeric chai latte on the terrace of an Ibizan wellness spa.

Apart from the circumstances of the retreatants I met – the monks, meditators, stressed-out executives, drop-out *sadhakas* and bedroom-bound gaming addicts – I have drawn extensively on the cognitive and social scientists, philosophers, writers, artists and religious thinkers who have experienced or examined what it is to withdraw from society. The aim is vaguely paradoxical: a richly peopled portrait of the world forsaken. An anatomy of retreat. Which is not to make any claims at exhaustiveness. The tradition of meditative retreat in the Jewish Kabbalah, for instance, is one of the many areas I have excluded for no better reason than to keep the scope of the book manageable. But it is, I hope, a representative study, a glimpse through the distorting lens of my subjectivity at the idea in its breadth – and, while it's at it, an account of my own immersion in a mode of behaviour I had been increasingly drawn to without quite being aware of it.

According to the *ashrama* system, the division of life in Hindu philosophy into four successive stages, as a man in my late forties I had reached number three, *Vanaprastha*, the 'forest-dwelling' stage that involves the gradual withdrawal from worldly concerns. It is the ancient Indian response to the mid-life crisis. (*Vanaprastha* is followed by the fourth and final stage, *Sannyasa*, renunciation, where you retire to a hut to live out your years in contemplation.) Up to that point, whenever a conversation turned to spiritual matters, I would mark myself down as a humanist and hold out for a change of subject. I saw no reason to question my belief that life was love, for my wife and children, my parents, my friends, nature, art, work when it was going well, and that I neither expected nor wanted anything else, even in the event that they were taken from me. I was similarly bemused by the principle of non-attachment common to Hinduism and Buddhism: surely you attached yourself, passionately, and accepted loss and bereavement as the price you paid for those attachments, without which life would not be worth living? As to dwelling in the forest – well, as a father of young children, with what I at least thought of as a preference for peopled places, a city disposition, gradually withdrawing from worldly concerns was neither possible nor desirable.

These were the articles of my faithlessness, although, as the years went by, I had to admit to a subtly contradictory feeling, that my secularism might be a little reflexive, a position that as I aged was in danger of annealing into a prejudice, something that I thought that I thought. A feeling that something was up, that there was change in the air, that change was necessary. The best way to test this, I supposed, would be to take a step back. It only remained to be seen what form this stepping back would take, and to what extent I was cut out for it.

If I was ambivalent about retreat it might have had something to do with my parents' decision to leave the city when I was one. By the time I was born my father was commuting four hours a day to teach art at a comprehensive school in Essex. And so the decision was taken to sell the house in London, move to a cheaper place in the country, and spend the difference on a retail property that would bring in a decent rent. That way Dad could afford not to teach and spend his time painting. It didn't work out. In the midst of the oil crisis the rent from the shop barely kept us afloat. From our cheaper place in the country we moved to a *really* cheap place, in rural west Wales, where, in the seventies, you could pick up a two-bedroom cottage, with a few acres of land, for next to nothing. Not only was the land cheap, but with space to keep goats, chickens, pigs, geese, even the occasional heifer, the family could economise by becoming self-sufficient. Growing up in Peekskill, a small city by the Hudson forty miles north of New York, my father had loved *Walden*, Henry David Thoreau's account of the two years, two months and two days he spent living alone in the woods by Walden Pond in Massachusetts. Thoreau's utopian ruralism must have held a special appeal for a kid growing up in the grimy, industrial sprawl where my grandfather had worked as a foreman.

Now was Dad's chance: not to increase our wealth but to make our poverty matter less. We would grow our own vegetables and protein. A pig in the chest freezer could keep us in pork and ham and sausages for well over a year. Anything we didn't grow we could barter for. It was a farming community. There was a mill up the road. We could trade goat's milk for flour, globe artichokes for horse manure. And this 'partial specialisation', as John Seymour, the great guru of countercultural self-sufficiency, put it, this give-and-take participation in a loose collective of interdependent producers would free up resources for the higher life. Sidestepping the vicious circle of industrialised labour, working all hours to buy stuff we could do without or produce more cheaply ourselves, there would be time to do what life in London had precluded – to make art.

That this was idealistic verging on naïve became clear very quickly. The idea of our small corner of Wales as some form of Celtic kibbutz was an absurdity for starters. The cheap real estate had attracted its fair share of drop-outs and social utopians, but they were too widely distributed to be much use as fellow participants in a functioning barter system, leaving the immediate vicinity much as it had been for centuries: Welsh-speaking, socially conservative, welcoming to incomers yet subtly excluding of them, and as hospitable to notions of sustainability and anarcho-primitivism as might be expected. Going back to the land, it turned out, was hard work. In the absence of an adequate network of self-supporting neighbours, producing enough food for three involved getting up at 5.30 to milk the goats, and working like a dog until nightfall, digging and sowing and feeding and shovelling shit, noble and sometimes fulfilling and in fleeting sunlit moments even rapturous, but far, very far from the leisurely utopia promised by Thoreau. 'Sometimes, in a summer morning,' he writes, 'having taken my accustomed bath, I sat in my sunny doorway from sunrise till noon, rapt in a revery, amidst the pines and hickories and sumachs, in undisturbed solitude and stillness ... until by the sun falling in at my west window ... I was reminded of the lapse of time.' Well, bully for you, Henry David. *Walden* had sold us a pup.

Over the months, then years, that we stayed in the cottage my father's inability to devote enough time to his painting was compounded by our isolation, the distance in miles and sensibility of rural Wales from the metropolitan art world he had found confining and superficial and now regretted leaving. The effect was to throw my parents back on themselves, on us, our tight little unit, more self-sufficient than had ever been foreseen, a close-to-heavenly arrangement for five-year-old me, but limiting for them in a way I only understood in retrospect. Everything would change, eventually, but irrespective of all that happened in the interim I am unable, as an adult, to separate my attraction to isolated places from my fear of them, the dread of isolation that had prompted me, no doubt, to bring up my own children next to a main road in the middle of the city.

The inkling I'd had of a more general turning-inward was certainly borne out closer at hand. Clearly, one's friends came and went, but lately, at least scaled to my circle – and with the caveat that from a planetary perspective my circle was an uncommonly privileged one – the usual pattern of absences had started to coalesce into something more permanent or determined. A friend had just given up her job and moved to the Peak District to breed Golden Retrievers, which was surely the ultimate retreat: a dog was what you got when you'd had it with humanity. And she was *breeding* them. Another friend was in Ouarzazate, on the edge of the Sahara Desert, doing his 300-hour yoga-teacher training with the intention of moving his family to Morocco and establishing a retreat centre there. One of my very closest friends, Phil, having narrowly decided against being ordained as a Theravadan Buddhist monk in Rangoon, had recently returned to a hut in Nepal for three months of silent, solitary meditation. If they weren't physically absent, several more friends were training themselves in mental defection: mindfulness at home, meditation on the morning train. A sort of mass stepping-back, a vanishing, prompted by the pressures of work, by a vague but persistent sense of dissatisfaction, by fear of environmental collapse or the darkening political weather.

And then there was Oscar. It was in his early twenties that the urge to disappear had become too strong to suppress. He had felt something like it in his teens, the kind of painful self-consciousness or discomfort in company familiar to many adolescents, but rather than fade with the onset of adulthood the urge became stronger, close to obliterating. As a boy he had been on family holidays to the Greek islands, and remembering something consolatory in the light there, something in the hazy gradation from water to sky, the summer he left college he returned to the northern Aegean, travelling from island to island in search of something he could only identify as peace.

He couldn't find it. The islands weren't as he remembered them.

'There were people everywhere,' Oscar told me.

To this day the southern coast of Crete remains relatively unspoilt, the summers too hot, and the terrain too rocky, to be hospitable to anything but the most half-hearted development. Oscar arrived there in early September, after two months working his way south, via Chios and the Cyclades, that sense of renewal, of the jolt that comes of distancing yourself from the familiar, eluding him with each stop. Now he had reached the end, of Europe at least. Only the tiny, parched island of Gavdos lay between him and the North African coast, a rumour beyond the white-hot horizon. Setting off from Elafonisi, in the south-west corner, he walked east, where the bare limestone peaks of the White Mountains descend to the sea, until, after twenty-five or thirty miles, somewhere between Sougia and Agia Roumeli, he found it: exactly what he had been looking for, even if it took arriving there to lend form to what had until then been no more than a feeling. Thirty feet above a small, secluded bay, a cave, standing height at the entrance and fifteen feet deep, hollowed out of the limestone by one of the hundreds of springs that render this stretch of coast, with its Saharan blasts of wind off the Libyan Sea, basically habitable.

He settled in. Walked four miles to the nearest village and came back with five kilos of oranges and a family pack of peanuts. Slept on the bare rock covered by a sheet he had brought in his backpack. And very quickly found himself slipping into a routine: not because he had intended to, particularly, nor because he was especially orderly back home. It was more that the austerity of his circumstances seemed to demand some form of structure, a grid to lay over the void. Breakfast at sun-up. An hour of yoga. Often as much as three hours' swim, exploring the neighbouring coves or heading out to sea, far enough for the shoreline to grow pale and dissolve into the sky. A walk along the cliffs after lunch, followed by an hour or two of reading – he had brought a tatty paperback *War and Peace* with him that summer, tearing out the pages as he read them, so his burden grew lighter the more story he absorbed – and a late afternoon meditating on the beach, as the sun beat its slow, smouldering retreat. On the rare occasion a walker or canoeist came by he might nod, or smile, but no more, confident that the totality of his stillness was its own guarantee, would repel any further attempt at human contact. A trip for supplies every other day or less. And so five days became ten, a fortnight, the temptation to move on dwindling with each tide, along with his appetite for anything but water, his investment in the anxieties that had sent him here, his interest in anything other than the weird Aeolian music the wind made in the cave.

That was twenty-nine years ago. With a couple of exceptions, he has been back to the cave every year, staying for up to five weeks at a time. I know Oscar as a bon viveur, a talker, a funny, rather eccentric extrovert whose tendency to dominate rooms has partly to do with how much air he displaces – he is six foot five, barrel-chested like a Victorian strongman. He was, in other words, more than averagely *there*, indisputably present, and yet, over the years, I have come to understand his conviviality as the carefully constructed persona of someone socially inclined who is nonetheless sorely tempted by solitude. Withdrawing to his cave allowed some respite from the effort of self-impersonation. Those long weeks of silence, the way Oscar spoke of them, were less a chance to reflect than to empty his mind, leave off worrying about work or relationships or who exactly he was in the expectation that these problems, when he returned to the world, might be the more soluble for not having been consciously addressed.

Five weeks were generally enough. Any more and he felt the lure of never returning like an undertow. The year he stayed for two months – ten years ago now, not long after he and Rowena first met – he remembered thinking he would never come back, floating far out to sea, feeling the nothingness, an immersion in the world that was also a renunciation of it, a grasping that was at once a letting go. Then suddenly he felt cold and swam as fast as he could back to shore.

Devon was not my first experience of meditation. A few months earlier I had signed up for a course of eight mindfulness classes lasting two hours each. Compared to Phil's experiences in Myanmar and Nepal, a secular mindfulness class twenty minutes by bus from my house was as tentative a toe in the water as could be imagined. Still, mindfulness training was both widely recommended as preparation for lengthier and more intense retreats, and, especially via meditation apps like Headspace and Calm, the way retreat was experienced by many would-be retreatants too busy or broke to take the time off.

The classes were held on the top floor of a Georgian town-house whose elegant proportions were hard to keep in mind under the polystyrene ceiling tiles and insectoid hum of the strip lights. Our teacher was Vanessa, a tall, slender psycho-therapist in her early fifties, with trace elements of Scouse in her accent, red in her hair, and, in her otherwise gentle and generous manner, a slightly disconcerting imperturbability: the paradoxical absence of the very present. Each week she took us through a different approach to the same task – paying attention, whether that be via mindful eating, mindfulness of breathing, a body scan, walking meditation, or learning to respond more dispassionately to stressful or uncomfortable stimuli. On the Sunday between classes six and seven there would be a 'retreat day', from 10 a.m. to 4 p.m., when the group got the chance to practise our newly acquired techniques in near-total silence.

There were ten of us on the course, representing a fairly broad spectrum of interest and engagement. Nasreen, for example, always had something specific and insightful to say about the previous week's home practice. Paula, on the other hand, emitted a general arms-folded air of exemption. What she lacked in enthusiasm she made up for in circular arguments.

'The fact that it didn't even occur to me to practise,' she admitted, at the start of class on week three, 'just goes to show that it hasn't taken hold in my life.'

The rest of us fell somewhere in the middle. Kwame and Brett were both thoughtful and eager to learn, if not always very forthcoming. Harry was articulate but often late, arriving in the room with the chinstrap of his cycle helmet loose and a little skid in his socks on the parquet floor. On our second session he had excused his failure to record his home-practice observations in his workbook on the grounds that he was a 'hacker' whose mind recoiled at authority.

'It was the same at college,' he announced. He never did his homework there either. 'And I always did very well.'

And then there was Rachel, inscrutable, self-contained Rachel, an Anglican chaplain at a west London hospital, with her crisp, asymmetrical bob, her hands folded in the lap of her plaid wool skirt, and, more often than not, her chin set inquisitively at twenty-five to the hour. Still, for all our differences we were a pretty cohesive group. There was, despite the atmosphere of half-attention, the custard-cream mundanity of the adult-education course, an otherworldliness about those Tuesday afternoons. Even the less committed meditators amongst us were there, it seemed, for the same reason: to step back, to slow down, to sit in the silence and reflect.

Mindfulness in its present, popularised form has its roots in the US countercultural movement. From the 1950s onwards, Buddhism held increasing appeal for a generation of young Americans chafing against the confines of Christianity; it chimed with the emerging spirit of anti-authoritarianism that Buddhists place faith in no God. Teachers like the Zen monk Shunryu Suzuki Roshi and the Tibetan meditation master Chögyam Trungpa Rinpoche emigrated to the US to set up centres of Buddhist practice, like the San Francisco Zen Center and Vajradhatu, later known as Shambhala International. Meanwhile, young American teachers were heading in the opposite direction. Both Joseph Goldstein and Jack Kornfield, founders of the massively influential Insight Meditation Society in Barre, Massachusetts, spent their time as Peace Corps volunteers in Thailand, applying what they learned under the forest masters there, and later in India and Burma, to what became known as the 'vipassana movement', first in Barre and subsequently (in Kornfield's case) at the Spirit Rock Meditation Center, across the bay from San Francisco in Marin County, California.

The emphasis of vipassana – or at least the 'New Burmese' variety passed to Goldstein and Kornfield by the Theravadan Buddhist monk Mahasi Sayadaw and his student U Pandita – is on gaining insight through the practice of *satipaṭṭhāna*, 'the foundation of mindfulness', involving minute observation of changes in one's sensory and mental experience. Goldstein and Kornfield's innovation was to adapt the practice to American tastes, downplaying the more explicitly devotional or ritualistic parts, like the chanting of the suttas, in favour of the meditative element.

Jon Kabat-Zinn was to go a step further. In 1965, while studying for his PhD in molecular biology at MIT, Kabat-Zinn attended a talk on meditation by Roshi Philip Kapleau, an American-born teacher of Zen Buddhism. Over the coming decade, Kabat-Zinn would become ever more intrigued by the potential, and as yet untested, applications of Kapleau's teachings. If meditation encouraged greater awareness of body and mind, what effect might it have on apparently intractable conditions like chronic pain and depression? Kabat-Zinn's challenge was to bridge the two cultures. In the academic circles that he moved in, to propose an essentially religious approach to a medical problem would have had you laughed out of the lecture theatre. His solution was simple: remove the religious part. By 1979, he had developed a technique he called mindfulness-based stress reduction, or MBSR, combining elements of hatha yoga with mindfulness meditation, and, crucially, divesting it of its religious trappings. Kabat-Zinn has since objected to the idea that his work amounts to the 'secularisation' of Eastern religious principles, when, after all, the ultimate aim of modern mindfulness is still to connect the individual with a universal, compassionate oneness. Nonetheless, it's easy to see how MBSR, with the emphasis it places on the rational benefits of meditation, had to a large extent armoured itself against accusations of hocus-pocus.

It was a decisive step in the normalisation of what had until then been firmly located in the hippie-esoteric margins of Western culture. MBSR bloomed on ground made fertile by the vipassana movement. The eight-week training programme devised by Kabat-Zinn at his clinic at the University of Massachusetts in Amherst has since been taken by more than 20,000 people. Mindfulness training now accounts for 7.4 per cent of an alternative-care market worth \$15.1 billion in the US. MBSR and related therapeutic approaches are offered by healthcare systems the world over. Relieved of its religious baggage, mindfulness became a fit subject for scientific study. Hundreds of randomised controlled trials have since shown the effectiveness of MBSR and related techniques in reducing levels of stress-producing cortisol, improving executive functioning, working memory and visuo-spatial processing, as well as suppressing the brain areas involved in the unstructured, wandering thought patterns that characterise depression and poor focus. Nirvana could wait. Mindfulness was now academically respectable, the materialist's panacea.

Big business began to take notice. In 2007, Chade-Meng Tan, a software engineer and Google employee #107, co-founded Search Inside Yourself, a mindfulness training programme designed to help his fellow Googlers deal with work-related stress and improve their focus. The programme has since been spun off into an independent non-profit organisation, the Search Inside Yourself Leadership Institute, promoting mindfulness in companies and other non-profits all over the world. What was once the preserve of monks and gap-year dharma bums was now sound business practice, mysticism with a measurable return on investment. (In Buddhism, incidentally, 'dharma' refers to the eternal truths taught by the Buddha). And where Silicon Valley leads, the rest of culture follows. A 2017 report by the US National Center for Complementary and Integrative Health found that 14.2 per cent of adult Americans – more than 36 million people – now report practising meditation. Mindfulness was no longer alternative. You were a bit weird if you *didn't* do it.

Vanessa pinged her cymbals and the meditation began. In the 'sitting practice', at least at this introductory level, we were invited either to sit on the floor or stay in our chairs. No-one went for the floor option. I sat so my spine was no longer in contact with the back of my chair. If I wasn't going to endure the discomfort of the lotus position, I could at least sit up straight. I tried to counteract the natural tendency of my shoulders to creep up towards my ears, and, as instructed, focused on an imaginary mark on the floor, using the slope of my nose as a rifle sight.

'Breathe in,' said Vanessa. The idea was to do this naturally, unselfconsciously, without forcing or willing it. 'Simply let the breath breathe itself.'

I did as I was told, focusing on the in- and out-breaths for their full duration. The breath and nothing else. In, out. And then the thought arose: what *was* my breath? What precisely was it I was supposed to be focusing *on*? The texture of air in my nostrils? In my larynx? My lungs? The sound it made? The rising and falling of my chest? And before I knew it I was off, on one of the abstracted mental saunters that would soon become familiar, realising maybe ten, fifteen seconds later that I'd become entirely absorbed in an aimless rumination on the nature of experience, the phenomenology of breath, while the breath itself had slipped from my attention. The same thing would happen in Devon. However hard I tried – *bad* mind – to return my attention to the breath, it refused, or obeyed only momentarily before wandering off again. And the longer these thoughts continued, the more physically uncomfortable I got, which gave rise to two further thoughts, neither of which I bothered to note then let pass. One, that I was an old crock, and two, that my errant mind might indicate a deeply ingrained reluctance to dwell in my body, to vacate my head – that, in other words, however much Vanessa reiterated that mind-wandering was normal and nothing to beat yourself up about, mindfulness was a disposition, and that there were some people who simply didn't have it.

After class, by the shoe rack at reception, I eavesdropped on a conversation between Paula and Rachel. From what I could make out they were discussing the retreat day between weeks six and seven.

'It's going to be tough,' Paula was saying. 'A whole day! Really tough.'

As I bent to tie my shoelaces, I found myself feeling defensive on Rachel's behalf, pressured by the class rebel into disowning the practice. Of us all, I was sure, Rachel was the stillest, the most acquainted with silence. The natural contemplative.

Rachel shrugged on her coat.

'It's going to be hell,' she said. 'I might jump out of the window.'

*

The ability to dwell in your body – an ability Vanessa's mind-fulness classes had amply demonstrated I lacked – is a key area of interest for Giuseppe Pagnoni, a professor of neuroscience at the University of Modena and Reggio Emilia in northern Italy. Giuseppe is himself an embodiment of his interests. Tall, lithe tending to gaunt, he has the shaved head and tranquil manner of the Zen Buddhist monks he has spent much of his academic life studying. 'During meditation there is high attention on pro-prioception,' he told me. Proprioception is the sense we have of where the parts of our body are situated relative to one another – of our posture, in this instance. 'And my feeling is that this may, in time, actually optimise those parts of the internal model that are related to the more embodied and situated aspects of cognition.'

Paying attention to our posture tells the brain not only to be more alert to our bodies, but to where they are in the world – to our immediate surroundings. 'And this,' Giuseppe said, 'helps counteract the depersonalised, disembodied modality of brain function that occurs when we are distracted.'

We've all experienced this: forgetting where we are for a mo-ment, being away with the fairies. When we're lost in thought, the brain areas devoted to processing signals from our envir-onment stop working with such precision. We begin to rely less on observable reality and more on the internal models we've built of the world. And if we're stressed, or anxious, or depressed, it's all too easy for us to enter a self-perpetuating cycle of habitual, negative thought, based not on reality but on our stubborn preconceptions of it. We become rigid, stuck in our ways, less responsive to what the world might throw at us, less quick on our feet.

Meditation aims to reverse this. In Giuseppe's view, it is something best done on retreat – at a monastery or meditation centre – and a form of retreat in itself, wherever we are, in a traffic jam or the cleaning-products aisle of the supermarket, in that it entails a stepping back from our stale habits of thought. The consensus among contemporary neuroscientists is that the brain works as a kind of prediction machine. 'All living organisms try to minimise the long-term, average probability of finding themselves in a surprising state,' Giuseppe said. 'And it turns out that the optimal way to do this is to build an internal model of how things occur in our environment, trying to predict the next sensory state and minimising the prediction error.'

Over time, we use our experiences of the environment to build predictive models of the situations we are likely to encounter, accommodating any errors – the discrepancies between our internal model and reality – so that the model is perpetually refined, and the errors minimised. When we perceive something – a cup of coffee, say, on the table in front of us – our perception strikes a balance between our prior knowledge of cups of coffee and the sensory input from this specific cup of coffee, the steam and smell of roasted beans reaching our neural pathways via our eyes and olfactory receptors. From an evolutionary perspective, the benefits of the predictive component of perception are obvious. It prevents us from burning our tongues.

But there are disadvantages, particularly when one considers that our reliance on foreknowledge – on our internal models – tends to increase as we age. If we accept that our internal models get better the more prediction errors we accommodate, then it follows, somewhat paradoxically, that the viability of our internal models depends on their disruption. To minimise surprise we must seek surprise, or else, as Giuseppe put it, 'our internal model may become overfitting, in a sense – very precise and efficient in a stable environment, but somewhat brittle and inadequate should conditions change.' Errors keep our minds alive. As any artist or athlete knows, to get things right, we need to get them wrong again and again. Conversely, the more rigid we become, the more disinclined to surprise, the more our internal models diminish in accuracy.

What Giuseppe's research demonstrates is that meditation seems to dial down activity in those brain areas devoted to prediction. Further, because like many meditative disciplines, *zazen*, the main meditative practice in Zen Buddhist tradition, involves heightened attentional focus but restricted movement, the brain expects the signals coming in both from the external world, and your own body, to be extremely precise. To put it another way, if you sit very still and remain highly attentive, the credibility of that sensory input is increased. This has the effect of weakening your priors, that is, switching your perceptual resources from your foreknowledge of the world to your current experience of it.

'The net result,' explained Giuseppe, 'is that you become a little freer from your habitual patterns of thought.' Again, somewhat paradoxically, the resolute discipline of meditation – the kind Vanessa was trying to instil in us – is designed to make you looser, freer, more open to experience. More alive to the infinite.

There are profound differences between Christian contemplative practice, on the one hand, and the practices derived from Buddhist meditative tradition on the other. Still, the similarities between certain Christian practices and mindfulness meditation are worth noting. In the Eastern Orthodox Church, the term 'hesychasm' refers to the core practice of silent prayer. The mystical theology of the early Eastern Church, particularly as developed by the fourth-century bishop St Gregory of Nyssa, was 'apophatic': that is, wedded to an essentially negative conception of the Divine. God exists beyond knowledge, and can therefore only be described in terms of what He isn't.

Negative theology is a strain that runs through mystic poetry from John of the Cross to the metaphysical poets. It is the burden of a poem like John Donne's 'Negative Love' (known in some manuscript versions as 'The Nothing'), where, by refusing to name what cannot be named – the object of his carnal desire – the speaker metaphorically invokes the Divine love that surpasses all understanding. 'If that be simply perfectest / Which can by no way be expressed / But negatives, my love is so.' If you can describe what it is about your beloved that you love, it isn't worth loving. Apophasis is the language of the unsayable, but its referent is not absence but the infinite.

The ineffability of God is the basis of hesychasm. The term is derived from *esychía*, the Greek for 'stillness', 'silence', and refers to the separation of prayer from deliberate or discursive thought. Far from putting Him out of reach, the impossibility of addressing God directly provides an opportunity for 'theosis', or mystical union with God, via a form of prayer that rids itself of all visual or conceptual content.

The worshipper prays not with their lips or minds but with their entire being. To this end, hesychasts recite the Jesus Prayer, the mantra-like repetition of the words 'Lord Jesus Christ, Son of God, have mercy on me, a sinner.' This is a step on from the apophatic rhetoric of Donne. Rather than describing God's ineffability, it enacts it, operating at a level where language itself breaks down. It's a bit like the psychological phenomenon of semantic satiation, repeating a word, like, say, 'retreat', over and over again until it loses all meaning – except that, in the case of hesychasm, the Jesus Prayer is repeated until its meaning escapes mere consciousness to imbue the whole person, mind, body and soul.

Again, it's important to bear in mind the fundamental differences between the gestures of Christian prayer and Buddhist meditation: the one towards union with a creator God, the other towards an apprehension of nothingness. But – in the case of hesychastic prayer and mindfulness meditation – the means to those different ends coincide to a remarkable degree. In repeating the Jesus Prayer, hesychasts are taught to regulate their breathing, while sitting with their head bowed and gaze 'fixed on the place of the heart'. Both hesychastic prayer and mindfulness entail a subordination of thought to watchful attention, and the dissolution of the border between body and mind. The body itself becomes mindful. You pray with your entire being: you *are* prayer. The physical elements that invite comparison with mindfulness practice – the bowed posture, the fixed gaze, the regulation of the breath – are designed to aid concentration, what Buddhists would call *samadhi*, oneness with the object of meditation. Theosis is in God's gift, but it's as well to get yourself ready to receive it.

Sister Nectaria had been getting ready since the age of eleven. She was now seventy-three. We met a few months before my Devon trip, in the midst of my mindfulness course, when I flew to Greece for a few days, catching the hydrofoil from Piraeus to Hydra, a small, rocky outcrop separated from the Peloponnese mainland by little more than a narrow channel. Sister Nectaria's monastery, Agia Matrona, was accessible only on foot, via a switchback mountain path that climbed for two kilometres above Hydra port, the island's only town. In the sixty-two years since Nectaria had first walked up the path, forsaking her illiterate parents for a life of pious contemplation, the monastery had struggled to attract new or lasting vocations, and now only Nectaria and Sister Matrona – out back, apparently, polishing the silverware – remained, alone in their mountain sanctuary.

Five of us – myself, Nectaria, Harriet the translator and a young French couple whose arrival had coincided with ours – were seated around the dining table in a long, underlit reception room, hung on one side with icons and framed photographs of priests in full liturgical vestments, the other side dominated by the kind of heavy-brown, wood-effect kitchen units you might find in a holiday rental. Amid the gloom, three small windows gave like sudden visions onto ecstatic blue dreamscapes of sea and sky. Outside, something metal was clanking. I took a sip of my Greek coffee and asked via Harriet if Nectaria remembered much of her life before the monastery.

'Not a lot,' relayed Harriet. Nectaria's voice sounded both girlish and aged, like a flute heard over a crackly radio – perhaps all the more so, to me, for the unintelligibility of the words. All I could hear was the music. 'She was at school,' Harriet went on. 'After that there were night schools, church schools. That's about it.'

'And isn't eleven an unusually young age to enter a monastery?'

'It is quite unusual, yes.' Nectaria seemed a little annoyed at the question. 'Some other people would come up a lot older, when they were adults. It's just whatever people felt like at the time.'

I had come to Agia Matrona partly to find out what had attracted Sister Nectaria to a life of hesychastic prayer – or, viewed another way, whether there was anything identifiable in her temperament that had equipped her for such a life. If my performance at Vanessa's mindfulness classes was anything to go by, the idea of sitting in silent contemplation for more than ten minutes seemed like a pretty solid achievement. On the hydrofoil from Piraeus, I had managed about ninety seconds of an 'Anxiety Release' meditation on my Calm app before my mind had wandered out of the grubby, spray-spotted windows to the Aegean beyond, to Oscar on Crete, to Rowena in London, to my own wife and kids and the defensibility or otherwise of leaving them behind.

Harriet had guided me up the mountain from Hydra port early the following morning. Aesthetically, the monastery was nothing special, a rather functional assembly of hefty white rectangles clinging to the mountainside, somewhere between a villa and a correction facility. Below it a large area of scrub had been fenced off for chickens. From up here you could see how immaculate the island was, how empty, the cluster of the port, yachts bristling from the jetties like white bivalves, and then nothing very much, the odd sheepfold or outcrop of juniper amid the dry, scree-strewn slopes that led down to the sea. Although less than five miles from the mainland, Hydra felt quite remote enough to begin with, distant in time if not in nautical miles, in part because of the absence of cars. Other than the rubbish trucks down at the port, no motorised vehicles were allowed on the island.

What sort of person, I wondered, would find this degree of tranquillity wanting – to the extent of retreating to a mountain-top monastery for sixty-two years? In place of a robe or *isorassa* Nectaria was wearing her workaday clothes, a shapeless grey tunic, a grubby grey skirt spattered with white paint, and a pair of black Crocs, the sole concession to formality being the hijab-like veil, or *apostolnik*, that left an oval aperture for the face. And what a face it was: skin dark and remarkably un-lined, as if smoothed by the sea breezes, deep-set eyes and an emphatic, downward-pointing nose like an hour hand, setting her features for evensong. How did the Sisters fill their days, I asked?

'They get up at five-thirty and go straight to prayers,' said Harriet. 'After that they'll have their breakfast and do another little prayer reading.' A long day of chores would follow – cook-ing, cleaning, maintaining the building, tending to the donkeys and chickens – followed by an hour and a half of prayer, dinner, and a further two hours of personal prayer before bed. 'They never stop,' said Harriet. She gestured at the room and the corridor beyond. 'You'll see how huge the place is, and how immaculately clean. All the man labour, they do it themselves. And they're old ladies now.'

What about time spent away from the monastery? Did Sister Nectaria ever leave?

'She walks down to the port maybe once a fortnight. To buy biscuits, coffee.'

'And what about off the island?'

'Once.'

'She's only been off the island once?'

'For a cataract operation. It had to be done in Athens.'

'And how did she find the big city?'

Nectaria went quiet for a moment before answering. 'It was a little bit difficult,' translated Harriet. 'She's so used to here, it being so quiet. It was a little difficult, being in the city.'

'Any other impressions?'

'She liked the flower shops.'

The quiet. The clanking. The whispery sound of the French guy shifting in his seat. 'And was it strange, after all that excitement? Coming back here?'

Nectaria shrugged and appealed to Harriet. 'It's a few years ago now,' said Harriet. 'She can't really remember.' If Nectaria wasn't openly scornful of my questions, she was certainly playing them with a dead bat. I was, in fact, under the increasing impression that she was neither addressing me, nor Harriet, but the French couple, listening to my questions then aiming her responses at them, perhaps for the simple reason that they weren't saying anything. With my iPhone voice-recorder app and list of irrelevant questions I was the opposite of retreat. I was noise.

Hesychasm *is* retreat: a turning-inward, a withdrawal from external and internal noise towards the silence of theosis. In this respect, entering a monastery is only a means to an end, furnishing the conditions favourable to the deeper retreat of silent prayer. To ask Nectaria to comment on her faith, I began to realise, was to suggest, incorrectly, that she was exterior to it, a person who prayed rather than a living, breathing, invocation of God.

Still, I asked. Didn't she ever get lonely?

'No,' translated Harriet. 'They'd quite like it if somebody new wanted to come up here and be with them as a nun. But they don't really miss big groups.' And with that, Nectaria rose, and beckoning to the French couple offered to show them through to the monastery chapel, leaving Harriet and me alone with our cups of sludgy coffee grounds and the listless clanking outside, beating out eternity at a snail's pace.

We retreat to pay closer attention. The silence it affords, the lack of distraction, enables a level of concentration that soon enters a virtuous circle. Mindfulness and meditation are appealingly recursive like that: their main purpose is their own intensification. Concentrate on practising the piano and chances are you'll become a better pianist. Concentrate on mindfulness and you'll get better at concentrating. Among neurologists like Giuseppe Pagnoni, opinion is divided as to quite how profound and long-lasting the attentional benefits of meditation may be. Giuseppe and his fellow researchers at Emory University in Atlanta, Georgia, conducted fMRI scans of twelve seasoned Zen meditators, each with more than three years of daily practice, alongside twelve control subjects with no experience of meditation. Admittedly, these are small samples. As with many meditation studies, the findings are preliminary – but tantalising. In the meditators, the grey-matter density in their basal ganglia, deep-brain structures implicated among other functions in attentional processes and reward mechanisms, showed little or no signs of age-related decline. Normally, grey-matter density begins its downward trajectory as soon as we reach the age of twenty. Ventricles enlarge, the volume of water in our skulls increases at the expense of brain matter. We become dilute. Not so in the meditators, according to Giuseppe's study.

Neurologists make the distinction between short-term 'state effects' and long-term or permanent 'trait effects' that may involve structural changes in the brain. In 2005, Sara Lazar, a researcher at Harvard Medical School, scanned the brains of twenty experienced vipassana meditators, using non-meditators matched for age and gender as controls. The meditators showed greater cortical thickness in prefrontal areas implicated in attentional focus. Other longitudinal studies have suggested better connectivity, in long-term meditators, between the amygdala – the primitive group of nuclei, deep within the temporal lobes, that regulates our fight-or-flight response – and the prefrontal cortex, the region, newer in evolutionary terms, that governs more complex cognitive behaviour. This, in turn, suggests an enhanced ability to bring their more primal fear and stress responses under rational control. To remain cool, calm, focused. Further studies are needed to confirm these 'neuroplastic' trait effects, but the possibility remains that meditation might not only reduce stress and render us more open to experience. It might make us brainier.

What's more, the benefits can accrue quickly. Some studies suggest that even we L-plate meditators under Vanessa's watch could expect marked improvements in attentional focus after as little as eight minutes of mindfulness practice. Two weeks and our minds would be less prone to wandering and our working memory enhanced. Giuseppe is convinced that with a little more effort still, structural changes detectable to neuroimaging techniques can take place in our grey matter. 'There is strong evidence,' he said, 'that intensive practice for a period of only a few months can in fact induce anatomical plasticity.'

Some scientists believe the effects may in fact be more discernible in beginners than in experienced meditators. 'Novices often report a stronger effect, perhaps because they are very sensitive to change,' explained Giuseppe. 'They experience this new thing and it may be very different from what they usually experience.'

There's little doubt, however, that the most durable changes require sustained effort. At mindfulness class, the idea that I might have been improving my attentional focus, let alone altering my brain on the anatomical level, seemed to recede with each attempt. I began to read a malign disingenuousness into the instructions in my mindfulness workbook. 'Let the breath breathe itself' now seemed like a taunt, a swimming tip for a man with no arms. 'It's as valuable to become aware that your mind has wandered, and to bring it back to the breath, as it is to remain aware of the breath.' Well, fine, if you *could* bring it back to the breath.

Try as I might, even the most basic level of concentration, the most fleeting feeling of awareness in the present moment, seemed as unreachable as sleep when your body was tired but your mind wouldn't settle. Fausto Taiten Guareschi, abbot of the Fudenji Zen Monastery near Parma, and a friend and sometimes collaborator of Giuseppe Pagnoni, has spoken of the 'great effort' required if meditative retreat is to have any effect – an effort that is, at once, not consciously willed, but arrived at only through intense practice and submission to the body.

'You can't get there with the mind alone,' agreed Giuseppe. 'It's just something that you need to discover.'

I was yet to discover it, to feel my way through practice and postural awareness to the sweet spot between vigilance and relaxation. It remained possible that I never would – that *samadhi*, true concentration, was not a state attainable by everyone. There was, I supposed, only one way to find out: to keep practising, to practise harder, a habit I reckoned might be instilled on the forthcoming six-day, intensive yoga and meditation retreat in Ibiza I'd briefly considered booking myself onto, but had rejected on the grounds that it was more time spent away from my wife and kids. Who needed 'profound renewal in an exquisite island setting'? I could practise at home. Some scientists believe that the introspection inherent in contemplative retreat can be actively harmful, and not just for those with pre-existing mental-health conditions. It was exactly as I'd suspected at mindfulness class. You were either cut out for retreat or you weren't. And I had my doubts that I was.

Taiten Guareschi speaks of the 'stillness and internal silence' – the *hesychía* – of contemplative retreat as a calling, arising on 'the background of a vast narrative of religious nature'. We are able truly to sit, thinks Guareschi, only if this narrative has somehow called us personally. Hesychasts expend great effort in prayer, but only to render themselves receptive to a union bestowed by the grace of God. In Caravaggio's *The Calling of St Matthew*, Christ enters the customs house and points at Matthew the tax collector, sitting at a table with four others. It's left ambiguous which of the figures is Matthew, the bearded man gesturing at himself, as if to say, 'Who, *me*?', or the clean-shaven youth counting coins at the head of the table. Whichever is Matthew, the implication is clear: that the impulse to stillness, religious or not, falls upon us like the beam of white light cast across the room to illuminate the men's faces, a sudden access of clarity amid the gloom.

At Agia Matrona, after Sister Nectaria had shown the French couple through to the chapel, leaving Harriet and me alone in the reception room, I dithered for a bit before stepping out through a low doorway into the courtyard. There Sister Matrona, Nectaria's sole companion at the monastery since Matrona had taken her vows in 1977, was sitting by a low wall polishing a pile of church ornaments with a tin of Brasso. She looked up and acknowledged me with the barest of nods. If anything, Matrona seemed to have taken her vow of poverty even more seriously than Nectaria. Her skirt was filthy, and strands of matted grey hair straggled loose from her veil. Like Nectaria, like Vanessa, in her way, she had the charisma that came of unavailability – I was drawn to her even as she held me at bay. I muttered a *kalispera* and entered the chapel.

Nectaria and the French couple had left. Even for such a cramped space the chapel felt cavernous, abandoned. On the night-blue walls above the ranks of *stacidia*, wooden leaning-chairs with armrests at standing height, the saints stood arrayed in bright reds, oranges, purples and greens. Ornate silver censers hung on chains from the ceiling. On the iconostasis was a gilded image of Matrona of Chios, the monastery's titular saint. The visual noise of Orthodox church interiors exists in a sort of complementary opposition to the silence of hesychastic prayer, bathing the eye in what the ear is denied, the divine truth rendered visible by the iconostasis. On 20th October, Saint Matrona's feast day, two hundred Hydriots would climb up to the monastery to honour its patron. Then the crowds would recede and the monastery sink back into silence. Returning to the reception room, I found it empty. Harriet was outside with Nectaria, feeding the donkeys. I was about to slip out unnoticed when I saw a laminated picture, the size of a credit card, left on the dining table where I had been sitting. It was a gift from Sister Nectaria – a reproduction of the icon in the church, Saint Matrona with her hand raised in benediction, her gaze perfectly still and a fraction averted, over my shoulder towards the invisible.

✳

I thought of Nectaria and her gift to me as I drove home from the retreat centre in Devon. I kept the card of Saint Matrona in my wallet and took it out from time to time. It seemed an answer to my questions, asked and unasked. Silence. Stillness. Patience. By the time I was nearing Stonehenge the sun was setting behind me, cheering the stones against the dun of the surrounding fields, blinding the opposing traffic, heading west to their retreats with their shades on and their sun visors down. Cars were our meditation spaces, our monastic cells, our speeding retreat centres, offering some respite, for however long the journey lasted, from the world we were moving through, while we focused our attention on the road, soothed by silence or music. The road dipped and Stonehenge disappeared for a moment before looming back into view. And then it happened – quite suddenly, something beyond or beneath thought, or feeling, a simple if bottomless and profoundly calming occupation of my body and the car, the ochre glow in the rear-view, the tidal hush of tyres on tarmac, the stretched shadows in the fields. And in the instant the feeling was circumscribed by a thought, the instant I noticed I had felt something, I forgot to let it go, and the feeling vanished so abruptly I couldn't be entirely sure I'd felt it in the first place.

2.

The Vacation Response, Squared

'Just drop in right here,' said Gemma. 'Drop into your body, into your breath.' After a run of cloudless days Ibiza had finally acquiesced to autumn. I closed my eyes, and shuffled on my sitting bones so each foot was tucked firmly under the opposite thigh. My hands were in the *jnana mudra*, resting palms up-ward on my knees, with each thumb and index finger forming a circle. In Hinduism the thumb represents Brahman, the su-preme reality, the index finger *jiva* or the individual soul. From somewhere outside I heard the gulp of rain received by standing water. The purpose of this meditation was preparatory: to regu-late the breathing, calm the mind, so that we might attempt the asanas, or poses, with an awareness of our bodies in the present moment.

'Just observing your body this morning, right now,' intoned Gemma. 'Not five minutes ago. Right now.'

Gemma was Scottish, from Kilmarnock, and with her Yoga Voice on – soothing, incantatory, like audible incense – her vowels, elongated anyway, stretched like premonitions of the poses we would shortly endure. *Raight noooow. Drop intae yir breeeaath*. I had come to Casa Parvati to step up my practice, but was beginning to wonder if there was an intermediate level I'd missed out by mistake. The yoga on offer was either in the 'yin' style – slow, still, meditative, deeply taxing to the liga-ments – or, as with this morning's session, in the more dynamic 'vinyasa' style, where you passed from one asana to the next, without holding them for long or stopping to correct any mis-alignments. It was yoga in cursive: flowing, balletic, at least if you knew what you were doing. The first time I did it, at the Devon retreat, I found myself standing in a pool of my own sweat, while the ladies to either side of me, several of them in their late sixties, floated through the poses like dandelion clocks. It was exhausting, but did at least benefit from its relentlessness. There was no time to reflect on how much pain you were in.

We stepped to the front of our mats for the Sun Salutation.

'The more you breathe,' said Gemma, 'the more you charge up your body with this vital force, this prana that you're cre-ating, this energy, this goodness that you're doing for your body.'

Prana is breath in the sense of 'life force', roughly analogous to the Chinese principle of *qi*. We moved through the asanas. Warrior II. *Phalakasana*, the petrified push-up better known as the Plank. My abdominal muscles began to shudder. We moved into the Tree – standing on one leg with the other foot nestled into your upper thigh – and I began to tremble so violently the idea of remaining upright seemed absurd. But something stilled me.

'We can do all of these postures,' said Gemma, 'but without the focus, the attention, the awareness and your *in*tention, it's all just gymnastics. It's all just shapes on the mat.'

We lay on the floor for *shavasana*. The Corpse. Feet apart, arms relaxed to either side. Eyes closed. Breathe. 'Just melt,' said Gemma. 'Let go.' And letting go was like coming round. Every part of the body alive, vibrating almost, inseparable from mind. Euphoric. Simply there.

Ibiza has a long history of harbouring escapees, retreatants, cul-tural refugees of one sort or another. In the 1930s, the island became a haven for European artists and intellectuals fleeing fascism. The great German-Jewish thinker Walter Benjamin spent the spring of 1932 and summer of 1933 here, attracted by the cheap rents and the sense that this undeveloped 'outpost of Europe', as he referred to it, had escaped the atrophying effects of modernity. In 1936, of course, the Balearics fell to the Nationalists, but by the 1960s the isolation the island suffered under Franco had encouraged a second great bohemian invasion. As the writer Paul Richardson has noted, part of the appeal for the hordes of hippies, drop-outs and Vietnam draft-dodgers that descended on Ibiza was the pagan charisma of a culture that still, at least outside Ibiza Town, observed ritual practices dating back to the island's settlement by the Carthaginians in the seventh century BC.

All that is long gone, but an echo of the island's mystical history is present, perhaps, in its greater than average hospitality to alternative practices. Casa Parvati was a handsome, impeccably restored old finca at the end of a long, rutted track uphill through the mountains. My six-day 'Rejuvenate' retreat was a chance both to develop the techniques I had picked up in Devon and on Vanessa's mindfulness course – to take them up a gear or two – and to experience them in a more commercialised context. Could the benefits of retreat be bought – or rather, did more benefits accrue the more money you spent? Were the sort of 'deep healing' and 'ancient yogic philosophies' on offer the real deal or a canny recasting of indulgence as spiritual search? Casa Parvati was definitely at the luxury end of the market, with its dreamy blue-and-white website and five-star reviews in upscale travel magazines. I had arrived expecting my fellow retreatants to be drawn from the West London linen-wearing classes – well-heeled, yoga-toned, deeply schooled in soulcraft and airhead esoterica. It certainly looked the part: the kind of place you'd go to have your colon irrigated now you were definitively too old to go clubbing. A shade sail cast the terrace in softly filtered sunlight. An L-shaped set of outdoor sofas looked out over the infinity pool and a long view of forested hills.

The company behind the retreat was run by Sophie, a well-spoken Englishwoman in her forties, who, sure enough, had graduated from PR and partying to devote herself to the 'higher purpose' of healing herself and others.

'Retreats are so much more intimate here,' she told me, as we sat eating tortilla and salad by the pool.

Compared to the big wellness institutes, like Esalen in Big Sur, California, that dominate the self-development sector in the US, independent retreat centres in Ibiza and elsewhere in Europe tend to be considerably smaller in scale. The upside is intimacy. Numbers at Casa Parvati are capped at twelve.

'You're seen as an individual here,' said Sophie. 'So you can be personally supported throughout your experience.'

A pine-scented breeze grooved the pool-water and sent the unopened parasols fluttering like phantom monks on their stands. Talking to Sophie was having an effect that would soon become familiar: a sort of extremely relaxed unease. There was so much to like here, the rational attractions of exercise, sunshine, tranquillity, that Sophie's more radical assertions – at one point the conversation turned from 'energy masters' healing the centre of earthquakes to the use of kriya yoga to 'clear and heal HIV' – often caught me off guard. For all the worldliness of places like Casa Parvati, they revealed, in the chinks of their agonised secularism, a level of belief no less intense than the mystical zeal I would encounter on Mount Athos.

Tony was the first of my fellow retreatants to arrive. 'Sorry,' he said. 'I'll chill out in a minute.' Tony had got lost in the tangle of patchily tarmacked lanes that wound up the mountain from the main road. If I had my concerns about Casa Parvati, Tony did a lot to allay them. Stocky, with a South London accent and a pair of thick-rimmed glasses that looked like the portholes in a jazz-funk submarine, Tony had come on retreat to recover from the break-up of his marriage. He had only clicked on the link for Casa Parvati after going cold on a solo trip to Ko Samui.

'You can't be going to Thailand as a single bloke in your forties,' he said. 'It just looks wrong.'

Of the other six retreatants, four were Italian. Three, if you didn't count Gianni, a dapper young breakfast-cereal executive from Milan who would spend almost the entire retreat in his room, suffering from an unspecified illness that cleared up, miraculously, a couple of hours before the farewell dinner on day five. That left Jo and Fran, best friends in their mid-fifties. Fran was a return customer seeking an alternative to self-medication.

'When I'm stressed,' she told me, 'I down a bottle of wine in about an hour.' Fran was MD of a company that manufactured high-quality horse-riding equipment. Last time she came on retreat, the effects – the profound sense of well-being, the healthy eating, the easing up on the booze – lasted for about six weeks. 'Then the racing season started,' she said. 'It's great fun, but then you start slipping into these bad habits again, then the stress of work, and it's hoo, wine! Yeah, that'll sort it all out.' What Fran most valued in retreat was distance, not just geographic, but from the habits that were alienating her from herself, were making her unwell. A stepping away that was also a return.

According to the Hindu sage Patanjali, author of the *Yoga Sutras*, the ultimate goal of yoga is *kaivalya*: isolation. It's open to question precisely when Patanjali lived – estimates range from the second century BC to the fourth century AD – or whether the texts commonly attributed to him are the work of one man or a Homeric succession. It seems likely, however, that the *Sutras* were compiled somewhere between AD 325 and 425, by a single author working with older sources now lost to us. By *kaivalya*, Patanjali actually means the isolation of spirit from matter, but in the attainment of pure spirit the yogi undergoes his own form of isolation, from the world and its concerns, the materiality that stands between him and omniscience.

It's a notion common to Hindu and Buddhist metaphysics: liberation as the effacement of the self. Yoga as we know it in the West – that is, primarily as the sequence of postures known as the asanas – is thus a means to an end, a preparation of the body for the rigours of meditation. (Gemma at Casa Parvati had it the other way round: meditation as a preparation for the asanas). Strictly speaking, yoga *is* the end, synonymous in the foundational texts with *samadhi*, the state of complete meditative absorption that leads to the emancipation of the spirit. A term like 'hatha yoga', for instance, is now generally understood to connote a gentler, less dynamic style, although in fact it refers to the practice of all physical yoga methods as distinct from more devotional forms like mantra-repetition. Either way, in the majority of the ancient texts, *haṭhayoga* does not describe a technique but a state – yoga – attained by means of *hatha* (which roughly translates as 'force'). Yoga is not an activity but the aim of it, the withdrawal from the external world and, ultimately, the self.

Sat Bir Singh Khalsa is an assistant professor of medicine at Harvard Medical School. His special area of interest is yoga therapy – that is, the effectiveness of yoga and meditation in treating conditions like insomnia, chronic stress, PTSD and anxiety. How might the self-effacement enabled by yoga help to counteract stress-related disorders? Sat Bir's work relates to the emerging field of 'neurotheology', that is, the attempt to explain the highly subjective phenomena of religious and spiritual experience in more objective neurological terms. It's essentially what Giuseppe Pagnoni does: trace the neural correlates of the numinous.

'I view spirituality as a biologically based experience,' said Sat Bir, when we spoke via Zoom. Transcendence, the feeling of unity with a universal consciousness: all are functions of neurobiological processes that can be enhanced by varieties of physical and mental exercise. Sat Bir is in his late sixties, with a sober academic manner belied by the joyous extravagance of his beard, silvery white and worn long in accordance with *kesh*, the discipline of keeping the hair uncut, upheld by Sikhs to honour the perfection of God's creation. Since his early twenties, Sat Bir has been a practitioner of kundalini yoga, a style that through a combination of asanas, pranayama (breathwork), meditation and mantras is said to awaken a divine energy – or *shakti* – located at the base of the spine.

'Of course, on the physical side, we know that yoga improves flexibility and muscular endurance.' The mental effects are just as significant – not that Sat Bir has much patience with the distinction. 'In modern medicine we've dissociated the mind and the body. You've got psychiatrists on one side, physical doctors on the other side, and they don't talk to each other. It's ridiculous.' Mind and body are inseparable. Have a massage or a hot bath and the physical and mental effects enter a positive feedback loop. Relaxing the body relaxes the mind, which further relaxes the body.

'Yoga does the same thing,' said Sat Bir. 'Particularly through the stretching, the awareness of tension in your body.'

Quite what's going on in the brain here is uncertain. In 2017, researchers at the University of Southern California studied the effects on thirty-eight individuals of a three-month yoga and meditation retreat. The results showed a significant increase in blood-plasma levels of BDNF: brain-derived neurotrophic factor, a protein that supports the growth and survival of neurons, and plays a crucial role in the regulation of inflammation, stress response and mood. A comparable increase was noted in a type of anti-inflammatory 'cytokine' or protein known as Interleukin-10, along with a decrease in the pro-inflammatory cytokine Interleukin-12. That inflammation is a risk factor in depression, anxiety and stress is well established. A study led by Dr Chris Streeter, of Boston University's School of Medicine, found that practising yoga may increase levels of GABA, gamma-aminobutyric acid, a neurotransmitter also boosted by certain anti-anxiety medications and alcohol. The effect is to inhibit neuronal excitability, that is, to calm us down.

In the USC study, it was hypothesised that the effects on BDNF and cytokine levels derived more from the meditative element than the asanas. However, no one has been able to rule out the role the physical element – insofar as it can be treated separately from the mental – might play in the stress-reducing benefits of yoga. One possible explanation relates to the vagus nerve, a long cranial nerve involved in the functioning of the autonomic nervous system. The ANS is the part of our nervous system over which we have little or no control. It regulates heart rate, breathing, digestion, sexual arousal, and the fight-or-flight response, all the functions that need to keep going whether our conscious mind is alert to them or not – the civil service to our conscious mind's executive. 'Vagal tone', a measure of vagus-nerve activity, implicated among other things in heart-rate regulation and gastrointestinal motility, is known to be affected by yoga practices and deep breathing; vagal-nerve stimulation may be a contributory factor in the increases in both BDNF and GABA levels.

Breathing is key here. It's thought that respiratory frequency has direct control over the ANS. The main branches of the ANS are known as the sympathetic and parasympathetic nervous systems, the former responsible for our fight-or-fight response – as Sat Bir puts it, 'the one that prepares you to fight with the bear in the woods' – the latter for stimulating resting-state activities like sexual arousal, salivation, digestion, defecation and so on. Sympathetic winds us up, parasympathetic runs a bath and lights a scented candle. The two systems are complementary, contributing, in a healthy individual, towards what neurologists call 'sympathovagal balance': a compromise between our urge to fight bears and kick back on the sofa in our onesies.

'In modern society, most people have a sympathovagal balance that's very much tilted towards the sympathetic side,' explained Sat Bir. 'You're out on the street, you're dodging cars, you're trying to balance your chequebook. That's why chronic stress is such a big issue in modern society. We don't have the strategies to cope with it.' The effect of yoga and meditation on the ANS is to redress the balance. 'You're reducing the sympathetic drive and enhancing parasympathetic activity. Breath has an immediate impact on that.'

In the long term, Sat Bir believes, the practice of managing the stress response can lead to permanent structural changes in the brain. 'You're no longer triggering your amygdala,' – the mass of deep-brain nuclei involved in the perception and processing of fear. 'So your amygdala actually gets smaller, because you're not using it as much.' The effects in the short term are transient but appreciable. Just as Giuseppe Pagnoni and others claim for meditative practice, Sat Bir maintains that beginners can experience the benefits of yoga almost immediately. 'Their monkey mind quietens down,' he said. 'They're no longer stressed. They're no longer *reactive* to stress.'

Over time, the state effect of reduced stress becomes the trait effect of permanently altered psychology. 'People who practise for months and years on a regular basis – who adopt a meditative or yogic lifestyle – a lot of these people start to experience a deeper, ongoing state of peace and calm.' What begins as a relaxation technique shades over time into self-transcendence. 'After a couple of years of practice, some may say, "Yoga changed my life."'

This frequently entails 'a change from a materialistic set of life goals to a set of higher life goals', like 'becoming a more compassionate individual'. Such positive psychological changes are, in effect, the neurobiological consequences of calming the mind, moving it 'into a contemplative state', 'creating the conditions in the central nervous system and the brain' to 'experience the universe more as a oneness'. We are kinder for our lessening attachment to selfhood. 'If you want to call that spirituality,' said Sat Bir, 'that's okay with me.'

The naked young man was telling the naked young Asian-American woman about the six-day workshop he was here to attend. 'It's called "Bio-hacking the Language of Intimacy",' he said.

'Uh-huh,' said the Asian-American woman. She directed this less at the young man than the kelp forest floating offshore. We were in the outdoor sulphur springs, clinging to the cliff-side at the Esalen Institute, a spiritual retreat centre in Big Sur, California. As at Casa Parvati, and the countless other commercial retreat centres worldwide that have followed in Esalen's wake, the programme here offers the chance to step back from your materialist life-goals at a distinctly materialist price.

The young man pressed on. What he particularly liked about the bio-hacking workshop was the ability to talk about stuff he couldn't talk about at work. Relationships and so forth. 'You know,' he said. 'Really make that human connection.'

She gave him the sort of bright, dead-eyed smile Californians deploy when they're about to violently disagree with you. 'I find I can make human connections in lots of different contexts.'

The young man went quiet. In all but one sense it was a typically, even touchingly American courtship ritual: the man no less diffident or deferential than his grandfather might have been, the young woman resistant, off-handedly wielding her power over him, yet to be impressed. The only difference was the nakedness – the effect redoubled, in the woman's case, by the fact that she was standing up in the water, exposing herself in full-frontal immodesty to the young man and the fresh Pacific breezes. It was like a night-before-the-prom anxiety dream from the 1950s. At Esalen, naked sharing is as commonplace and sapped of erotic charge as it might be at a naturist campsite – which was just as well, as I was naked, too, the gooseberry in the hot tub, desperately aiming at an air of easy-going self-composure as I scanned the visual field for a corner without exposed flesh in it.

Previously a disreputable spa resort – since the 1950s, 'Slate's Hot Springs' had catered to rough trade from LA and San Francisco, for a brief spell under the armed invigilation of a young Hunter S. Thompson – Esalen was founded in 1962 as a centre for the new 'Human Potential Movement'.

The intention of the founders, Stanford psychology graduates Michael Murphy and Dick Price, was to hold a series
of seminars and 'experiential sessions' exploring the capaci-
ties they believed lay unrealised in human consciousness. It's
thought that the geothermal springs on this craggy, intensely
beautiful stretch of the central Californian coast have been
in some form of ritual or therapeutic use for at least 6,000
years, when the Esselen, the native-American tribe that gave
the Institute its name, migrated south from the Bay Area, and
saw in the meeting of waters – ocean, mineral and fresh from
the neighbouring creek – a fitting place to worship and bury
their dead. Now Murphy and Price foresaw a new confluence,
a focal point for the era's preoccupations with psychedelics,
Eastern mysticism and self-actualisation. Under their watch
Esalen became a mother church for what Frederic Spiegelberg,
a professor of Michael Murphy's at Stanford, called 'the religion of no religion'.

If Esalen owed its growing prominence to a single event, it
was the arrival, in 1963, of the Berlin-born psychoanalyst Fritz
Perls. Initially a classical Freudian – he had visited the great man
in Vienna in 1936, although the encounter was not a success –
Perls had grown disillusioned with his former idol's focus on
repressed memories, drawing instead on existential psychology
and Zen Buddhism to develop a technique that prioritised the
present. This he called 'Gestalt therapy', from the German for
'shape' or 'form'. What mattered was not childhood trauma
but the here and now, the subject's construction of reality as
experienced in the moment.

For the subject the approach could be bruising. Ten to fifteen of them would gather in a room: 'the encounter group'.
If long-repressed traumas were no longer relevant, Perls would
happily arrange some fresh ones. Hot-tempered, oversexed and
potty-mouthed – his motto was 'I am who I am, I fuck when
I can, I'm Popeye the Sailor Man' – Perls liked to 'hot-seat'
his subjects, showing them to a chair then, in full view of the
group, dismantling their personalities trait by trait, subjecting

each rhetorical defence mechanism and unconscious tic to mocking and often violent critique. Take it or leave it, this was the treatment: to compel the individual to forget the past and confront the reality, however painful, of their self-projections at the very instant they occurred, thereby helping to integrate them into some sort of coherent whole or 'Gestalt'.

Word of the new miracle cure soon spread. Perls had the walls of his office decorated with the eyeglasses of clients whose 20/20 vision he claimed had been restored by his interventions. In 1967, the psychologist Will Schutz joined the faculty, developing Perls's Gestalt practice but transferring therapeutic responsibility from the therapist to the subject's fellow group members. Again, drawing on the Hindu notion of *ananda*, or bliss, Schutz's thesis was that all human beings were born into a state of unbridled, full-body joy, subsequently repressed and distorted by society. Gestalt in the Schutz manner was designed to reinstate that primal joyousness.

Perls dismissed Schutz and his followers as the 'instant joy boys', but their approaches were of a piece, dependent as they both were on a synthesis of Western psychology and Asian meditation, with the stress the latter places on awareness in the present moment. The result was a sort of demysticised mysticism, contemptuous of organised religion (or 'the black mud of occultism', as Perls called it), rooted in observable reality but alert to the consciousness beyond it. Perls and Schutz's Gestalt was a new and peculiarly Californian assimilation of ancient spiritual practices, rewired for instant gratification.

By the late sixties, Esalen had become world famous for Gestalt and the complementary practices – yoga, meditation, massage, getting high – that placed similar emphasis on the intense occupation of the here and now. Esalen was the place to be, in more senses than one. George Harrison flew in by helicopter for a sitar jam with Ravi Shankar. Sharon Tate was there for a session with Perls the night before her murder. Hordes of hippies moved down from the Bay Area, as the

Esselen had, to camp – and consume vast amounts of hallucinogens – in the grounds.

'The spiritual centre of the world moves every few hundred
years,' said Ben Tauber, a former Google product manager who
was appointed as executive director of Esalen in 2017. 'There
was a time in the sixties when that was San Francisco. And
then if you looked at where that was for San Francisco – that
was Esalen.'

Nearly sixty years on, the radical vision espoused at Esalen
has become part of the mainstream. These days the majority
of retreatants, or 'seminarians', come to attend a five- or seven-
day residential workshop, developing their yoga or meditation
practice, deepening their understanding of the esoteric traditions
that underpin Esalen's agenda ('The Path of Buddhist Tantra
and Mahamudra'), or confronting psychological blocks in
encounter-group settings ('Trauma, Memory and Restoration
of Self', 'It Won't Hurt Forever'). Fritz Perls died in 1970, Will
Schutz in 2002, and Gestalt as practised nowadays is a much
gentler, more consensual, respectful affair. An alternative to the
workshops is to come for the weekend and choose from the
drop-in classes on offer – yin yoga, qi gong, Gestalt movement
(helping guests to 'realize, express, shape and dance patterns of
their lives'.) Roughly half the guests come from the Bay Area
and LA, drawn from a demographic as diverse in age as it is
socio-economically homogeneous: young, middle-class college
graduates with time and money on their hands, spiritually
inclined retirees unpersuaded by the luxury cruise, and the
sprawling, moneyed middle, stressed-out professionals seeking
a more self-improving means of R&R. Esalen is merely a more
conspicuous instance of a reality I would confront in Ibiza and
elsewhere: that retreat, at least in the commercialised form promoted by the wellness industry, is the preserve of the privileged.

In a bamboo-floored meeting room named for Aldous Huxley
– with the exception of the psychologist Abraham Maslow,

perhaps the most important intellectual influence on Esalen's founders – I lay under a blanket on some velveteen cushions as a healer called Deva padded around gonging her collection of tuning forks, crystal singing bowls and 'tingshas', the miniature cymbals, joined with a leather strap, that I remembered from Vanessa's mindfulness class. 'Huxley' was upstairs from the main lodge and had the look of a luxurious barn. At Esalen, the doors of perception are bespoke and hand crafted. Along with the forty other seminarians prostrate on the floor around me, I was on a 'Sacred Sound Journey', borne on an auditory carpet towards a state of pure alignment and awareness. The theory, as I understood it, was that stress and anxiety cause our cells to vibrate at suboptimal frequencies, and that the sound of the bowls and other instruments would restore them to vibrational harmony.

In practice it was a bit like trying to get to sleep on a washing machine. When Deva really got going you could feel your cheeks begin to blur. The aim was to use the sound as you would your breath in a breathing meditation, as an attentional foothold, secure enough to let the to-do lists and random flashbacks and general mental detritus fall away. But as with this morning's body-scan meditation, I was finding the cushions and the incense a little *too* relaxing, and I drifted off until there was a ping from the tingshas and we were all sitting up and sharing our awareness in a quarter lotus.

'In the world that I live in,' said the smiling man opposite me, 'everything is *delicious*.'

After the Sound Journey I got talking to Krista, a marketing executive from Washington, DC. 'Experiencing this beautiful place, it's sensory,' she told me, as we walked from the main lodge to the Buddha Garden. 'It's the cool winds off the ocean, it's the sound of the waves crashing on the rocks, it's the heat of the baths. It's a sensory place that opens you up. And I realise I don't make very much time for that.'

It was a perfect afternoon, sunny with a caressing breeze, and Krista and I took to a couple of benches hemmed in by pink cosmos and tidy rows of salad greens and herbs. Ahead, beyond the produce garden, and the expanse of well-tended – but not *too* well-tended – grass that enveloped the estate, the land ended abruptly, at a split-rail fence a hundred feet above a shoreline you couldn't see. The effect was mesmerising-tending-to-queasy: an infinity lawn. Krista admitted a tendency to 'extreme workaholism', staying at her desk till midnight, neglecting her personal life, fulfilling her duties on autopilot. 'I'm that person that gets to work, and then all of a sudden it's one o'clock, and you haven't eaten, and you forgot to go to the bathroom. You just *work*.'

Now she was in her early fifties, Krista's promise to herself was a new 'intentionality': not to let life slip by unnoticed. 'I feel that the next twenty-five years, Act Three, could be a wondrous time,' she said. 'But only if I'm paying attention.' For Krista, the 'experiential, sensory' qualities of Esalen permitted precisely that: an alertness to the present. 'It's not about learning something new. It's not about expanding your mind. It's just being.'

In recent years Esalen has been accused of selling out, of betraying the countercultural principles it both emerged from and helped to shape. In part this is due to the particular burden of authenticity borne by such places. What constitutes the real thing is of course a vexed question in all forms of tourism, particularly those catering to the middle class, but weighs especially heavily when the product on offer is authenticity itself. You go to a place like Esalen to have your physical, emotional or spiritual integrity restored. You need, in turn, to be assured of the integrity of what you're getting: any whiff of exploitation or inauthenticity and the deal is off. The problem is compounded by the mongrel nature of modern self-development, its mishmash of Dharmic religion and Western therapeutic practices. Does it matter that the form of yoga, meditation or primordial qi gong you signed up for was concocted in California last Tuesday? Is this quackery or adaptation? It's a question I'd encounter again and again on retreat, in India as much as in the US or Europe. How to be sure – given the intense and thus infinitely exploit-able need people have to believe in the possibility of their own redemption – that you aren't being taken for a ride.

The other, related accusation was that Esalen had begun to cater exclusively to the middle classes. This criticism was nothing new. The counterculture was always a deal less egali-tarian than its apologists liked to make out. Abraham Maslow – who taught at Esalen, and like Aldous Huxley has a room named after him – lays it out in his famous 'Hierarchy of Needs'. Self-actualisation is only possible when the basic human needs of food, warmth, water and rest have been met. Accordingly, it was for the most part the young, white, college-educated beneficiaries of the post-war economic boom that had the leisure time to indulge in psychedelics and soulcraft. Tom Wolfe was calling it as far back as 1964. 'Esalen,' he writes in *The Electric Kool-Aid Acid Test*, 'was a place where educated middle-class adults came in the summer to try to get out of The Rut and wiggle their fannies a bit.' In 1990 some graffiti appeared on the Esalen entry sign on Highway 1: 'Jive shit for rich white folk'.

It has also been to Esalen's commercial advantage that the marginal demographic it was founded to serve – those hippies and Eastern-influenced seekers that described themselves as 'spiritual, but not religious', or SBNR – is no longer so mar-ginal. The space vacated by Judaeo-Christian religion has been colonised by metaphysical hedge-betting. Gordon Wheeler, a Gestalt psychologist and president of Esalen since the early noughties, describes the SBNR as 'the modal group in Western society': not a majority, but a larger group than the liberal Christians, fundamentalists, or atheists. Every other manage-ment consultant now has a healing crystal bracelet. In 2017, a mudslide on Highway 1 caused the closure of the Institute for eight months. After the resulting financial hit, reported to have run at more than $1 million a month, the accusation gathered force that Esalen was pandering to the wealthier end of its client pool, had become a corporate retreat whose cosmetic hippiedom rendered it indistinguishable from all the other upscale resorts borrowing from ancient spiritual practice and repackaging it for the secular wellness tourist. It was a familiar story: the steady absorption of the counterculture by capital.

It can certainly cost a fair bit to hang out here. A weekend can set you back as much as $3,000. Come for the week and you're looking at close to $7,000. The appointment of Ben Tauber, with his ties to big tech, and a subtle shift in the programme from the numinous to the digital – the catalogue at the time of my visit listed workshops on 'Conscious AI' and 'Blockchain & Cryptocurrency' – invited suspicions that Esalen was becoming the therapeutic wing of Silicon Valley, a rehab centre for tech bros with misgivings about their industry, and the money to assuage them. Esalen, the feeling went, had become about as countercultural as the newly installed Tesla charging stations in the parking lot.

Terry Gilbey, Ben Tauber's successor as executive director, disputes this. 'You can come to Esalen for $400 for the weekend,' he told me. 'Granted, that's a sleeping-bag space, but you get your food, you get your workshop, you get the opportunity to retreat.' The higher-end accommodation – private suites with ocean views, redwood decks, outdoor clawfoot tubs and open fireplaces – subsidises the scrimp-and-save seminarians bunking down on the meeting-room floors. Esalen exists to meet a need, to provide refuge from a society grown ever more materialistic, atomised, brutalising, and if fulfilling that mission involves a degree of doublethink – submitting to precisely those mammon-worshipping forces Esalen is supposedly there to resist – Terry was sanguine about it. Post-mudslide, the choice for Esalen was stark: 'rebuild the operational model' or hit the buffers.

Like Ben Tauber, Terry straddled the worlds of spirituality and tech – as a serial Esalen seminarian and former IT director at the health-insurance conglomerate Kaiser Permanente – and spoke, accordingly, in a peculiar hybrid of hippie mysticism and management-speak. Ultimately, if Esalen is to continue offering guests the chance 'to slow down, disconnect ... and connect with others on a different level', to 'sit in the quietness and reflect', then the focus for its leaders is clear: 'driving higher mission impact'.

After dinner I took the short, sandy path back down to the hot tubs. In the changing rooms I disrobed, showered, then slipped into the communal, jacuzzi-style plunge pool I had shared with the naked couple earlier that afternoon. A vast sky pricked with pin-sharp stars vaulted from the horizon to the dark mountains inland. There was a mild but pervasive smell of rotten eggs. I got chatting to Amethyst, a professional trapeze artist and healer from Fresno. Quite what Amethyst looked like was hard to say, as the bathhouse was largely unlit, and my fellow bathers were discernible only in pale convexities picked out by the moonlight – a jawbone here, a collarbone there. Despite or because of the nudity, the baths were especially popular after nightfall, lending the sharing that went on here an air of the secular confessional.

I asked Amethyst what she was here for.

'Oh,' she said, 'I'm here for the Wild Woman's Way?'

'And what does that involve?'

'It's a five-day workshop,' explained Amethyst. 'Basically it's devoted to an archetype of liberated womanhood? You know what I mean?'

'Not really.'

'Okay. It's about connecting to the earth? Feeling the movement of the tides and stars, stuff like that? Just basically giving expression to the wild woman we don't always get the chance to be.'

'And how do you do that exactly?'

'It's all about feeling and embodying the archetype?' said Amethyst, with a new confidence in her voice. 'So you might for example give it a song? Or move the body by checking in and asking it, like, what are you feeling?'

'You ask your body that.'

'Right. Then you let that feeling have expression in movement.'

As quickly as it had come about Amethyst's conviction seemed to have waned. Several of the conversations I had at Esalen had this quality – that neither I nor the other person had a very firm idea of what we were talking about, that meaning, here in the sulphurous warmth before the invisible ocean, was as phantasmal as the moonlight on Amethyst's cheekbones. Essentially, she explained, the task with these retreats was to remain open, alive to the unknown.

'It's a good way to go in,' she said, 'and see what comes up.'

After the baths I returned to the light and warmth of the lodge, where I bumped into the young man from the hot tub, leaning on a balustrade looking out to sea. He introduced himself as Eric. I asked him what 'Bio-hacking the Language of Intimacy' entailed.

He wasn't sure. 'I'm making an educated guess that it's going to consist of exercises, lectures.'

With his tidy hair and J. Crew-ish open-neck shirt, Eric looked like the kind of guy you might run into at a sports bar or an executive airport lounge. To an extent it seemed like, for him, the specifics of the workshop were of secondary importance. 'A big part of the benefit here is meeting like-minded people,' he said. Eric was a real-estate broker from Sacramento. In his spare time he tended to 'hang out at the country club and play golf'. Esalen was an outlet for an otherwise occluded side of him. He looked out beyond the uplit trees to the now indivisible blackness of ocean and sky.

'At my country club I'm the only guy asking if the soup is gluten-free,' he said. 'I guess I'm a bit of a different drummer in some respects. But here I feel like, this is my tribe, you know?'

Clearly, a significant part of the benefit in short-term retreat is what Sat Bir Singh Khalsa calls 'the vacation response' – getting away from it all. 'You're no longer walking into the kitchen and looking at your chequebook on the table. Nobody's shouting at you, nobody's screaming, your ex-wife is not calling you on the phone.' In this sense a retreat is no different from a week sunning yourself in a deckchair. 'All of the images and sounds that are generating a stress response in your home environment are missing.' There is a large body of research that confirms what common sense would tell us: for example, that immersion in nature can have a calming effect. Of the colours in the visible spectrum, green light has a medium wavelength, blue the lowest of all. Some studies suggest this makes them easier to perceive, with the consequence that views of foliage or sea have a sedative effect on the nervous system.

What, then, of the *extra* benefits supposedly conferred by a retreat at Casa Parvati or Esalen? Are there any, or would I have been just as well off in a hammock with a good book? Isolating the specific effects of yoga and meditation – or qi gong, or sacred sound baths, or dancing stereotypes of liberated womanhood – is notoriously difficult, but the studies undertaken by Sat Bir and others do suggest that the 'vacation response' to a quieter, greener (or bluer) environment can be multiplied many times over by intensive practice of the asanas and meditation techniques.

There is also, of course, the benefit of structure. With a full schedule, we are relieved of the paradoxical burden of nothing to do. A retreat is a holiday from choice – from the ordeal of choosing where to eat, which beach to go to, whether to visit the flea market or the mud volcano or the surprisingly interesting doll's house museum. A week by the sea may or may not make you calmer. By Sat Bir's lights, a week by the sea practising yoga is considerably more likely to, and may, of course, be the starting point of a longer-term practice that could induce permanent trait changes at the anatomical level. A retreat is like a holiday but more so: a vacation squared.

*

Lunch on our penultimate day in Ibiza. Hazel the mostly vegan chef had prepared fried tofu on gluten-free noodles, an avocado salad, some unspeakable shiitake pâté and a platter of thinly sliced Manchego (okay because 'the molecules in sheep's milk are smaller'). I pulled up a chair next to Jo and Fran. What did they reckon, now the retreat was all but over? Had they enjoyed themselves?

'I've loved everything about it,' said Jo, then, in an undertone: 'Apart from the food.' Last night Hazel had served a salad containing strands of slimy blue spirulina. (As far as Fran was concerned there was a pondy, algae-ish note in pretty much everything Hazel prepared. 'It turns my stomach, to be honest.')

'What have you missed?' That night we were booked in to a nearby Italian restaurant to mark the last night of the retreat. All dietary restrictions, we were promised, would be lifted. 'Food-wise, I mean.'

'Bread,' said Jo. 'With wheat in it.'

'Wine,' said Fran. 'Does that count as food? Wine.'

'Okay,' I said. 'Let's play "Least Hazel-ish food imaginable". Fran first.'

'What are those McDonald's things called? The ice-creamy ones.'

'McFlurries,' said Jo.

'A Reese's Peanut-Butter Cup McFlurry.'

'I've got one,' said Jo. 'A Gregg's sausage-roll sandwich.'

'A Ginsters all-day-breakfast-pasty sandwich.' I said. 'On white Mother's Pride.'

Later Jo and I discussed giving up our jobs to start a chain of yoga pubs. The Chest, Knees and Chin. The Downward Dog. There was a sense that this low-level satire, this outbreak of back-of-the-bus insurgency, was in fact a measure of our appreciation. We were all enjoying the retreat so much that certain of its pieties could be teased without sounding ungrateful. That morning I had held a pose I found particularly difficult – *chakrasana*, the wheel pose, a backbend with your palms flat on the ground – for a good thirty seconds.

My endurance was improving. There was no doubt about it: I felt calm. Relaxed in body and mind. We all did. What had particularly taken Jo aback was how quickly she had felt at ease in everyone's company.

'You've got this common ground,' she said. 'And I think then you're quite open with each other because you're all here for a reason. I probably get to know people better on a retreat in a few days than I might with some of my friends back home.'

Jo, it has to be said, didn't strike me as given to this sort of admission. If anything, what I enjoyed about her company was the edge of scepticism in her friendliness, the salt in her sweet disposition that validated – in that very English way – the geniality by keeping it in check. It was a sentiment I would encounter again and again on retreat: the pleasure taken in stepping back, not to get away from people, but to spend more time with people like you. The tribal gratifications of the common pursuit: the more you relaxed, the more you let your guard down, the larger your tribe grew. The more 'like you' people became. It was our defences that kept us apart. 'I just think it's so restorative,' Jo went on. 'It gives you that kind of – not faith, but pleasure in humankind again.'

Scattered on the sofas and side tables throughout the finca were laminated menus of the treatments on offer. Reflexology, Ayurvedic massage, spiritual and shamanic healing. All sounded like exactly the sort of saw-you-coming quackery I had been expecting to find on Ibiza – and which, admittedly, formed a marginal enough part of the whole Casa Parvati experience as to be safely ignorable. That said, the treatment that set off the loudest bullshit alarm – something called 'Somatic Transformation Therapy', priced at 180 euros an hour and conducted by a mysterious Swiss woman called Sonja – was also the one everyone seemed to swear by. It had come up at lunch with Jo, who was booked in for a session.

'Really?' I'd said. 'Doesn't it sound a bit – bollocksy?'

Jo raised an agnostic hand. 'I've heard it's good.'

Later that afternoon I found Jo staring into the distance on a pool-side recliner. Precisely what had gone on between her and Sonja – there had been something about Jo's smoking, and her use of it as an emotional prop – was unclear, mainly because Jo was scarcely capable of speech.

'You've got to try it,' she gasped, which, coming from someone as dry and unillusioned as Jo, was tricky to dismiss altogether. I had nothing to lose – apart, of course, from the small matter of 180 euros.

Sonja was tall, slender, at once groomed and wild-looking with her long, tousled beach hair and wide, sea-green, mesmerist's eyes. Everyone at Casa Parvati had a soothing manner – it went with the territory – but Sonja's was so soothing it all but flipped into its opposite. She was feverishly laid-back, manically relaxed, to the extent that my first instinct was to bolt for the door. There seemed good reason to believe I was about to be inducted into a cult. Sonja told me to strip to my underwear and lie back on the treatment table.

'How can I help you?'

It's a moot question when you're prostrate on a table in your Y-fronts. I told her about my back operation and the persistent pins and needles it had caused in my lower legs and feet. As I spoke, Sonja began to massage my right foot, gently at first, concentrating on the toes. And then she struck – pressed the tip of her thumb into my big toe, not very forcefully, but suddenly, inducing a pain the like of which I had never experienced, as if it wasn't her thumb she were using but a skewer pushed through my flesh directly into my central nervous system, a sort of neurological shriek that was at once at the upper limit of tolerability, and, I had to admit, kind of nice.

'Is that okay?'

No. Yes. Both. 'Gnf.'

'Just keep breathing,' said Sonja. '*Breathe* into it.'

Sonja pressed her thumb into the muscles above my hamstrings. Whee: a high C of pure pain. And so on up my body, seeking out and stimulating pressure points in my legs, back and neck, each time inducing that same close-to-unendurable, sub-orgasmic pain that lessened not one bit in intensity the more it occurred, and in time had me bucking on the treatment table as if Sonja had attached electrodes to my skin. There was a line of tension or 'energy blockages', Sonja concluded, originating somewhere under my breastbone. It was true that from about half an hour in I had felt a faint vibration there, which at first I thought might be hyperventilation, what with all the deep breathing, but wasn't, it was deeper, less dizzying and, growing ever stronger, had moved up from my chest into my face, like an Apache-stripe of vibration across the bridge of my nose.

'How old were you when you first felt this tension?' asked Sonja.

'Eleven,' I lied. Or was it a lie? It's what I found myself saying – perhaps, in retrospect, because eleven was when I'd passed the exam to get into grammar school, moving, thereby, from the happy egality of childhood to my first experience of rank, with all the new pressures that brought, to be clever, not to disappoint. The awful jeopardy in my parents being so pleased. Perhaps eleven was the first time I could remember wanting to withdraw into myself. But there I was again: off on one. 'Let it go,' said Sonja, and I tried to, although what precisely there was to let go depended, of course, on whether I'd ad-libbed the grammar-school stuff or dislodged an actual memory. The vibrations were now loud and exerting a sort of hydrostatic pressure behind the bridge of my nose. Half an hour later the vibrations passed out through the tips of my toes and the session was over. I croaked a feeble thank-you and retreated to my room, tempted to call it a day and skip the goodbye dinner.

I thought better of it, after a nap. The restaurant was a couple of miles away, downhill through the pine forests on a metalled track. My fellow retreatants, including the rapidly recovered Gianni, had squeezed into the party's two small cars, but as it was such a beautiful evening, the warm air powdery in the failing light, I had decided to walk. A few hundred yards down the track Gianni pulled up beside me in his rusty-red Fiat 500.

'Get in, hippie.'

'Piss off, Gianni.'

'Ah, *che pazzo*.'

With a gravelly crunch the Fiat disappeared from view and my ears readjusted to the forest: the breeze in the needles, the disregarded dial-tone of the cicadas. From the valley below came the sound of a dog barking. In retrospect I was a little annoyed, or embarrassed, to have overruled my inner sceptic and lain on the table for Sonja – but I felt so good, in the warm evening air, after six days of exercise, healthy food and no booze, that my irritation soon gave way to a scatterbrained happiness. A bell started tolling in the valley. Walter Benjamin had a particular fascination with the bell tower of Ibiza cathedral, in the Dalt Vila, the Old Town, with the minatory inscription on its clock: *Ultima Multis*. 'The last day for many'. And I found myself thinking of his last day, in 1940, aged forty-eight – my age – overweight, asthmatic, having escaped the Nazis on foot, over the Pyrenees from Banyuls-sur-Mer, only to be refused entry into Spain. If he walked the ten miles back to France the Nazis would arrest him. Walter Benjamin, the great scholar-poet of wandering, stuck, unable to move. So he took a fatal dose of morphine. Whichever way he retreated meant death.

The hot-and-cold feeling in my feet had gone. I wasn't sure at first, but as I emerged from the forest and turned right towards the church, its bell gable silhouetted against the sky, I realised something wonderful: that for the last half-mile, while my mind had wandered off with Walter Benjamin, I hadn't felt so much as a tingle. The joy of it. I had to check: a body scan, focus my attention on my feet. It was true. For the first time in more than a year they felt normal – that is, only just perceptibly there.

Sonja would say that by stimulating my pressure points she had unblocked trapped energy, and that by doing so she was addressing a lifelong tendency to 'hold tension' that my back operation had only exacerbated. Somehow, and in conjunction with the yoga and meditation, I had learned to let go, to lessen the feeling not by ignoring my body, but, on the contrary, by paying focused attention to it. Conventional medicine would cite 'hyperstimulation analgesia', which holds that intense stimulation may activate brain areas that inhibit pain-signalling mechanisms. You induce intense local pain to reduce it more generally. Which story did I buy? Mysticism or materialism? East or West? Sonja's touch or the textbook? The textbook, probably, although as I walked on past the church, the bells so loud now I had to press my fingers to my ears, I felt a flicker of what drew people to these retreats: the need to believe.

It was dark now. A hundred yards beyond the church I passed a dilapidated farmhouse. The dog began to bark again, and in the gloomy, deserted valley its metallic echo sent a volt of mild anxiety up my spine. The mutt was at my heels before I saw the sign: *perro peligroso*. And then another dog came running from the other side of the track, then another, and another, until pack instinct had drawn seven, eight of them into the chase, not *perro* but *perros peligrosos*, vicious little dust-coloured mongrels pouring down the verges, yipping and snarling and drooling at the prospect of sinking their fangs into my newly tingle-free ankles. And rather than run – should I run? They wanted me to run – I turned to face the pack leader, a small, black, red-eyed goblin of a dog, ears pricked like horns, whiskers spiky with saliva – and did the only thing I could: raised a finger and over the tolling of the church bells bellowed 'No. *No.*'

3.

The Preparation for an Encounter

This close you felt each toll in the bones. I had walked to the abbey in parodically gothic conditions: driving rain, sky so dark it was hard to believe it was only three in the afternoon. In medieval theology it was believed that monasteries were marked out for demonic attack. The Devil was wasting his time dispatching his minions to the city. There, everyone was won over to the cause already. Monasteries and convents were a different matter, impregnable redoubts against evil it would take a pitiless and unflagging onslaught to overwhelm. Come nightfall, the sky above the cloisters would have swarmed with winged monstrosities. Apart from summoning and dismissing the faithful, the church bells were like bird spikes or burglar alarms: their function was to drive off the demons. Now, as the congregation filed out from Vespers, night had fallen for real, and although the rain had eased up, the gloom was so intense as to be exhilarating, each bell-toll a warning aimed as much at us, it seemed, as the fiends scuttling over the parapets.

The Abbey of Solesmes, half an hour's walk along the river from Sablé-sur-Sarthe, in north-western France, was founded in 1010 as a Benedictine priory. ('Solesmes' is pronounced like 'solemn', but with the stress on the second syllable.) It's had its ups and downs. Destroyed by the English in the Hundred Years War, the priory was rebuilt on a more modest scale, then emptied of its monks when the National Assembly abolished all religious orders in 1790. By the 1830s, what remained of the old priory was on the brink of demolition when a priest, Prosper Guéranger, native to the area but then living in Le Mans, took advantage of the diminished anti-clericalism of the Bourbon restoration to raise enough funds to buy the ruins. One thing that distinguishes the Benedictines from other Catholic orders is the independence of their monasteries. Much of the guidance in the Rule of St Benedict, laid out in 516 either by the Italian monk Benedict of Nursia – or, conceivably, by a group operating under a collective pseudonym – is devoted to the establishment of an autonomous community of monks answerable only to their abbot. This gave Guéranger the freedom to pursue his own highly ambitious vision, and within five years of his installation as prior, from near-obsolescence Solesmes had risen not only to abbey status but to the head of the French Benedictine Congregation, second only to the first house of the order, Monte Cassino, established by St Benedict himself.

At the end of the nineteenth century the jumble of old priory buildings was replaced by the massive structure that stands to this day, looming over the Sarthe like the Ministry for Spiritual Rectitude. In the 1950s, when the writer Patrick Leigh Fermor made regular retreats at French monasteries – recounted in his brilliant short travelogue, *A Time to Keep Silence* – Guéranger's fourth successor presided over a flourishing brotherhood of more than a hundred monks. In common with monasteries across Christendom, numbers have dwindled since, but thanks to its status and international reputation for Gregorian chant, Solesmes is still the largest abbey in France, with forty-five monks and a healthy proportion of new vocations.

Now as in the sixth century, for the Benedictines, prayer hangs on the taut line between sound and silence. In the Rule, Benedict warns against idle speech, quoting from Proverbs: 'You will not escape sin if you talk too much.' Loose talk costs souls. Silence promotes humility and discourages the sort of carping that might threaten the cohesiveness of the community. Benedictines are 'cenobitic' monks, as opposed to hermits, meaning that they have chosen to withdraw from society not to live alone but among others of their kind. They need to get along. It's often underestimated how influential medieval religious orders were on the development of European democracy. As Rowan Williams points out, the procedures of the first English parliaments in the thirteenth century were modelled on the Dominican system of representation and decision-making. Rules like Benedict's were designed to keep everyone rubbing along together; keeping quiet was crucial to the common spirit. Beyond that, to be silent is to be closer to God, at whose perfection the spoken word stutters and fails. The great outbreaks of noise that characterise the monastic round, the clamour of bells and the singing of the liturgy, are both acts of praise and delineators of the silence that surrounds them. Attend Mass, and the hush that follows the Alleluia feels like an opening on another dimension.

Another bell sounded for the evening meal. There were six of us on retreat, and in the cloisters by the monks' refectory we lined up to have our hands washed by the prior, Father Geoffroy, a serious-looking young man with oval wire-rimmed glasses and a pronounced browbone, as if fortified for contemplation. (In an abbey, the prior is second in command to the abbot, who would have done the hand-washing had he not been away 'on business'. Accepting the top job means taking a step back into the world. As abbot, Dom Philippe Dupont is not only the head of the monastery but its representative in the wider community.)

From a silver ewer Father Geoffroy poured water over our hands into a stone basin, set into a niche in the cloister wall known as the lavabo. ('Lavabo' is also the name of the hand-washing ritual.) We processed into the refectory, heads bowed and hands crossed in front of us like mourners. The sense that, however hard I tried, I was only play-acting the appropriate seriousness was intensified by the melodrama of the room, divided into two elaborately vaulted naves by five granite columns the girth of ancient trees. The guests sat at a central table, the monks to either side, on tables abutting the heavy Beaux-Arts pilasters that ran the length of the room. Again, the effect was both austere and a little theatrical, a place both for quiet contemplation and, as Patrick Leigh Fermor suggests, a kind of stage set of monastic solemnity, a Romantic quotation of the medieval ideal, with the grey stone and the monumental fireplaces and the figures in black habits bent over their soup bowls.

Meals are taken in silence, or almost. Once Grace was said, a monk ascended to the lectern and began, via a head-mike, to read from what I later learned was the book of the week: a history, in French, of Charles VII, king at the time the English were laying waste to this part of France. It was a little like listening to a podcast, albeit an exceptionally avant-garde one, as the monk was not speaking but singing the text, *recto tono*, that is, on a single repeated note. Less like a podcast, perhaps, than an audible news crawl, running under the acoustic minutiae revealed by silence – the creak of the benches, the scrape of cutlery on plates, as we chewed on buckwheat pancakes filled with an austere but rather delicious mix of fish paste and cabbage.

At Cluny, the great powerhouse of medieval monasticism, so deep was the commitment to silence that the monks developed a complex system of hand signs, later picked up and developed by other silent orders like the Trappists and Carthusians. To sign for honey a monk would lick his fingers. The sign for a layman involved miming a beard – as, of course, in contrast to Orthodox tradition, Western monks were clean-shaven. To indicate anything other than a religious text, a monk would scratch at his ear, the implication being that only a dog would descend to such impiety. No such system exists in contemporary Benedictine practice, so we did our best, pointing at the salt, mouthing *merci*, and resorting to mime only in cases of ambiguity – as when I passed the elderly gentleman opposite the wine, and, shaking his head, he began making a vigorous sawing motion before munching on an imaginary slice of bread. *Du vin* and *du pain*, it turned out, were hard to tell apart when they were being mouthed with Gallic insouciance across a table.

The monks ate quickly, without looking up. And underneath it all, unflagging, the history ticker, this sorry tale of war and greed and Burgundian intrigue, drifting in and out of my understanding, and sung without the slightest inflection in a monotone that forced your attention onto the words, at the expense of the singer, subtracting himself as best he could from the sound he was making.

Benedictine hospitality is written into the statutes. 'All guests who arrive,' says Benedict in the Rule, 'should be received as if they were Christ.' The tradition of welcoming guests – within reason – dates back even to the forbiddingly austere monastics of the Egyptian desert. 'Forgive me, father, for I have made thee break thy rule,' says a visitor to an old hermit in the *Sayings of the Desert Fathers*. 'My rule', replies the hermit, 'is to receive thee with hospitality and send thee away in peace.' With the flourishing of the monasteries in the Middle Ages, welcoming guests became a crucial way of maintaining healthy donor re-lations. Underneath the monks' refectory at Mont St Michel, for example, was the Knights' Hall, set aside for aristocratic drop-ins. At Solesmes, Christians and non-believers alike can stay in the guest house for anything between one and seven days, reading, walking in the enclosure, attending the Holy Offices or seeking spiritual solace, either alone or under the guidance of a monk.

It's a point worth bearing in mind that, by comparison to retreats in other religious traditions, the freedom afforded to the retreatant at a Christian monastery tends to encourage more, not less, of an encounter with the intangible. Attend a Hindu or Buddhist retreat, and, whatever your level of spiritual engagement, the material advantages of yoga or meditation – flexibility, calmness – remain. At a place like Solesmes, there is so little to do other than pray, and sit or walk in contemplation, that it would be odd to show up for any other reason. Silence is available elsewhere. When I visited Mount St Bernard Abbey, the last remaining Trappist monastery in England, a family of six Irish travellers pulled up in their battered white van, 'Three Little Birds' blasting at distortion level from its open windows. They were seeking shelter after a feud with another family had threatened to get out of hand. However pragmatic their reasons for retreat, they were inseparable, you felt, from their need for more immaterial refuge.

At Solesmes, the responsibilities for greeting retreatants fell to the guestmaster, Father Michael Bozell, originally from Connecticut, who entered Solesmes aged twenty-five in 1978.

'Making a retreat at the monastery acts upon people in ways they often don't really understand,' said Father Michael, as we sat in his small office on the ground floor of the guesthouse. With his cowl down, and his comfortable black shoes poking out from the hem of his habit, Father Michael seemed both in and out of the world, something further confirmed by his speech: warm, colloquial, but just that little bit removed, as if for all his presence he were also elsewhere.

'A lot of them come here very tired, very washed out, down. And the experience has a very beneficial effect upon them. Upon the heart, upon the mind, upon even the body. Part of it is the eating well, part of it is the beautiful liturgy, part of it is the comfortable bed. But it's also much more than that.'

There was no doubt in Father Michael's mind that a retreat here, no matter how short, could offer something akin to the full-blown monastic experience: a monk's life in microcosm. 'I would say that 95 per cent of the people who come here want in some way to plug into what it is we're doing.' Some were well versed in the solemnities. 'They know how to follow the Offices, the prayers, they can get right into the liturgy.' Others were drawn for more nebulous reasons. 'People going up and down the highway, they'll see the signs for Solesmes. And they'll say, oh my God, there are still monks? In the twenty-first century? They're actually still there?'

When I spoke to Dr Max Sternberg, an expert in monastic architecture at Cambridge, he told me that 'monasteries are much more about retreat now than they were back then,' – 'back then' being the high point of Western monasticism in the twelfth and early thirteenth centuries. For all the seclusion of the monks, the great abbeys were part of the communal fabric, living examples of the piety expected of everyone. The monasteries' need for money and land, and the willingness of the local aristocracy to donate them in exchange for intercessory prayer, created a culture of exchange symbolised by the narthex, the lobby or entrance area to the abbey church, often made of wood to broadcast the monks' simplicity, and open to lay donors, sometimes including women, if they were rich enough. 'The narthex was basically the space that communicated with the world,' explained Max. It was both in and out, sacred and secular. With the decline in monastic influence, and, since the nineteenth century, of institutional religion per se, monasteries have moved from the centre to the margins of their communities, places of retreat more than exchange, unintegrated, truly apart. As Father Michael described it, for the outsider the function of a place like Solesmes was as an 'eschatological sign' – not so much a reminder of bodily death, a memento mori writ in stone and bell metal, as a living example of the Life overarching this one, the joyous eternity of God's love. What might strike us as archaic or absurd becomes, at closer quarters, a mystery worth looking into.

'A lot of people who've never been to a monastery before, upon leaving they'll say – as if we've never heard this before – you know, I'm going to tell you something. You guys here, *this* is the real world. What's going on out there is not the real world.'

For Father Michael, the gap between that realisation and deciding to enter the monastery proved unexpectedly brief. He came here on retreat after graduating from college. 'Not for one second did I imagine myself becoming a monk.' It was only after the retreat, back home in the US, that he realised the effect it had had on him: a nagging dissatisfaction with life on the outside. What Solesmes offered was clarity, an unimpeded path to God. 'For some religious traditions, silence is an end in itself,' he said. 'Whereas for us it's a means, a preparation for an encounter. You can't pray if there's too much going on outside or inside you.'

Catholic religious orders might be said to represent a sliding scale of withdrawal, from the mendicant orders, like the Dominicans and Franciscans, engaged in evangelism and ministry – that is, out in the world – to the most austere and insular of the enclosed orders, silent in their cells like the Camaldolese. Roughly speaking, the Benedictines fall somewhere to the insular side of the middle, enclosed but (in many cases) outward-facing in their pastoral work and involvement in schools and parishes. That said, there are degrees of insularity within the order, too. Some Benedictine monasteries tend to active ministry, while others, Solesmes included, are closer to the Cistercians in their confinement. The focus here is on contemplation.

For the monks, the day begins at 5.30 a.m. with the Office of Vigils, sung *recto tono* to the words of Psalm 94: 'Understand, ye brutish among the people: and ye fools, when will ye be wise?' Lauds, the service of morning prayer, is at 7.30 a.m., followed by Mass at 10 a.m., 'Sext' and 'None' either side of lunch at 1 and 1.50 p.m., Vespers at 5 p.m. and, at 8.30 p.m., before the Great Silence descends, Compline, the ancient propitiation against the darkness, warding off, like the bells, the evil spirits cackling in the eaves, poised for a moment's weakness. Between the Offices, the monks adhere to the Benedictine motto, '*ora et labora*', pray and work. Far from distracting from prayer, so the Benedictines believe, manual labour enhances it – is itself prayerful – in that it encourages silence, humility and obedience, and by promoting collective effort and a level of self-sufficiency, helps strengthen the bonds of the community. Under the watchful eye of the cellarer – the monastery's quartermaster – a monk might be charged with maintaining the grounds, manning the kitchen, binding books, or mending torn vestments in the tailor's workshop.

Nonetheless, the emphasis is on prayer, both personal and through *lectio divina*, a form of prayerful reading whereby a passage from the scriptures is scrutinised, not as a means of analysing it in any theological or literary sense, but so that the reader might enter into it, dwell within the living Word, participate in the peace of Christ that it embodies. It's an attitude to worship anyone whose exposure to Christianity is limited to christenings and jumble sales would find deeply exotic, the sort of ardent, if not to say amorous appeal to the Divine you would have to turn to the metaphysical poets to understand, still drenched, like Donne, in the intensities of the old faith. Life at Solesmes was only austere from the outside. For the monks, what might strike us as renunciation was only a clearing-away, the removal of an irrelevance or obstacle to a realm of incomparable richness and fulfilment.

The next morning, at Mass, I sat far back in the nave, the oldest part of the abbey church, while the monks took their places in the choir. Behind me, what was once a great stained-glass window had been bricked in to accommodate the organ, so that, in the morning, the nave got progressively brighter, from the gloom near the back to the choir, flooded with light that fell diagonally from the side windows like ghostly buttresses, chiselled in long grooves where the tracery cast its shadow. The monks sat in silence, their shaved heads bowed. At the time of Patrick Leigh Fermor's visit, a distinction still applied between 'lay brothers', otherwise known as 'claustral monks' and often recruited from the lower, agricultural classes, and the 'choir monks', generally more educated and drawn from the bourgeoisie and landed gentry. The choir monks – addressed as 'Father,' not 'Brother' – were also ordained as priests, and thus able to administer sacraments. The lay brothers bore the brunt of the manual labour. After Vatican II – the Second Vatican

Council of 1962–5, which attempted to reform the Catholic church in line with social and technological change – a new spirit of egalitarianism softened the distinction between priests and the unordained. The terms 'claustral' and 'choir' monks fell out of use, and ordination became less a matter of class than the needs of the community. A monk took holy orders if that was what he had been called to do.

At Mass, monk-priests are still aesthetically distinct. Rather than the black habits worn by the Brothers, they wear white, under a chasuble whose colour depends on the liturgical season. (We were in Advent, so the chasubles were purple.) Among the congregation, maybe twenty-strong that morning, were three nuns from the nearby Abbey of Sainte-Cécile, established by Dom Guéranger as a sister foundation to Solesmes; my five fellow retreatants, mostly middle-aged men soberly dressed in flannels and quilted car coats or kagoules; and, from the village, I presumed, a shifty-looking bloke in combat fatigues, jabbing with a blackened finger at his ancient Nokia and reeking so strongly of booze I could have given tasting notes on his last bottle of wine.

Save for the occasional creaking of pews, the silence was of the absolute sort that's really quite loud, the high-pitched whine of the auditory system turned in on itself, hearing itself hearing. And then with a rustle of vestments the monks rose and sang. In the earliest days of public Christian worship, the chanting of the liturgy would have fallen to a single, specialist cleric called the cantor. With the adoption of Christianity as the official religion of the Roman Empire, and the subsequent appearance of ever grander and more voluminous basilicas, a sacred music was developed commensurate to the space it was required to fill. The cantor lost ground to the *schola cantorum*, the choir, singing pieces of an ever greater complexity to match the elaboration and solemnity of the rituals they accompanied. In the eighth and ninth centuries, this Roman corpus of mono-phonic chant – sung in unison, by contrast to polyphony, composed of two or more differing melodic lines – began to merge with the Gallican repertory, originating in Roman Gaul, to form what we now refer to as Gregorian chant.

One of its innovations was the introduction to Christian chant of the melisma, where several notes are sung to one syllable, familiar from earlier traditions like Torah chanting, Indian raga and the muezzin's call to prayer. It's familiar from later ones too: Mariah Carey's nine-second 'all' in the final chorus of 'Vision of Love' is nothing if not melismatic. To borrow from St Augustine, melisma helps the chant 'cut itself free from the shackles of its syllables'. Important as the words are, to hear the monks sing the *Gloria* in long, unravelling ribbons of pure tone is to hear them gesture at a divinity beyond anything that can be articulated verbally, the last cry before the silence it emerged from, and that will follow it.

Singing is, of course, also a handy way of keeping your monks in line. With the shift, in the eighth century, from the cantor to the massed choir, came the practice of singing the Psalms not only during the Holy Offices, but at work in the fields, meaning the abbot could rest assured his monks were not caught up in idle daydreaming – still less chatting among themselves – but focused on God. Whistle while you work: as in Eastern meditative practice, body and mind were subject to the same repetitive discipline to the exclusion of all irrelevance and distraction.

Monasticism in its organised form dates back to third-century Egypt, although there is evidence of eremitic practice in Syria at least a hundred years earlier. (Syrian trade in the first centuries AD would have brought local Christians into contact with Hindu and Buddhist merchants from India and central Asia, with their much older traditions of worldly renunciation. Spiritual retreat may be as old as humanity.) In or around 270, Antony, a young man from Coma in Lower Egypt, gave away the land he had inherited from his prosperous parents and retired to a hut in the Nitrian Desert, west of the Nile Delta. As the historian Diarmaid MacCulloch points out, the geography of Egypt was itself an inducement to ascesis. From Alexandria to Aswan, the country is a narrow fertile strip surrounded by desert. Wherever you lived, the wilderness was at your back door.

'If thou wilt be perfect,' says Jesus in the Gospel of Matthew, 'go and sell that thou hast, and give to the poor, and thou shalt have treasure in heaven: and come and follow me.' What made Antony's withdrawal exceptional was also its undoing. People *did* follow him, the paradoxical problem for all inspirational isolates. Soon aspiring hermits were flocking to worship at his side, driven from civilisation by oppressive Roman taxes and the continuing persecution of Christians under the emperor Diocletian. The conversion to Christianity of Constantine, Diocletian's successor-but-one, gave Christians a new motivation for retreat. The precise extent of their earlier persecution is debated, but now Christianity had become the state religion its adherents needed a new form of martyrdom. To withdraw to the desert was to martyr oneself when excruciating torture at the hands of a Roman soldier was no longer available. St Jerome called it 'white martyrdom': social as opposed to literal death.

Under the former soldier Pachomius the Great, Antony's contemporary and fellow Egyptian, the fashion for solitary monasticism gave way to the 'cenobitic' or communal style: a group of monks living together under a common rule and the authority of an abbot. The earliest Pachomian monasteries were established in the ruins of abandoned villages – abandoned due to the same punitive Roman taxes that had, along with the Diocletian atrocities, driven Antony's followers into the desert. In re-establishing community where it had been destroyed, Pachomius instilled a mixture of discipline and esprit de corps whose peculiarly military flavour we might recognise in cenobitic monasteries to this day.

Either way, solitary or communal, the monks' purpose was the same: to desertify their material selves. In this they showed the influence of the third-century scholar Origen of Alexandria, who stressed the importance of spiritual combat to the Christian way of life. Soldiers of God vs soldiers of the devil: early Christian monasticism was a battlefront of competitive austerity. Syrian and Egyptian monks vied to out-renounce one another. To tamp down his carnal desires, Ammonius, the third great Egyptian ascetic after Antony and Pachomius, is said to have applied a red-hot iron to his genitals. (History fails to record if this had the intended effect or the opposite.) The anchorites of East Syria were renowned for their squalor, prompting St Jerome – who had tried retreating to the Syrian desert as an ascetic, and concluded he wasn't cut out for it – to comment that they were just as concerned with the dirtiness of their bodies as the cleanliness of their hearts. Monks slept for an hour a night lashed to a post or lived in wooden boxes. All family ties were to be severed, as the 'remembrance of kinsfolk' was the devil's work. To be saved, you must become a dead man: die to the world.

In a sense, the lifelong retreat represented by monasticism is incongruous in Christianity. In the case of Buddhism, for instance, it follows that a religion whose central tenet is *anatta*, the non-existence of self, should have taken to a self-abnegating practice like monasticism. Annihilation of the self is the duty of all practising Buddhists. To do it according to the *pratimoksa*, the set of rules governing Buddhist monasticism, is merely a surer means to the same end. This constitutes a fundamental difference with the Abrahamic religions. Both Judaism and Islam take a dim view of celibacy, and while there are ascetic and mystical traditions on the margins of both faiths, they fall a long way short of institutionalised monasticism, which is forbidden in Islam. Excessive self-denial is un-Islamic. 'Moderation, moderation!' goes a hadith spoken by the Prophet. 'Through this will you attain your goal.'

For all that Christ preached self-sacrifice – 'go and sell that thou hast' – the goal was never the dissolution of self. Far from it: the incarnation privileges the flesh, the bodily integrity of the individual, whose selfhood in a Christian context is something foundational and God-given. There are no mentions of monasticism in either the Old or the New Testaments. It's perhaps helpful, therefore, to conceive of Christian monasticism as a form of revolt, a reaction, as MacCulloch suggests, to the religion going mainstream. When Christianity was still an obscure Judaic cult, subject to regular bouts of persecution, it was easier for its followers to number themselves among the elect, a small group granted special knowledge of Christ's death and resurrection.

As the religion spread, in the Apostolic Age and afterwards, an appetite for spiritual athleticism developed as a means of distinguishing the ascetic from the pious masses. To renounce all possessions and sensory pleasures, to kick away the crutches of conviviality and connubial love, was to argue for oneself as a Christian apart, superhuman in self-sacrifice. In pre-Christian Rome, the gods were open-access, available to anyone versed in the rituals. Invoke Ceres and she was there. Where Christianity began to depart from this was in privatising the supernatural, arrogating access to the divine to a rarefied class of intercessionary figures, holy men who had proved their closeness to God by relinquishing almost everything that made them mortal.

In this light, monastic silence takes on the character of a radical act, a refusal to engage in the everyday discourse of the Episcopal Church authorities. To choose not to speak is to assert your independence. Abba Agathon, who was at Scetis with Macarius, was said to have kept a stone in his mouth for three years, until he had acquired the skill of keeping his counsel. Silence may be a medium, the oil in the microscope slide of prayer, but it is also a retreat, an unanswering and unanswerable riposte to worldly authority.

'I like desert silence better than any other sort,' said Sara, lighting a cigarette. 'Because it is very, INTENSELY silent.'

Sara and I sat on the pebbles as little Zoë skittered ahead on her sharp claws, and, like a spiritual goal, disappeared at intervals, where the beach dipped or a boulder proved too ir-resistible a surface not to pee on. I had come to south-western Scotland to talk to Sara Maitland – writer, Catholic convert and recluse – about her decision, aged forty-seven, to break with family and friends and move to an isolated shepherd's cottage on the Galloway–Ayrshire borders. Rather as Sister Nectaria had found the isolation of a car-free island in the Aegean insufficient, so Sara sometimes yearned for a depth of silence greater than she could find even on her remote Scottish moor. She had recently returned from her second forty-day silent retreat in the Sinai desert, site of St Catherine's Monastery, one of the world's earliest Christian monasteries, and the oldest to be continually inhabited. Sartorially she looked the part: wild salt-and-pepper hair, pre-modern teeth, nails left to curl over her fingertips like talons.

'The Desert Fathers were very particular about sound,' said Sara. 'Are you familiar with the distinction between geophonic, biophonic and anthrophonic sound?'

Geophonic sound, Sara went on to explain, is sound made by natural forces – wind, thunder, running water. Biophonic sound is made by animals, anthrophonic by humans. Sensitivity to the three types varies from person to person, but generally speaking it is anthrophonic sound – speech, snoring, drum and bass leaking from somebody's earphones – that drives us up the wall. Before moving to Galloway, Sara spent forty days alone in a remote cottage on Skye, built beside a burn whose succession of thunderous waterfalls ('like distant aeroplane engines') failed to disturb her silence one bit. Geophonic sound seemed com-patible with, or absorbable into, silence in a way its man-made counterpart rarely was. Not so for the earliest ascetics, however. As recounted in the *Sayings of the Desert Fathers*, the commit-ment to silence of the great fifth-century hermit Arsenius, for example, brooked no interruption, anthrophonic or otherwise.

'It's quite funny.' Sara laughed. 'Arsenius goes to visit these monks, and they're living beside some very noisy reedbeds. Or at least *he* thinks they're noisy. And he says,' – here, to evoke

Arsenius's indignation, Sara cranked up the volume a notch or three further – 'HOW CAN YOU POSSIBLY HAVE A GREAT SILENCE IF YOU'RE SITTING BY THESE REEDBEDS ALL THE TIME?!'

Sara didn't trust herself on the pebbles, so I left her to finish her cigarette as I pushed on up the beach, following Zoë to the cliff face at its north-western corner. 'Ninian's Cave' was said to be the personal retreat of a fifth-century missionary who had built a stone church four miles from here at Whithorn. Bede referred to Ninian's church as the 'Candida Casa' – the 'shining white house,' and the toponymic root of 'Whithorn' – as it stood out so dramatically amid the Pictish gloom. 'Whatever you think you know about Christianity being founded in Scotland by Columba is very simply WRONG!' Sara had told me. The Candida Casa predated St Columba's abbey on Iona by at least a hundred and fifty years. It was the birthplace of Scottish Christianity, the cave its founder's hermitage, a place, as he is said to have referred to it, 'of terrible blackness' where he could find himself closer to God.

I stepped inside. The cave was a dripping, narrow cleft, twenty feet deep by ten wide, its walls glistening with moisture and covered in votive crosses deftly carved into the rock. As the first Christian mission north of Hadrian's wall, and later, a seminary for the apostles who took monasticism to Ireland, in the Middle Ages the Candida Casa became a major destination for pilgrims, many of whom would have stopped to pray where I was standing now. The crosses were theirs, along, it had to be said, with a millennium's worth of less high-minded graffiti, 'Ælfweard was here' and so on.

I stepped back into the open. Just above the horizon, roughly where I reckoned Ireland ought to be, the January sun had diffused into a smear of blinding light, transmuting the stony beach into gold. Zoë was nosing at something dead and feathery at the foot of the cliff face. Sara was where I had left her, at the far end of the beach, staring out to sea. For a moment I stood and listened to the waves bid the shoreline be quiet.

Breathe: the *relief* of it. Much as I loved living where we did, I often longed for such calm, for the unceasing din of traffic outside our house to be stilled, if only temporarily. From somewhere inland, a bird, a sandpiper or something, made its high-pitched cry, registering, it was true, less as sound than as part of the silence.

Even without her radical commitment to solitude, Sara's résumé would be impressive. Her first novel, *Daughter of Jerusalem*, won the Somerset Maugham Award for the best novel by an author under thirty. Since then she has published twenty-five volumes of religious fantasy, short stories and (mostly theological) non-fiction, all as fiercely intelligent as she is in person. She was born in 1950, into a large, 'dead posh' military family with Scottish roots. The second child of six, Sara, along with her siblings, was 'blatantly encouraged' by her loving, 'deeply sociable' parents 'to be highly articulate, contentious, witty, and to hold all authority except theirs in a certain degree of contempt'. In a sense, Sara's trajectory over the intervening sixty-nine years had been a gradual emancipation from sound. At Oxford, she moved in Anglo-Catholic circles, in the days before Anglo-Catholicism became a byword for the misogyny and reactionary politics Sara has spent her writing life resisting. In her early forties, she converted to Roman Catholicism, but waited until the second of her two children had left home before fully embracing the contemplative life she had longed for. In 1990, her marriage at an end, she moved to an isolated cottage above Weardale in County Durham. At Solesmes, I had been struck by how the monastic austerities amounted, for Father Michael and others, to the systematic removal of impediments to prayer. Similarly, for Sara, to seek silence was to aspire to direct confrontation.

'Silence is the place, the focus, of the radical encounter with the divine,' as she puts it in *A Book of Silence*, her 2008 memoir-cum-intellectual history. 'The desire to break the silence with constant human noise is, I believe, precisely an avoidance of the sacred terror of that divine encounter.'

We make noise for fear of not living up to what silence might reveal in us. It was only ironic that, for a writer whose goal and great subject was silence, Sara had such problems with volume control. 'Everyone else can FUCK OFF!' she said, when I asked her how the local Catholic community viewed her life of seclusion. We were back at the house now, and if Sara was raising her voice again, it was, in fairness, partly to be heard above the spit and sizzle of our supper frying. Outside a moonless night pressed like lagging against the windows. Sara's cottage occupied an elevated position on moorland about four miles from the nearest village, but sitting at her kitchen table it felt, in the absence of neighbouring lights, like we might as well be stranded in some barren wadi, a capsule of light and warmth in a terrible blackness. With a yawn, Zoë rose from the sofa and padded over to sniff at a wastepaper basket overflowing with empty cigarette and crisp packets.

'Of course,' said Sara, 'there's a rhythm to the contemplative life.' Sara reserved particular admiration for Tenzin Palmo, the English-born Tibetan Buddhist nun famous for spending twelve years in silent, solitary retreat, in a Himalayan cave 13,200 feet above sea level. 'Tenzin Palmo believes that when you're being silent, you are absolutely silent, and when, for instance, you're in Italy teaching elderly nuns how to contemplate, then you engage with that.'

'You engage with what's engaging you at the moment.'

'Precisely. And that's the thing about Tenzin Palmo. She will NOT MAKE hard lines. I have difficulty with people who make hard lines and then don't seem to keep them. And, of course, the reason that it upsets me is that it describes me PERFECTLY!'

Sara's laugh – and she laughed a lot – sounded like something cold being dropped in hot oil. I wondered, in the light of what she'd said about Tenzin Palmo, if Sara's tendency to loud speech was as ironic as it seemed. It wasn't simply that, after twenty-two years of living on a peat moor with no-one but a dog for company, she was prone to sudden crescendos she might not in normal circumstances have vocalised. It was more that the urge to shout, to make herself heard, as you might well do growing up with five highly educated, self-confident siblings, was the flipside of her urge to solitude and silence, its equal in intense engagement. Silence was the way you made yourself heard to God. If she couldn't sit quietly, she would bloody well thump the table and bark obscenities. If silence *was* available – in the desert, or here, when it wasn't being broken by visitors like me – she would pursue it with a conviction commensurate to her desire for union with the divine.

At its heart, Sara's view of eremitic silence was as close to the Buddhist ideal as Christian observance can get. As in the early Eastern Church, 'apophatic' prayer seeks to address God by negation, reaching at knowledge of Him by affirming all it can affirm – that is, what He is not. It is wordless, devoid of thought or image, and for the practitioner involves a gradual emptying, or 'kenosis': not the dissolution of the ego but the softening of its boundaries, as the soul feels its way towards eternity. It is the meaning of silence, the good stuff, the goal of throwing off all worldly concerns and embracing the emptiness of the desert.

Sara had turned from the hob and planted her wooden spoon on the sideboard.

'When it is going well,' she said, 'I REALLY ENJOY PRAYING!' A gust of wind rattled the windows against their frames. 'Who'd want to do anything else? Knocks sex into a cocked hat.'

It was the joy, the *jouissance* – that ecstatic bubbling-over of the pan of mere pleasure – offered by silent prayer that lay behind Sara's objection to the term 'retreat', at least as used to describe a permanent commitment like hers. 'I don't think it's retreating. I think it's advancing.'

'Aren't you retreating from noise, though?' I asked. 'From vulgarity? Distraction?'

'But you're NOT retreating, are you? You're advancing to a better space.'

For the first time I felt an edge of reprimand in Sara's voice. She was in no two minds about this. 'I think retreat is a perfectly proper word to describe people who have a different vocation – they're a doctor, a teacher, a candlestick maker, and they give that up for a few days to look at some other aspect of their lives. When they really are retreating from something, in order to create space for something else.'

For a monk, or a nun, or an independent contemplative like Sara, it was the other way round. To re-enter secular life, the world of noise and stress and frenzied stimulation, would represent the stepping-back, the giving of ground, the knuckling under. 'Probably it's from growing up in too military a family,' she said. 'But retreat does for me equal defeat.'

The Battle of Chosin Reservoir was one of the most gruelling of the twentieth century, let alone of the Korean War. Thirty thousand UN troops were stationed at Chosin, a man-made lake supplying the north-east of the Korean peninsula with hydroelectric power. In November 1950, Mao Zedong ordered 120,000 troops of the Chinese People's Volunteer Army to encircle the reservoir and crush the UN forces. But the PVA fell short in one crucial regard. They failed to close the circle, allowing UN troops under Major General Oliver P. Smith to retreat along the icy mountain defiles that led to the port city of Hungnam, seventy miles to the south, where they could be evacuated below the 38th parallel.

Casualties were horrendous, and not only because of the relentless onslaught by PVA forces. Temperatures that regularly dropped below minus thirty degrees jammed weapons and froze vital blood-plasma supplies into solid blocks. For want of foxholes – the ground was too hard to dig them – soldiers used their comrades' frozen corpses as sandbags. Over the course of the sixteen-day retreat, an estimated 18,000 of 30,000 American and allied soldiers lost their lives, were wounded, or went missing in action. After their evacuation from Hungnam, UN forces would never set foot in North Korea again. Meanwhile, of course, the North had begun the cultural and economic retreat that would make it the most isolated and unknowable country in the world.

That the retreat from Chosin is considered as a tactical withdrawal, rather than a defeat, is down to a simple fact. The Chinese casualties were worse. Of its 150,000 troops, the PVA 9th Army was estimated to have lost just under a third, nearly 20,000 of them due to the freezing conditions and broken supply routes. Two of the eight elite PVA divisions were so diminished they were forced to disband. The UN forces had lost North Korea, but the losses the PVA suffered helped to protect the South from invasion.

'Retreat, hell!' said Smith, as the 5th and 7th Marines pulled back along the road south from the reservoir. 'We're not re-treating, we're just advancing in a different direction.'

For every humiliating military retreat – Napoleon's from Moscow, Robert E. Lee's after Gettysburg – there is a tactical one, a marshalling of resources, or canny luring of the enemy, in the interests of eventual victory. The ancient Iranian people known as the Parthians were renowned for their feigned re-treats, drawing the enemy into pursuit before twisting in the saddle – no mean feat, in the days before the stirrup was in-vented – and riddling them with arrows. Hence the 'Parthian shot' – the parting zinger that we wish we'd thought of in time.

'Retreat' in the sense of military withdrawal probably dates to the late fourteenth century. The earliest recorded reference to 'beating a retreat', that is, the formalised withdrawal, to a drumbeat, of troops from the field at nightfall, is in an order issued in 1690, by an officer in the army of the deposed James II. 'The generalle to be beate att 3 clock in ye morning ... Ye retreate to beate att 9 att night.' (The 'generalle' was what we now might refer to as 'reveille', the morning call to arms.) The ceremony is still observed. In US army installations, 'retreat' marks the end of the duty day, heralded by a bugle call, the firing of a cannon, and the playing of 'To the Colours' as the flag is lowered. Clearly, no sense of defeat is implied in these rituals of retreat. Rather, they proceed from the quaint under-standing, upheld in the early days of organised warfare, that both sides needed a good night's rest before bayonetting each other's guts out in the morning.

The French have a useful term: *'reculer pour mieux sauter'*, 'to back off in order to jump better', which we might more idiomatically translate as 'stepping back to move forward', albeit at the loss of that sense of potential energy, of elasticity, the string pulled back against the bow.

The use of 'retreat' to denote a period spent in spiritual self-examination or discernment dates from the mid-eighteenth century, but the idea goes back two centuries further, to the *Spiritual Exercises* of St Ignatius Loyola, co-founder of the Jesuits, whose own spiritual awakening sprang from military misadventure: he heard the call to the religious life while con-valescing from a cannonball injury sustained at the Battle of Pamplona in 1521. The *Exercises*, composed over several years, are a series of prayers and meditations, traditionally observed over a continuous thirty days of silence and solitude. Gradually, via this process of bringing himself into intimate relationship with the Divine, the Jesuit acquires 'discernment', the ability to distinguish his true feelings as they pertain to God.

You stepped back from life to return better equipped for it. By founding an order whose followers begged and evangelised in public, St Francis of Assisi inverted the model of Western monastic retreat. Nonetheless, throughout his life, Francis with-drew from mission work to spend periods of contemplative prayer in the caves of the Eremo delle Carceri, high in the mountains above Assisi.

You might argue, *pace* Sara Maitland, that this sense of retreat as a drawn bow with renewal in its sights is related to a radical contrariness at the heart of Christianity. 'If slander has become the same to you as praise, poverty as riches, deprivation as abundance,' promises the Desert Father Macarius the Great, 'you will not die.' 'Love your enemy,' commands Jesus in the Gospel of Matthew. 'Bless them that curse you.' Jesus ups the ante in Luke: 'If any man ... *hate* not his father, and mother, and wife, and children, and brethren, and sisters, yea, and his own life also, he cannot be my disciple.' In Buddhism, when a layperson steps back from the world to join a community of *bhikkhus*, or monks, the rite is known as *pabbajjā* – 'going forth'. In this light, retreat *is* advance, as it was for Jesus himself in his forty days' fast in the wilderness, for Muhammad in the cave of al-Hira, where the archangel Gabriel revealed the Qu'ran to him, for Gautama Buddha, meditating under the Bodhi tree for forty-nine days. Retreat was advance for the Desert Fathers as much as for St Benedict, holed up in his cave for three years, mistaken, so St Gregory tell us, for 'some beast' by the shepherds that found him, before he emerged to found his monasteries and write the Rule that its inheritors live by to this day.

I was all for renunciation, but the situation with the towels was beyond a joke. The shower was across the corridor from my room, and lacking a bath towel, I had to tiptoe back, with dew-spangled collarbones, wearing a hand towel whose top corners barely met at my hip, leaving one or other buttock exposed. Not a good look in a monastery. In *A Time to Keep Silence*, Patrick Leigh Fermor recalls how hard it was adjusting to the routine at St Wandrille, a fellow member of the Solesmes Congregation further to the north near Le Havre. Partly it was the lack of alcohol. (Not a problem at Solesmes: a good, sturdy red was served in label-less bottles at lunch and dinner, and, I confess, there were a few times during my stay that I popped over to the bar across the road from the abbey.) Mainly, though, it was the dishabituation, the entry into a world of light, sound and mood 'not only unlike' the world outside the abbey, as he described it, but seemingly 'its exact reverse'.

I could see what he meant. For all the warmth of the welcome I'd received from Father Michael and the others I found Solesmes not a little bleak. I had said as much in a WhatsApp message home on my first evening. ('Go with it,' replied my wife, wisely. 'Absorb it.') Compared to Ibiza and Esalen, a retreat here was a step up in self-reliance. Without the distractions of company, or the structure lent by exercise and meditation, I was thrown back on the empty space I suppose my faith would have occupied. In the absence of God, the silence was frightening. We make noise for fear of what silence might reveal in us. Hence the fussing over the towels, my seeming inability, outside of the Holy Offices, to sit still for more than a minute, the general headachy sort of sense that I had been copied then pasted a little to one side of myself.

In Patrick Leigh Fermor's case, the answer was sleep. For the first couple of days, he would spend more time in bed than awake, as if retreating to the abbey had involved crossing a time zone, a form of spiritual jetlag. In mine, the beers at the bar across the street were some solace. La Solesmienne was one of those unimprovable *bars-tabac* that could almost have been state run: half-shop (local papers, *Paris Match*, tinned asparagus), half-bar, with vaguely eighties décor and fluorescent lighting so stark and impoverishing of skin tone that we drinkers could easily have been mistaken for the dead. If so, we were in a kind of paradise, a sanctum of French civility of the kind long absent (if ever present) in public life back home. Whenever a local came in they would stop, notice me sitting in the corner with my *demi* of Kronenbourg and packet of peanuts bought from the shop part, and either greet me with a nod and a '*bonsoir, m'sieur*' or actively acknowledge, and absolve me of, my outsider status by coming over and shaking my hand. It was a retreat from my retreat: a retreat back into life. And so I would sit there and wait for the beer to do what Dr Chris Streeter had promised it would: inhibit my neuronal excitability, calm me down, allow me the meditative ill discipline of an uninterrupted mind wander.

My friend Phil was a bit like this with alcohol. At university, while the rest of us drank to get high, to wind ourselves up, there was a definite sense of Phil using booze as a sedative. His default mode was so sharp, so intense, that I guess he needed something to soften the edges. You could tell this by the way he smoked – he would pull on a roll-up as if there was another roll-up beyond it, a platonically ideal uber-cigarette whose nourishment he could never quite attain. He was after the hit, the hard stuff. If I thought of him as my closest friend, it was perhaps because I had the sense it couldn't last, that he would be off one day, that if you were going to enjoy Phil's company you had better get on with it, while it was still available.

So when Phil emailed to say that he had undergone *pabbajjā* at a Buddhist monastery in Rangoon I wasn't exactly surprised. Saddened, certainly, and envious if not of the hardships of the life he had chosen, but of his escape from indeterminacy, from the dole queue of overeducated aimlessness. But not surprised. Judging by Phil's emails, 'going forth' into the life of a Theravadan renunciate was a respite so complete as to be life-saving. Having passed the psychological screener – as, years later, I would find out for myself, Buddhist and Christian monasteries alike attracted their fair share of lunatics, drawn to the life as if to some psycho-spiritual Foreign Legion – he began the long years of study and meditation a Buddhist *sāmanera*, or novice monk, must undergo before being considered for full ordination as a *bhikkhu*.

And then the emails stopped coming. I could only assume he had made up his mind, entered the process that began with the novitiate and would progress, over the next two or three years, to *upasampadā*, the higher ordination that would bind him to the community for life. As it turned out my assumption was wrong. A couple of years later Phil returned to the UK, retrained as a teacher and started a family. It was left perhaps deliberately unclear whether his time in Rangoon had answered a specific need, had done the job, or whether he simply wasn't ready for a life of retreat and renunciation. 'As a youth I had been woefully at fault,' Saint Augustine tells God in his

Confessions. 'I had prayed to you for chastity and said, "Give me chastity and continence. But not yet."'

After my first few days flitting between Solesmes and La Solesmienne I began to adjust to the rhythms of life at the abbey. After None, the short Office that followed lunch, coffee was served in a room adjoining the refectory, giving us retreatants the rare chance for a chat. Otherwise, our interactions had been restricted to gestures at dinnertime and the odd, amiable nod as we passed on the gravel paths. Clément Boisseau had done a week's retreat at Solesmes every year for the past forty-seven years. In part he came for the Gregorian chant, but it was the structure of Benedict's Rule that he found the most fulfilling.

'Observer la Règle', he said, 'me permet de vivre ma vie Chrétienne plus fort.'

Observing the Rule let him live his Christian life more fully. With a gracious half-bow Clément made his excuses. In the fourth and fifth centuries, those pilgrims the Desert Fathers deemed sufficiently pious were known as 'visitors from Jerusalem'. The merely curious, on the other hand – the rubber-neckers, the spiritual tourists – were known as 'visitors from Babylon', and would generally be given a bowl of soup and sent on their way. Clément was a visitor from Jerusalem. And I began to wonder if the difference between him and visitors from Babylon came down to their respective perception of time. Prolonged periods of silence and inactivity – or at least what a Babylonian like me might identify as inactive – are well known to disrupt our sense of time passing, something that is of course structural to the religious experience. If, as Sara Maitland observes, you believe in an eternal God, then the less attached you are to the temporal order, the closer you feel to Him, the more permeated you are by His timelessness.

There is, of course, another dimension to cenobitic monasticism: the structure imposed on silence by the practicalities of communal living. It was the way Clément liked it. Mass was at ten and not a minute later. But there was a sense in which the bells that summoned us to prayer further diminished our awareness of time passing. I, for one, began to rely on them – or the percussive click-ding, click-dong you heard in the rooms, which sounded as if operated by some underground monk at a vast Bakelite switchboard – to the extent that in the intervals between the Offices, particularly the yawning, post-prandial, three-hour gap between None and Vespers, I hardly if ever thought to check the time.

The disorientation this caused – the Dalí-clock sensation of time melting into inexistence – was at once the least fun thing about my stay at Solesmes, and, the more I got used to it, the source of its greatest satisfaction. On my fourth day, having asked Father Michael for a job to pass the time, I was given a rake and an enormous medieval-looking wooden cart and invited to clear up the leaves that had settled on the paths and flowerbeds in drifts of bright yellow and brown. After what may or may not have been an hour Father Antoine, a monk well into his eighties I had met briefly on my first day, stopped on his way to the guesthouse, surveyed the pile of leaves I had yet to load into the cart, and said, in heavily accented English, 'It's a reminder of the real.'

'Yes,' I said, and then, cheerily: '*Ora et labora!*'

A silence. Then: 'Excusez-moi?'

Maybe it was my Latin. '*Ora et labora*,' I repeated.

Father Antoine looked puzzled. 'Oui?'

I had a sudden, bowel-freezing apprehension of what I had done – quoted St Benedict at a Benedictine monk, and in the hail-fellow manner of a Sunday gardener leaning on his neighbour's fence.

'Ce n'est pas important,' I said. 'Bonne après-midi.'

'Oui, oui,' said Father Antoine, raising a stiff hand as he turned to leave. 'Amusez-vous bien.'

Yeah, you enjoy yourself. Owned by a monk! And although my embarrassment took a while to wear off, the *labora* actually did seem to be doing the trick, as I transferred great musty-smelling armfuls of leaves to my corpse-bearer's cart, and the river rushed past silently, under a sky whose deepening gloom was my only indication of how long I had left until Vespers.

'That one looks perfectly revolting,' said Sara, relieving me of my empty wine glass. 'Let me get you a nice one.'

The nice one, it turned out, was still semi-opaque but at least lacked the sense that something had been growing in it. Sarah ladled the chicken risotto she had been making onto my plate. I tried a forkful: very nice. We had been discussing whether or not she would ever have considered taking vows.

'If you don't mind me asking,' I said. 'If so much of your life is devoted to silence and prayer, why not go the whole hog and become a nun?'

'Luckily the new bishop [of Galloway, Sara's diocese] doesn't want me to,' she said. The old bishop did, but it was never quite clear how to proceed. 'The only form of vows I could possibly take at the moment would be to be a consecrated virgin.' According to Catholic doctrine, consecrated virgins are spouses of Christ, either living in a monastic community or out in the world under the supervision of a bishop. Regardless, as Sara pointed out, the stress was on virgin. 'And I'm not one. So the bishop said, "Oh, it doesn't mean it *literally*."'

'You can have children and qualify.'

'Yes,' said Sara. 'As long as the "virginity" applies from here on in.'

Church doctrine is nothing if not the creative interpretation of the rules. Still, it was hard to imagine any form of team membership, however nominal or decentralised, that Sara would put up with. Even the growing fashion for 'submitting your rule of life to the care of the bishop', a kind of vocational devo-max with few diocesan responsibilities, struck her as 'bloody pretentious'. Sometimes I wondered if Sara's nonconformity owed as much to her patrician upbringing as to her longing for mystical union with God, or, indeed, if the two considerations were usefully separable; either way, it amounted to a kind of spiritual libertarianism that both fed off and necessitated her solitude. No one was going to tell her how to live, or pray, or wash wine glasses. Even her appearance, the black teeth and the dirty, shapeless grey jumper, seemed to proceed less from an ascetic disdain for the body than from a single-minded refusal to be bossed about. I knew this because Sara was also a bit vain.

'I showed a friend a photograph of me at a wedding,' she told me, putting down her fork and lighting another cigarette. 'And he said, "I always forget this, Sara. You could always scrub up." A bit of me wanted to say fuck off. And another bit of me thought, I really don't want to be arsed. I mean, he's quite right, I'm nothing like as glamorous as I was thirty years ago, and I don't want to be. It's not a renunciation.' Maintaining your looks was 'hard work, you know. And it gets harder as you get older.'

The same went for her other vocation. 'Nobody fucking tells me what to write,' she said. 'And that includes God.'

'In that case,' I said, 'isn't writing a rival activity to prayer?'

'No,' said Sara. 'Or sometimes it is. But sometimes being alive is. Look, to be a living human being is to be endlessly separated from God, and to be trying to close that separation. I don't see that writing decent short stories separates me more from God than walking up a mountain, or, for that matter, bitching with my friends.'

Another eruption of crackly laughter. Ultimately, for Sara, writing and prayer were not opposed but in parallel, complementary even. 'Writing is a terrific ego activity,' she said. 'Prayer is a de-ego-ing.' Both entailed a letting go that was, in some senses, anything but. 'When I decided I was going to be a writer,' said Sara, 'I made some choices about income. I think it's realistic to say I could be earning more than I'm now earning. But I never thought for one second that it was a renunciation.'

The same went for her life of solitude and silence. 'Think of the sacrifices an athlete makes,' she said. 'They can't eat what they want, they can't drink what they want, they can't socialise how they want. They live a life that is totally renunciatory. How many of them want to give it up? Bloody few. Because they're going to get a reward, by winning a bronze medal in an Olympic Games four years in the future, which is more important to them.' Absenting yourself from society was no different, a reward in the guise of renunciation, a relinquishment of assets less valuable than the gains. I took a sip of wine and pushed back in my chair.

'Are you absolutely sure about this, Sara? That beyond material possessions there isn't a genuine renunciation, a loss we might measure in absolute terms, in giving up friends, family, physical intimacy?'

'Okay,' said Sara. 'I was stuck in a not very happy marriage for a very long time.' Then, so loud it distorted on the recording when I played it back later: 'I DON'T THINK I'VE RENOUNCED ANYTHING!' The 'anything' drawn out, contemptuous, close to triumphal. 'I really, really do see no renunciation in choosing a life of silence and prayer if it suits me a fucking sight better than what had gone before.'

In the Rule, St Benedict makes clear what sort of monk should occupy the role of guestmaster: 'a brother whose heart is filled with the fear of God'. As Patrick Leigh Fermor reminds us, it takes a particular firmness of religious purpose to come into daily contact with the outside world and remain immune to it. Like Sara Maitland, Father Michael came from a large, happy family he spoke of with great affection. What was it that led him to leave them behind?

'I don't know,' he said. All he did know was that he had 'found a new family here', a fractious one, sometimes, but a family nonetheless. In his biological family, Father Michael had been one of ten siblings. There had been an eleventh, Father

Michael's twin, who had died in the womb. I wondered if there was something in large families, like Sara's and Father Michael's, that cultivated an urge to be heard that no material presence could quite satisfy. In Father Michael's case, there was the additional factor of his double, his almost-self, being absent from the very beginning. It was like being born with one foot in eternity.

In *A Time to Keep Silence*, Patrick Leigh Fermor is impatient with any secular accusations of selfishness or escapism aimed at the monastic life. The Benedictines he meets at St Wandrille and Solesmes have withdrawn from the world in order to redeem it: 'they alone have confronted the terrifying problem of eternity, abandoning everything to help their fellow-men to meet it.' The first duty of the solitary, Sara had told me, was 'intercession', praying on behalf of others.

Likewise, Father Michael conceived of his vocation not as a stepping away from the world but as an intervention on its behalf, an occupation of higher ground, the better to take in the view. A monk's purpose – his *ponos*, in the words of the Desert Fathers, his work – is to seek sanctity, 'to emerge', as Father Michael put it, 'as the being that God sees him capable of becoming. And to the extent to which each one of us here, or in any monastery, does that, he's pulling up the world with him. He's not alone at all. He's a member of the human race who is doing this. He's bringing society up with him.'

Again, the monk leaves the world to be in it more intensely. 'My sister said something to me once,' he told me. 'She said, "Michael, you're away from the family, you've left us. But in a sense you're at its heart."'

As with Sara, the dividend of inwardness was joy. 'You don't see it when we're in the choir. You think, oh gosh, how austere can you get? But the fact of the matter is that there's an underlying joy that springs up when you have these moments of détente or getting together. It's a sort of explosion of joy. And the more rigid the life is, the more you have that.'

It was a controlling paradox of monasticism: the joy depends on what we might judge to be its absence. 'There's a particular type of Carmelite nun, very, very austere,' Father Michael continued. 'And there's nothing so joyous and incredibly beautiful as their moments of being together. It's a wonder to behold.'

That evening, at Compline, I watched from the stalls as the monks sang the hymn. *Precamur, sancte Domine, hac nocte nos custodias.* Oh holy Lord, we pray to thee, throughout the night our guardian be. Father Michael was right. You don't see it when they're in the choir. And it felt like the species of grief, or betrayal, that I would feel in other holy places, with other monks and ascetics I would get to know a little, and like: at their inaccessibility, for all Father Michael's talk of society and compassion. The half of them that had retreated out of reach. Then the monks filed out and the Great Silence descended.

4.

The Myrrh-Gusher of Mount Athos

No one had said a word since Karyes and I, for one, was beginning to find it oppressive. Every so often we'd hit a really deep pothole and be prostrated, arms outstretched, as if in veneration of the person beside us. On the track above Stavronikita there was a thump as the minibus tipped and a thickset man rammed his large, hairless head into my upper arm. Then the bus would right itself, my neighbour would detach, without so much as a mumbled apology, and we'd rattle on, in silence, until we hit another pothole and the bald guy would headbutt my shoulder again.

We were on our way to Great Lavra, oldest of the twenty surviving monasteries on Mount Athos, spiritual heart of the Eastern Orthodox Church. From the snatches of conversation I'd overhead as we boarded at Karyes, the unofficial capital of the peninsula, I guessed my dozen fellow passengers were Bulgarian – although that may, I had to admit, have been down to certain stereotypes of bull-necked muscularity imparted by the TV sports of my childhood. These guys were so massive I found myself worrying about the minibus's payload capacity. In the row of seats behind me a portly, young-ish priest in black robes and *skufia* sat tearing fistfuls of white bread from a paper bag, absent-mindedly chewing before swallowing each oversized mouthful with a grimace. To our left, a sheer drop gave onto a view of the glittering Aegean the absence of a crash barrier made it hard to enjoy.

Without warning, the minibus pulled into a layby cut into the mountainside to our right. The driver got out and slid the door open with such force that my first thought was that something had gone badly wrong, that in the silence I had somehow blasphemed by omission. Wordlessly, we processed down the track, the priest brushing breadcrumbs off his cassock. Through a gap in the trees, a small stone shrine stood where a spring ran off the mountainside and emerged via a mossy conduit into a narrow green pool. Beside the pool was a pile of empty plastic water bottles.

'For you.' Another of the Bulgarians – brawnier, if anything, than the bald guy, with a military crop and a Fila track jacket zipped to the neck – was offering me a crumpled bottle. I filled it and drank. The water was cold and tasted deliciously of nothing. 'Holy water,' said the man in the track jacket. A monk called Athanasios had met a woman here, he explained. 'And she told him, hit this rock with your staff.' He gestured at the conduit with his trainer. 'So he did. And the water came. It was Jesus' mother.'

'The woman who appeared to him.'

'Yes.' The man quickly crossed himself then held out his hand. 'Pleased to meet you.'

I shook his hand – or tried to. It was one of those hands so stuffed with muscle that you couldn't actually get your own hand around it. 'Nice to meet you too. Where are you from?'

'Romania.'

'I thought as much. I'm Nat.'

'Nat.' I had not yet been able to retrieve my hand. 'Michael Caine.'

'Michael Caine?'

'Yes, Michael Caine.'

'Like the actor.'

'Yes!' The man had brightened. 'Mihai Baston! "Baston" means cane!'

'As in a walking-stick cane?'

'Yes! So I am Michael Cane! Like the actor!'

'Your name. Is Michael Caine.'

'Yes! Ha ha! My name is Michael Caine!'

Back in the minibus the mood had dramatically improved. The priest had opened a large can of lager and was offering round his bag of bread. They were prison guards, Michael Caine and his friends, from a medium-security penitentiary in Timişoara, near the border with Serbia. The priest, Ştefan, was their prison chaplain. According to the 2011 census, more than 85 per cent of Romanians belong to the Orthodox Church. It had become the custom for this group of colleagues to visit Athos at least once a year. (Ştefan had been twice.) From the surly vibe pre-shrine, the pilgrimage had taken on something of the testosteronal jollity of a stag weekend. Christ knew what went on back home in Timişoara, what duties these indomitable bodies had been built to discharge. Here, however, cleansed by the Virginal spring, I was one of the lads, a communicant at Ştefan's informal eucharist of bread and Alfa lager, welcomed into the group with a warmth only fractionally undermined by their bemusement at what on earth an Englishman was doing here.

'You are brave,' said Michael Caine.

'Am I?' I said. 'Why?'

If he actually answered my question, it was in Romanian, and directed at his friends, but in the laughter that followed I discerned – or hoped I discerned – a mildly xenophobic spirit of blokeish banter more than the murderous scorn of a busload of hypersteroidal screws. And so we rattled on, the potholes a laugh now, the deeper ones drawing a cheer like a dropped glass outside the pub, the summit of Mount Athos itself, the Holy Mountain, veined with ice, veering in and out of view as the track mimed the indecisive shoreline.

*

'We Greeks are lucky', Panos held his arms up, 'to have this.' We were standing in Great Lavra's main courtyard, near the *katholikon*, the monastery church, a domed cruciform building painted the colour of deoxygenated blood. Patrick Leigh Fermor had spoken of the 'white-hot conviction' of the monks he encountered at St Wandrille and Solesmes. As one of the world's great centres of belief – the solar core of Orthodox conviction – Mount Athos seemed a good place both to witness lifelong retreat at its most devout, in the case of the monks, and the quieter devotion of those who, like Panos, came here to spend time in their midst. Panos was a judge in his mid-fifties from the city of Veria near Thessaloniki. 'It's a very responsible job,' he told me. He came to Athos twice or three times a year, relying on the 'calmness of the monks' minds' to help him 'lift the responsibility from my shoulders'.

The monastery, in truth, looked more like a fortified medieval town, a cluster of chapels, stone cottages and outhouses faced in cracked plaster and herringbone brick, surrounded by a battlemented wall set off in its south-west corner by a sturdy, castle-like keep known as the Tower of Tzimisces. Beyond the tower, the wooded foothills of the Holy Mountain deepened the sense of enclosure. For a thousand years the monks of Athos had been vulnerable to attack – by Saracen pirates, Frankish raiders, Catalan mercenaries, Turkish soldiers, secular modernity – with the result that the profound tranquillity of the contemplative life here carried with it an equal and opposite intimation of violence, that only the thickest walls could keep the world out, preserve the serenity of this Green Zone of monastic devotion.

It was a late afternoon in early April, and the shadows in the courtyard were lengthening. Vespers was in half an hour or so, followed by the evening meal. Normally we could look forward to a monk joining us after dinner, but as it was Lent, Panos reminded me, 'the monks observe an extra level of silence, preparing for the Resurrection.' Panos smiled. 'This is the meaning of Orthodoxy.' Resurrection. Renewal. 'People sense something here. You come here with an open mind, an open heart, something can happen,' said Panos. 'You just have to believe.'

People have been sensing something here since ancient times. Of the three spindly promontories of the Chalkidiki peninsula, sixty-five miles south-east of Thessaloniki, Mount Athos is the easternmost, roughly thirty miles long and named after the 2,000-metre peak at its southern tip. It's unclear when the first ascetics settled on Athos, but there is evidence that contemplative practice had taken root here by the seventh century, stimulated by circumstances similar to those that contributed, four centuries earlier, to the first flowering of monasticism in the Egyptian desert: societal breakdown in the neighbouring towns and villages. The world was ending. People fled for the hills. The development in the ninth century of cenobitic monasticism on Athos was partly in response to the threat of incursion, primarily by Saracen pirates with bases on Crete. Hermits were especially vulnerable: communal monasticism offered the safety of numbers. As with the Meteora monasteries, teetering on their rock columns to the west of Athos in Thessaly, the martial aspect of the new Athonite monasteries served as much to keep persecutors out as inhabitants in.

The founding in 963 of Great Lavra, by Athanasios the Athonite – the monk whose miraculous spring I had visited with Michael Caine, and a learned ally of the Byzantine Emperor Nikephoros Phokas – marked the decisive shift from the eremitical to the cenobitic, although not without the ruffling of local feathers. The Athonite monk Paul Xeropotaminos was the leader of a faction that cleaved to the ideal of maximum austerity and seclusion. To live and pray communally – in a building made of stone, no less, as opposed to mud and twigs – was for wimps, a submission to luxury, a retreat from retreat. With his imperial connections, Athanasios won out, but the tension between rigidity and reform is one that bears upon Athonite monasticism to this day.

Rigidity has the upper hand. Athos has special status as an autonomous region within the Greek state, meaning that visitors must apply for a temporary visa lasting only four days. Non-Orthodox visitors are restricted to ten per day. Women to zero. Since a chrysobull – a form of imperial decree – issued in the tenth century, the entire promontory has been out of bounds not only to women but to all female animals. (The monks turn a blind eye to cats: the monasteries have a mouse problem.) This may seem especially perverse in a place consecrated to the *Theotokos*, the Mother of God. The legend goes that Mary was blown off course en route to Cyprus, and, taken with the wild beauty of Athos, prayed that she might be given the Holy Mountain as her garden. It was the very perfection of the Virgin, however, that ruled the place out for her sex. No other female could possibly measure up. Women are not allowed within half a kilometre of the coastline.

In 1953, a young Thessalonian named Maria Poimenidou spent three days on Athos disguised as a man, whereupon the ancient chrysobull entered the statute book. From then on, any woman caught in the monastic state faced a maximum penalty of a year in jail. And so Athos stands as the world's largest gentleman's club, a retreat from femininity spanning 130 square miles, something the visitor might feel most acutely in Ouranopolis, where the ferry bypassing the uneventful north of the isthmus leaves for Dafni, the de facto entry point for Athonite pilgrims. On the morning of my arrival, I had breakfast in Ouranopolis, on a harbourside patio enclosed in flapping plastic and hazy with cigarette smoke. Groups of men and teenage boys huddled collar-up over their coffees while a waitress, middle-aged, Albanian, with brutally bleached hair showing black at the roots, slalomed the tables, taking orders, wiping down the melamine, ferrying plates of egg and bright-red sausage stacked two to each forearm, a vision of vitality in the wordless, early-morning gloom.

In a sense the extremity of Athos's conservatism is a function of its reduced status. Like Cluny in the early eleventh century,

Mount Athos under Byzantine rule enjoyed a level of intellectual and political influence out of scale with its ostensible function as a sanctuary for quiet contemplation. The intensity of its inwardness was precisely what gave it its outward heft, as a centre of scholarship renowned throughout the Eastern Empire. With the fall of Constantinople in 1453, its fortunes declined, but the canniness of the Athonite abbots in submitting to Sultan Mehmed II – and in paying him taxes – won them the tolerance of subsequent Sultanates and the survival of their way of life. Athos today is in many respects little changed, a relic of Byzantine magnificence frozen in time, as resistant to modern, ecumenical gestures towards Christian unity as it had been to medieval attempts to reunify the Eastern and Western churches. Its walls are thick. In recent years, the age-old tension between the rigorists, fanatically resistant to change, and the moderately more open-minded has flared into violence. In 2004 monks at Esphigmenou Monastery in the north-east of the promontory were filmed throwing punches and pulling each other's beards. A monk loyal to the Ecumenical Patriarch Bartholomew I, current *primus inter pares* of the Orthodox Church and an advocate of improved relations with the Vatican, had tried to gain admittance to the cloister. As ever, the rigorists prevailed.

Far from discouraging new vocations, however, the strictness of the Athonite *Typikon* – the rule book of liturgical practice – may lie behind the steady increase in the resident monk population since the 1980s, reversing years of decline and the continuing downward trend in Orthodox observance I glimpsed on Hydra. There is a surprisingly persistent appetite for the hard stuff. By 1971, there were fewer than 1,150 monks on Mount Athos. Now there are more than 2,000, drawn not only from Greece but from Serbia, Bulgaria, Romania, Moldova and Russia, impelled whether by the rigour of the *Typikon*, or weariness with the outside world, to a life of fervent prayer. Granted, 850 extra monks in fifty years doesn't sound like much, but I got the sense, nonetheless, of Athos as resurgent, galvanised by a renewed spirit that extended well beyond its territorial waters. It was only a hunch, but retreat felt like it was coming.

On the opposite coast of the peninsula from Great Lavra lies Simonopetra Monastery. Diakon Seraphim was Simonopetra's *archontaris*, or guestmaster, the Orthodox equivalent of Father Michael at Solesmes. After greeting me with the traditional offering of *loukoumi* (the Greek name for Turkish delight), a glass of water and a shot of a syrupy, anise-flavoured spirit called *raki*, Seraphim led me out onto a balcony clinging to the monastery's seaward face. Seraphim spoke so softly I had to lean in to catch what he was saying.

'I don't know if in your church you believe in relics,' he said.

I couldn't think of a way of answering this truthfully without giving offence. So I said nothing. Seraphim reached inside his cassock and retrieved a small Ziploc bag, the kind favoured by small-time dealers of hash or MDMA. Inside was a wad of cotton wool stained the reddish ochre of a weeping wound. 'Please,' he said, and pinching open the bag gestured at me to smell the contents. Pine sap, a bit musty or mushroomy. Sweet. A hint of citrus. With rubbery undertones.

'Very nice,' I said, as if Seraphim were handing out perfume samples in a department store, rather than demonstrating the pleasant smell of a venerated saint's post-mortem secretions. Simonopetra's founder, Saint Simon, was known as a Myroblete: a 'Myrrh-gusher', as after burial his relics were found to exude the aromatic oil I had just sniffed on Seraphim's tuft of cotton wool. Seraphim delved into his cassock again and retrieved a second, slightly larger Ziploc. This one was from Christ's tomb in Jerusalem. I took a sniff. It smelled exactly the same as Saint Simon's.

'When they found the holy grave,' said Seraphim, 'the computers and mobile phones of the engineers stopped working. Stopped. Just like that.'

Seraphim smiled and stashed the bags back in his cassock. Simonopetra is spectacular. 'Petra', of course, refers to the rock from which Simon's monastery rises, not so much perched on its cliff than seeming a miraculous extension of it, emerging like an unfinished sculpture from its block, spirit struggling to free itself from matter. The monastery was founded in the thirteenth century, when Simon, living in a cave nearby, saw a light shining on the ridge, interpreting it as an order from the Virgin to get building. So vertiginous was the site, the story goes, that the monks retained by Simon to build the monastery were about to abandon the project when one of their number, Isaiah, sent to fetch drinks for his mutinous colleagues, slipped and plunged down the mountainside, returning not only unscathed but without a drop spilled from his tray of refreshments. This, it turned out, was precisely the slapsticky type of miracle that appealed to the builders, and construction resumed.

Over the intervening eight centuries, a number of catastrophic fires has meant that the present structure dates largely from the late nineteenth century, albeit in the medieval idiom. Look down on the monastery from the footpath to Dafni, and it scarcely seems real, a sensory input no prior could have prepared me for. For Seraphim, life at the monastery was a step closer to Christ than the world outside it.

'If you love one person, you want always to be connected with him, to see him, to speak with him.' Seraphim quoted Jesus in the Gospel of Matthew: 'He that loveth father or mother more than me is not worthy of me: and he that loveth son or daughter more than me is not worthy of me.' The pledge was marital fidelity transferred to the Divine. The monks were married to Christ.

'If you cannot be a good husband,' said Seraphim, 'you cannot be a good monk.'

It was within those marital constraints that the monks found their freedom, a 'freedom from the passions', as Seraphim put it, that was its own form of passion, manifest in Seraphim's pouches of sweet-smelling extract-of-saint and the 2,000 genu-flections an Orthodox monk might perform in his cell.

'It's not really important,' said Seraphim, when I asked him what he did before taking vows. Faith had erased his past and requisitioned his future. A fly landed on the wooden railing between us, and I couldn't help but wonder if it was female, like the swallows I'd seen earlier, or the shoals of female fish no doubt flouting the 500 m rule even as we spoke. 'This life,' said Seraphim, 'the life we're living now, is just the first five or six pages. You know when you want to buy a book, you look at the first pages? If you like them, you take the book. The other pages are the eternal life.'

'And what of other people?' I asked. 'Visitors, I mean. What do they come here for?'

Seraphim nodded quietly to himself. 'Some people come because they are thirsty for something spiritual,' he said. 'They are searching, they want to know the truth, to understand something in their soul. Other people come like visitors, to see the nature, the buildings. They take the things they are looking for.'

Behind Seraphim the sunset had gilded the sea like the ground of an icon. 'Sometimes the soul can get ill, like the body,' he continued. 'It needs a doctor.'

At Great Lavra, Panos and I headed to the *katholikon* for Vespers. We took to neighbouring *stacidia* in the narthex, the outermost chamber of the church. Through a succession of arched doorways we could see the monks in their vestments performing the liturgical rites. At the heart of the church, the sanctuary, the visual field was so crowded with icons, wall paintings, candlesticks and pendant gold and silverware as to confound the eye's focus: figure was indistinguishable from ground. A melismatic chant rose and resolved on a distinctly Arabic-sounding dissonance. A hieromonk, the Orthodox equivalent of the Benedictine monk-priest, did the rounds with his *kadylo*, or censer, chinking the eleven bells on its chain – one for each apostle, minus Judas – and wafting clouds of sweet-smelling smoke that rose like the chanting of the psalms. And then through the doorway I spotted Ştefan, Michael Caine and the others, standing in the middle chamber, the nave, crossing themselves repeatedly, over and over again with such intensity I wondered for a moment if they might pass out.

There are two models for human society, according to the anthropologist Victor Turner. The first is 'structure', the tendency to differentiate, to organise society according to a hierarchical set of distinctions that assume one individual or group's higher status over another's. The second is what Turner calls 'communitas', society as an unstructured (or 'rudimentarily structured') free-for-all of equal individuals. Structure forms the basis of our judicial, political and economic systems. It is the principle behind property ownership, distinctions of rank, individualism, and kinship rights and obligations. It also covers naming, self-ishness, secularity and the avoidance of pain and suffering. It is the scaffolding of a stable society. Communitas, on the other hand, represents the absence of property or status, uniformity of clothing or nakedness, and the suspension of kinship rights and obligations. Communitas also relates to anonymity, the submission of the individual to the communal good, sacredness and spirituality, and the acceptance of pain and suffering.

The two tendencies operate in a perpetual dialectic and cannot exist independently of one another. For example, among the Ndembu people of present-day Zambia, it was traditional, on the eve of his succession, for the chief-elect to be sent with either his senior wife, or a specially chosen female slave, to a simple hut about a mile from the village. The hut was known as a *kafwi*, a cognate of the Ndembu term for 'to die'. There they sat, in a humble crouching position, the chief-elect in nothing but a ragged waistcloth, and were subjected to the tribal equivalent of a celebrity roast. The rite of *Kumukindyila* – 'The Reviling of the Chief-Elect' – involved the headman of a subservient tribe berating his chief-to-be for his foolishness, ill temper, unjustness and dabbling in witchcraft. Any member of the tribe was then permitted to pile in and get any resentments off his chest.

During this the chief-elect had to remain silent, his head bowed in humility, even as the subservient headman periodically struck him with his buttocks. The purpose of this ritual, in its end-of-the-pier inversions of weakness and power, was, of course, to remind both the chief-elect and people that the authority about to be vested in him, and the status that came with it, were gifts of the community, not an opportunity to accumulate power for selfish gain.

There are limits to what can be drawn from an analysis undertaken in the 1960s of fieldwork from twenty years earlier. Still, there are elements of Turner's thesis that cast the impulse to withdraw in an intriguing light. An individual or group passing from low to high (or high to low) status is said to be in a 'liminal state', that is, without status, ambiguous, neither one thing nor another. An example would be the Ndembu chief-elect, caught between his ritual humiliation and accession to power. For as long as this lasts, he is liminal.

For the most part, liminality is a temporary state, the brief period of statuslessness that characterises a rite of passage, the revitalising jolt of communitas the chief-elect needs to fulfil his structural position more judiciously. On the societal level, outbreaks of liminality act as correctives to a culture grown rigid through over-reliance on its structures. A good example might be the destabilising effect that the hippie movement had on the crew-cut conformity of post-war America. As Turner stresses, however, 'the spontaneity and immediacy of communitas ... can seldom be maintained for very long.' Outbreaks of liminality overturn the structural positions before submitting to those structures themselves. The radicalism of places like Esalen has long since been assimilated into the corporate mainstream. Structure has its uses: without it, the complexities of social relations would quickly become unmanageable. We are set free by what binds us. There can be no permanent revolution, only a perpetual cycle of revolution and return to structure.

Where liminality persists, the organisation will tend either to disintegrate or develop its own structures, become institutionalised. A case in point is monasticism. The similarities between a monk's way of life and the liminal state of the Ndembu chief-elect are striking. Both abjure personal property, are (supposedly) sexually continent, abdicate their kinship rights and obligations – think of Father Michael Bozell and the family he left behind in Connecticut – affect maximum humility and accept pain and suffering. The difference is that in monasticism these qualities are made permanent, requiring, in turn, the development of institutional structures overseen by an abbot and codified, to cite the most obvious example, in documents like the Rule of St Benedict.

For the rest of us, to withdraw into the liminal environment of a monastery, a meditation centre, a commune or cabin in the woods is to be 'released from structure into communitas only to return to structure revitalized by their experience of communitas'. We withdraw from the world to return better equipped to live in it. It's tempting to draw a parallel between 'structure' as defined by Turner and the 'internal models' described by Giuseppe Pagnoni and others. Internal models, remember, are the pictures of the world our brains build up through experience. They are what we know already, our foreknowledge, dependent, like Turner's 'structure', on precedent and habitual pattern, customs of behaviour and thought developed over time. Remember also that intense meditative focus has the effect of switching off those models in favour of the direct input from our sensory organs. What communitas shares with the meditative state is the intense occupation of the present at the expense of stale habit.

Likewise, as structure and communitas exist in a perpetual, self-correcting dialectic, so our internal models are perpetuated and refined by our efforts to switch them off. The one adjusts the other. To spend time at Great Lavra or Solesmes is not only to refresh ourselves via silence and contemplation, but to be close to those who have chosen to do so for life, in hope a little of their immediacy, their exemption from status anxiety, might rub off on us. The more we're bound by structure, the more we yearn for communitas, for the chance to stand outside for a while, to take the boat to Dafni, to catch a flight to Rangoon, or Kathmandu, or Delhi, a bus to Rishikesh, a cab along the Karnprayag-Hardiwar Road towards Ram Jhula, past the stray cows with their conspicuous ribcages, the young men on their mopeds, the claggy-haired sadhus in saffron rags, on past the bridges and roadside fruit stalls to an ashram by the Ganges.

'For me,' said Sean, 'Nadi Kinare is a physical and spiritual boot camp.' The daily programme was tight, but there were a couple of hours after lunch where you could do your own thing, and Sean and I had decided to go for a walk along the Ganges west towards Shivpuri. Upstream from Rishikesh, the river was a milky, emerald green, placid near the banks and torrential in the middle. Every five minutes or so a raft packed with hel-meted adrenaline junkies, plump in their life jackets, would hurtle down the central channel, screaming in euphoric terror or waving in that look-at-me manner I had to summon all my fledgling powers of loving-forgiveness not to find annoying. On our side, the left bank, a long stretch of white sand, strewn with smooth boulders and chaotic ossuaries of bleached driftwood, had given way to a wildflower meadow, the grass long and in-filtrated by marigold. Mindful of scorpions, we picked our way along the indistinct path, Sean in his Birkenstocks, me in the cushioned running shoes I'd taken to wearing since the tingly feeling in my feet had returned, worse, if anything, than it had been pre-Ibiza. Ahead of us, the foothills receded like stages in a meditation, hinting at the pale enormities beyond.

'With Suhani-ji,' said Sean, 'we get the privilege of being with someone who is a true believer.' (Suhani-ji was our yoga teacher and the de facto leader of the ashram.) Sean came to India every year as a volunteer for Calcutta Rescue, a charity providing medical care and education for the disadvantaged in West Bengal. Rishikesh was respite. Much as he loved Calcutta, after a month of noise and smog and urban destitution he was ready not only for the peace and clean air of the Himalayas, but for the opportunity Nadi Kinare offered for vicarious devotion, for intimacy with, if not immersion in, belief.

'I've got a teacher in London who is much more sophisticated in the way she teaches yoga,' continued Sean. 'But I kind of love Suhani-ji's simplicity. And she's been very clear that the asanas are not really her thing. For her, it's the chanting. The *bhakti*.'

Of the four paths of yoga, *bhakti* is the most impassioned, closest to the ecstatic engagement with the Divine afforded to Sara Maitland by silent prayer, the bliss transcending all knowledge of St John of the Cross or the thirteenth-century Sufi mystic and poet Jalal ad-Din Rumi. It is the yoga of devotion, of spiritual love, of reverence for God expressed through chanting, prayer and ritual. The asanas – i.e. what much of the Western world understands by the term 'yoga' – constitute only a small part of a much larger and more heterogeneous group of meditative, physical and spiritual practices.

A retreat at an ashram like Nadi Kinare offered two distinct if related opportunities. One, to develop the postural and meditative techniques I had learned in Ibiza over a longer and more intense period. Two, to understand the asanas in their devotional context. Rishikesh is the world centre of yoga, a city of 100,000 people whose very name signifies retreat. 'Lord Hrishikesha' is an alias of Vishnu, and derives from the Sanskrit for 'the senses', *hṛṣīka*, and for 'lord', *īśa*, – that is, 'he who has mastery over the senses'. Holy men have come here to still their minds since ancient times, many of them in caves carved into the surrounding hills. Today hundreds of ashrams and secular yoga, meditation and wellbeing centres of varying integrity line the riverbank and back streets. Across the river from the main part of town is Parmarth Niketan, favourite of the trainee yoga teacher with more than a thousand rooms, pink like a utopian citadel imagined by my six-year-old daughter.

Nadi Kinare was set apart, a few miles upstream from Ram Jhula, and was thus peaceful in a way Rishikesh might once have been, before wellness tourism turned it into the number one spot on the international yoga trail. The present guru, Swami-ji, an Ayurvedic doctor who restricted his appearances, at least during my stay, to invigilating the evening mantra-chanting in an orange beanie, had handed over the running of the ashram to Suhani-ji, a yogini who had entered the ashram aged fifteen, severing all family ties just as Sister Nectaria had on Hydra.

According to Hindu lore, humanity has female ingenuity – or wounded male pride – to thank for the transmission of yogic knowledge. Parvati, the consort of Shiva, had grown ever more distressed at the stupidity and suffering of mankind, particularly as compared to the perpetual state of *ananda*, or divine ecstasy, she herself had experienced since Shiva had shown her the path of tantra, or self-transformation. Couldn't Shiva share this knowledge with mankind?

'No,' said Shiva.

He wouldn't budge. Mortals *enjoyed* their ignorance. If they truly wanted to haul themselves out of their pit of corruption and degeneracy, they had every opportunity to do so. Frustrated by Shiva's stubbornness, Parvati sought Vishnu's advice. And Vishnu said: Be his wife. So Parvati went to Shiva and lay with him. Afterwards, in his arms, Parvati brought up the subject of mankind and the raising of its consciousness. Forget I mentioned it, said Parvati. 'If it's beyond your capabilities, it really doesn't diminish you in my eyes.'

And that did the trick. Shiva held the world's first yoga retreat for seven rishis on the banks of Kanti Sarovar, now called Chorabari Tal, a Himalayan lake nearly 4,000 metres above sea level, where Mahatma Gandhi's ashes would one day be scattered. In the *Bhagavad Gita*, probably composed some time in the second century BC, the yogic principles gifted to humanity by Shiva are expounded in Krishna's advice to the warrior Arjuna, on the eve of war between the Pandavas, Arjuna's faction, and their usurper cousins the Kauravas. Many readers – including Gandhi, who was reputed to read the seven hundred verses of the *Gita* every day – have interpreted the battle at its heart as an allegory for the struggle between man's carnality and virtue, his ego and its subjugation, his clinging to things and the liberating spirit of non-attachment. Arjuna is horrified by the prospect of killing his kinfolk in battle. The thrust of Krishna's advice is that Arjuna must transcend his personal qualms in favour of dharma, that is, what is eternally, cosmically true. Better to kill your cousins in battle than not be righteous. And the apparatus of this righteousness is withdrawal.

'Leave all things behind,' Krishna tells Arjuna in the final chapter. Wisdom comes to those who practise *pratyahara*, the withdrawal of the senses, 'even as a tortoise withdraws all its limbs'. The aim is not to escape from reality but to step back and perceive it more clearly, to renounce external stimuli in the name of achieving *dharana*, or single focus. The fewer the stimuli, the easier this focus is to achieve.

'Day after day,' advises Krishna, 'let the Yogi practise the harmony of soul: in a secret place, in deep solitude, master of his mind, hoping for nothing, desiring nothing.' Bit by bit, our desires fall away, our attachments to worldly objects and phenomena, which in their impermanence can only bring dissatisfaction. The withdrawal is cognitive too, from the world of signs and concepts to a clarity of mind behind or beyond language, beyond discursive thought. We see afresh, no longer deceived by *maya*, the 'veil' or 'cloud of appearance' that descends whenever we conceive of reality via the conventional representations of language. It's just as Giuseppe Pagnoni speaks of our 'priors' or 'internal models', the predetermined categories assembled by our brains to minimise surprise. Switch them off and we see things as they are. Arjuna's death or those of his enemies no longer matter, Krishna tells us, as the life of the individual is inconsequential by comparison to *atman*, the true self. Our current, ego-bound embodiment is just a single, transient instance of a sequence of lives that stretches into eternity.

'When a man dwells in the solitude of silence, and meditation and contemplation are ever with him; when freedom from
passion is his constant will; and his selfishness and violence and
pride are gone, and he is free from the thought "this is mine";
then this man has risen on the mountain of the Highest: he is
worthy to be one with Brahman, with God.'

Crouching by a tree I cocked my head and inserted the plastic
spout in my nose. 'More breath more smell and so beautiful in
the garden,' said Suhani-ji. From the other side of the flower
beds Kai, the smaller of the two ashram dogs, had padded up
and was mimicking the tilt of my head. I found Kai unnerving,
perhaps because he reminded me of the demonic little mutt that
had chased me on Ibiza: the same mad eyes. It was stupid, as
Kai's main job was to ward off the monkeys that patrolled the
perimeter wall of the ashram like the demons at Solesmes. He
was a gargoyle, a compline bell: an *anti*-rabies dog. Still, I gave
him a look, perhaps a little undermined by the fact that I had
a miniature plastic watering can stuck up my left nostril. After
a brief delay a stream of tepid water fell from my right nostril
into the flower bed.

'Is a so nice,' said Suhani-ji. 'Now your nose hole is a become more open.'

Mornings at Nadi Kinare began with a silent meditation
followed by fifteen minutes of chanting, but for me, the *neti*-
pot ritual, at 6.45, out under the henna trees as the sun rose
above Mother Ganga, marked the real beginning of the day, not
least because it was hard to remain half-asleep with lukewarm
saline solution trickling through your sinuses. Afterwards, upstairs in the asana hall, we sat in the easy pose and began the
pranayama or breathwork session with some vigorous *bhastrika*. This involved filling your lungs with air then pumping
it out forcefully, and repeatedly, through your newly opened
nose holes. Some of us took to this more enthusiastically than
others. Vihaan, one of the two Indians on the retreat, usually

sat by the window, not visibly participating, his little rebellion confirmed by his insistence, when the rest of us had stripped to our t-shirts, on keeping his maroon leather jacket zipped to the neck. Abi, on the other hand, performed her *bhastrika* with such intensity it was as if she were trying to expel a crayon lodged in her nasal cavity. In truth it was in moments like these that I got the strongest whiff of fraudulence. According to Suhani-ji, by purifying our internal organs these breathing techniques were awakening the divine kundalini energy at the base of our spines. Maybe so. Sat Bir Singh Khalsa had said much the same thing. Nonetheless, there was a poignancy it was hard to deny about fifty well-travelled representatives of the industrialised first world, our little G20 of right-minded retreatants – dominated, in numbers, by the US, UK, and Israel, with only Vihaan and Sunil to represent India – yearning for rarity, for strange ritual, with such ardency that, viewed from another perspective, the value of this exercise seemed primarily to derive from the weirdness of spraying your yoga pants with vaporised snot.

My worry that we were being played was reawakened, briefly, one afternoon as I was passing through the ashram courtyard. In the middle was a small red and white temple topped with four onion domes, ribbed in bright red and rimmed around their bases with black and yellow cobra's heads. It was here that the short prayer ritual known as *pooja* took place each evening at sunset, beginning with a peal of bells and closed with the offering of a cone of burning incense to the worshippers. For the rest of the day the courtyard was a place for various elders related to Swami-ji to pass the time on plastic chairs. *Mauna* – silence – was observed from nine in the evening until after lunch, but even during the afternoon hours when talking was allowed, we were discouraged from interacting with staff or any visitors to the ashram not taking part in the retreat. Now, however, an old man in a grey kurta was making such unambiguous eye contact with me that I felt I had to respond.

'Hello,' I said. 'Do you live here?'

'Nah, boss,' he said. 'I live in Penge.'

For forty years he had run a corner shop in South London, coming to the ashram once a year to visit his relations. I asked him if he ever took part in *pooja* or the other observances.

'You must be joking.' To him, Swami-ji and the others were fraudulent 'god men'. 'Spiritual leeches, all of them. Taking advantage of people's weakness.'

The possibility that the old man had a point might, I suppose, have preyed more on my mind had I not been so determined to get better at the asanas. After pranayama came an hour and a half of hatha yoga, the gentler – or rather less aerobic – of the day's two asana sessions. Suhani-ji stood on a small stage enclosed in an alcove that meant her hands stroked the ceiling at the top of each sun salutation. She was compact, with her hair tied back in a long, thick plait, and had a fondness for yellow trousers and sweatshirts in salmon pink that bunched around her middle. It was as if by wearing such bright colours she were compensating for, or diverting attention from, the indistinctness of her eyes, set so deep in their sockets that it was often hard to gauge the affect of her expressions. She had a poker face even when smiling.

'Stand a straight with your legs wide apart. Arms now a straight out from shoulders. Stre-e-etching, stretching, stretching.'

As ever with the asanas, my chief difficulty was not really with pain but with the anticipation of it. It was an entirely self-defeating feedback loop. By taking me out of the present moment, my worry that the next pose, or the next five seconds holding the present one, would be painful, would in turn undermine the concentration that made the pain bearable. Expect pain and you were all but guaranteed to feel it. Expect nothing, dwell in the moment, and the pain would still come but would matter less, would no longer quite be what we understand as pain. I knew this, intellectually at least. It was just a lot easier in theory than in practice.

'*Leaning* to the right. Stre-e-etching, stretching. Is a so nice.'

Nice was one word for it. It didn't help that I generally set up my yoga mat next to Javier and Valentina, a young couple from Colombia. Valentina was a yoga instructor. Both of them moved through the poses with such grace I often felt like just sitting on my mat and watching. And then invariably something would change. At her yoga classes back home my long-term teacher, Monique, would often speak of the asanas, or the bodily awareness they brought about, as the closest we could get to the truth – how, for example, a minute focus on the position of your feet, and the knock-on effect that had on sensations elsewhere in the body, in the sacral area and so on, amounted to some respite from uncertainty, a frugal epistemology of the body. You might not know what the purpose of existence was, or why you insisted on swanning off to ashrams when you had a wife and two young children back at home. But you knew that your toes were there. You knew how they felt.

'Touching leg below the knee. Keep a arms straight. Stre-e-etching.'

It hurt. But I no longer minded. The asanas prepared you for meditation in a literal sense, in that it was good to be flexible if you were going to sit in the lotus position for hours on end, but also, I now realised, because they encouraged – demanded, in fact – a withdrawal both from your surroundings and the future you. It was the familiar paradox of retreat: you absented yourself to be more present.

With its prohibition on organised monasticism, the closest Islam gets to the forms of spiritual retreat familiar to Hindus, Christians and Buddhists is in certain practices associated with Sufi mysticism. *Khalwa* means 'seclusion' or 'separation': in the Sufi tradition, the faithful retire to an isolated place for a period of forty days to achieve a deeper understanding of the Divine will. This is usually done under the guidance of a *murshid* or spiritual advisor. One rainy evening shortly before leaving for India I attended a mini-*khalwa* at a terraced house just off the A12 in east London. We were perched on a sort of urban cliff: opposite the house was a high wall, preventing unmindful pedestrians from falling a hundred feet onto the six lanes of traffic the other side of it. My host and *murshid* for the evening was Abdul Ghaffur, an English convert to Islam previously known as Garry Doherty. Abdul and I sat on cushions in the sparsely furnished front room, along with the sole other meditator present, a glum-looking white Rasta called Adrian.

Sufi meditation is known as *muraqabah*, from the Arabic for 'to observe'. The idea is to watch over your heart, thereby discerning its worldly defilements and rising above them. Abdul reached up to switch off the standard lamp, and we sat in the sallow orange glow of streetlights filtered through net curtains.

'Concentrate on your metaphysical heart centre,' said Abdul. This was to be found two fingers' width below my left pec. 'After a while, you'll get a feeling there, a fluttering bird, a pressure. Let the thoughts come but return your attention to your heart centre, to that feeling.'

We sat in silence. I was fitfully aware of Adrian's breathing, which had a slight chesty purr to it. For the Sufi poet Rumi, to open the heart was to love God and receive His love in return, to be drenched in a love that ultimately dissolved all distinctions: 'That all "I's" and "thou's" should become one soul and at last should be submerged in the Beloved.' Love for all creation, the unitive state or 'oceanic feeling' the philosopher William James saw as the overcoming of 'all the usual barriers between the individual and the Absolute'.

I was reminded of Abdul and his love-drenched submersion during *kirtan*, the session of devotional chanting held at Nadi Kinare every evening before supper. This was Suhani-ji's moment. As Sean had said on our walk, the asanas weren't really her thing. What mattered was immersion. What mattered was belief. Suhani-ji would sit at the front with Swami-ji, hands pressed together in the *anjali mudra*. The marked movement, the brain telling itself to pay attention: in the physical grace of Suhani-ji's gestures I was reminded of the Romanians making the signs of the cross on Mount Athos. Suhani-ji would nestle the tablas between her knees and the chanting would begin. *Shiva, Shiva, Shiva Shambhu.* 'Shiva the auspicious.' Shiva is the *adiguru*, the first guru, who embodies enlightenment, the ultimate goal of yoga. Nadi Kinare was consecrated in his name. In the *Trimurti*, the Hindu trinity, he is the Destroyer – of evil, of illusion and ignorance. He annihilates the universe in order to remake it. *Mahadeva Shambhu.* 'Great God, the auspicious one.' Over and over again, Suhani-ji on the tablas, Swami-ji in his beanie, swaying gently with his eyes closed, the rest of us clapping or shaking our *jhikas*, a kind of rectangular wooden paddle enclosing two rows of miniature cymbals, the pitch and tempo gathering in intensity, dropping, on Suhani-ji's cue, to a crawling pianissimo, then gathering pace again, faster and faster, *ShivaShivaShivaShambuh-uh-uh-uh*, Suhani-ji's head thrown back, eyes to the light so you could finally see them, gleaming, exultant, but still unreadable. What can we ever read in eyes, or in anything?

Our penultimate day at Nadi Kinare coincided with Holi, the Hindu festival of forgiveness that marked the arrival of spring. After lunch I put on the white kurta and harem pants I had tried and failed to haggle over at a street market in Ram Jhula. ('They're 900 rupees. Take it or leave it.') Several of the younger Japanese and Israeli retreatants had gone into Rishikesh and come back smeared in coloured dye and either drunk or stoned or both. Nobody cared: it's what happened on Holi. In the dining hall overlooking the river, roofed but open to the elements through its colonnade of unglazed arches, the tables and chairs had been cleared aside for us to throw *abir* – the dye – at each other and dance to the electronic raga Suhani-ji had put on the stereo. The screams from the river were even more frenzied than usual. Namiko, one of the stoned young Japanese girls, came over and drew a pink target on my forehead with her finger. It was like a cross between a music festival and a stay-and-play session at the local children's centre, all fifty-odd of us, young and old and middle-aged, bucking and swirling and lobbing fistfuls of yellow and green and hot pink at each other's white outfits – all of us, that is, except Vihaan, who was sitting in an arch with his chin in the collar of his jacket, the corner of his mouth lifted either in contentment or contempt.

'What's up with Vihaan?' I had sidled over to Sunil, who was standing in the corner talking to Javier and Valentina.

'Don't ask me.' Sunil looked a bit embarrassed. 'I can't speak for him.'

'How are things?' I said, with half an eye on Vihaan as he pushed off his perch and left the party. 'You been enjoying yourself?'

Sunil, Javier and Valentina exchanged a look.

'It's just funny you should ask,' said Sunil. 'We were only just talking about the, uh, issues we have with the ashram.'

'Such as?'

'It's Suhani-ji, mainly,' said Sunil. 'Honestly I'm not very impressed. She's just so unclear in terms of how to take positions.'

It was true that compared to Monique's teaching style, or Gemma's at Casa Parvati, Suhani-ji's was strikingly approximate. In the case of *sarvangasana*, for instance, the shoulder stand, the instruction was to lie on our backs with our knees up, then rock back and forth until enough momentum had been achieved to hurl our legs in the air, without much attention to the strain this might place on the lower back or neck. But it hadn't occurred to me that anyone minded, particularly.

'Seriously,' said Valentina. 'I sit there thinking, what are you *doing* with these people? It's like, wow. I can get quite angry if I think about it.'

I found myself feeling defensive on Suhani-ji's behalf. 'She's got her work cut out, though, hasn't she?' I said. 'There are fifty of us in the room. She hasn't got a hope of going round and adjusting everyone's mistakes.'

Javier made an agnostic pout. 'Yeah, but you've got to understand that the Indian approach to yoga is very different. It's not
like going to a class in a Western country, or with a Western
teacher, where they approach the postures step-by-step. Indians
have a completely different conception of how to use their
bodies, a completely different configuration of the tensions.'

Sunil agreed. 'It's like a different language.'

A little later, needing a break from the music, I made my
excuses and walked down to the courtyard. Sitting on a plastic
chair in the shade cast by the temple was Helen, another of
the English retreatants. She looked upset.

'Vihaan was just here,' she explained. 'It was weird. He sat
down and immediately launched into this tirade. About how
inauthentic the ashram was and how we Westerners were mugs
for falling for it.'

'Maybe he's right.'

'Maybe,' said Helen. 'It's only that he seemed so amused by
it. What *idiots* we were.'

It's open to question how closely modern yoga – as practised
in India as much as in the West – relates to the principles laid
down in Patanjali's *Yoga Sutras* and the corpus of religious
texts. It's notable, in the primary sources, how little emphasis
is placed on the asanas compared to pranayama and the mental
disciplines of concentration and meditation. By the late nineteenth century, when the teachings of the Calcutta-born monk
Swami Vivekananda played a crucial role in disseminating yogic
principles in the West, the asanas had become stigmatised, first
as objects of Brahminical distaste for physical display, then, in
a European imagination stimulated by popular ethnographies
and lurid accounts in periodicals, as an exotic and morally
dubious street entertainment. Vivekananda himself prioritised
pranayama and meditation to the almost complete exclusion
of the asanas.

It was only in the 1920s and 30s, thanks in large part to the
work of gurus like Tirumalai Krishnamacharya, teacher of B.K.S.
Iyengar – instigator of postural yoga's true internationalisation

in the 1950s – that the postural elements of hatha began to be integrated into modern yoga as practised in India and subsequently abroad. As the yoga scholar Mark Singleton has shown, the revival of interest in ancient hatha practices coincided with the export to India of Scandinavian exercise regimes, the worldwide craze for bodybuilding as popularised by the German showman Eugen Sandow, and, especially, the spread of the physical-education movement by the YMCA, a significant presence in India by the 1930s.

A period of intense synthesis and cross-fertilisation followed, with the result that postural yoga as now understood worldwide is a hybrid of ancient (if adapted) Hindu practices and Western exercise routines. It is a product of cultural assimilation, and so Vihaan's accusation, plausible as it was – that we were a bunch of gullible authenticity tourists being sold a specious or sentimental version of Indianness – failed to take into account that yoga as taught pretty much everywhere was by its nature inauthentic, if by authentic you meant from a single, culturally circumscribable origin. Whether or not you bought the old guy's argument, on the other hand, that Swami-ji and Suhani-ji were trading on Western credulity in their non-asana observances, in *pooja* and *kirtan* and the mantras we chanted at sunrise, depended on the sounding you took of Suhani-ji's conviction, your belief in her belief.

I sat in the courtyard talking to Helen until the music stopped and our fellow retreatants appeared, exotic in their motley hair and kurtas, on the steps leading down from the dining hall. It was time to walk down to the river. That morning, after the 6 a.m. meditation, we had sat by the open windows in the asana hall and repeated, silently, in our heads, a mantra in praise of the Ganges. *Om Ganga Mai*. Om, the sacred word of the Vedas, sound in silence, the primordial noise, the cosmic vibration, representing *atman*, the eternal true self, which is Brahman, the ultimate reality. Om, Amen, Ameen. Ganga Mai,

Mother Ganges, the source of life. 'Its sacred bathing place is contemplation; its waters are truth; its banks are holiness; its waves are love,' says the ancient Sanskrit text, the *Hitopadesha*. In Buddhist terms we would be called 'stream-enterers': rookie contemplatives. 'Go to that river for purification: thy soul cannot be made pure by mere water.'

In single file we processed from the ashram past the ghat and lined up on the white sand at the river's edge. A raft barrelled past, its occupants screaming in unison, too focused to wave. Kai and the other ashram dog, a black-and-tan Alsatian, weaved in and out of our legs, snapping and pawing at each other and peeling off now and then to wrestle on the wet sand. Slipping off our sandals and shoes we pressed hands in the *anjali mudra* as Suhani-ji led us in prayer. *Om Jai Ganga Mata, Maiya Jai Ganga Mata*. Om praise to Mother Ganga, Mother Ganga hail to thee. I glanced up the line and saw Vihaan, eyes closed, hands pressed together, serene.

And then it happened: a glancing sharpness on my calf. My shout was more out of alarm than pain. Kai had bitten me. Playfully, but unmistakably. Suhani-ji cut the prayer short and hurried over.

'Show me.' The urgency in her voice was not encouraging. I lifted the injured leg and held the ankle in my hand. A new pose: the Demon Dog. Suhani-ji pushed a thumb into my calf and the wound bled a little. It was nothing. Or nothing much: the kind of scratch that in a country free of rabies you'd treat with a dab of Savlon and a sticking plaster.

'Is okay.'

'Are you sure?'

'Is a fine.'

Kai was an anti-rabies dog. I would be fine. Almost certainly. Side by side we entered the river up to our knees. Even this close to the bank the current felt strong, impermanence tugging at our ankles. I looked down and saw a cloud of red blooming from my trouser cuffs: *abir*, I trusted, not blood. With no shoes on, my tingly feet were at once irritated by the pebbly riverbed and soothed by the current. From a pile of red lily-heads in the crook of Suhani-ji's arm we each took a few petals. Another step in and my foot met a large, smooth boulder on the riverbed. I went under, and, for good measure, swallowed a mouthful of Mother Ganga.

In the Hindu Dharma, *kshama*, forgiveness, is classed as one of the six cardinal virtues. 'If in irreverence I was disrespectful,' says Arjuna to Krishna in the *Bhagavad Gita*, 'forgive me in thy mercy, O thou immeasurable!' Forgiveness holds the universe together. Treat everyone as if they were Divine. Did Vihaan have a point? Maybe. Worrying over whether he did or not, however, fretting over the authenticity or otherwise of the ashram experience, was surely to guarantee its inauthenticity, sabotaging as it did the single point of being there: not dwelling in the past or future. There was as much point worrying whether I was going to die of rabies or amoebic dysentery. Forgive. Forget. 'Forgiveness is the one supreme peace.' I had entered the stream: whatever life brings. I waded in chest-deep. Screams from mid-river. (Maybe *they* had a point, it occurred to me. What were *we* doing, wading into the river in our clothes? Rafting was fun: it was life.) In my hand, still, sodden from the dip, two red petals, one for a departed loved one, one for me. The first went for my mother. The second floated briefly then vanished in a gulp of white water, leaving me, purified or poisoned by Ganga Mai, quite still for a moment as the river rushed by.

5

Greg and the Tenth Army of Mara

It once came to the Buddha's attention that there was a group of monks living in the forest who weren't treating their meditative practice seriously. Walking the forest paths, the monks would look up at the sky or admire the birds perching in the trees. After a sitting meditation, they would rise to their feet unmindfully, yanking up their limbs without paying heed to the sensation in their muscles and joints. All this was to defile the dharma, to profane its teachings. So the Buddha sought out the monks. Practise meditation, he told them, as though you were carrying a bowl full to the brim with oil. Spill a drop and it's all over. Enlightenment came quickly to the monks after that.

Exaggerated slowness is an identifying characteristic of vipassana meditation in the Mahasi tradition. I had come to the Saraniya Meditation Centre in Salford, Greater Manchester, for a ten-day, silent Mahasi-style retreat. I had bargained on this being my most arduous experience of retreat yet – but not, apparently, on how drawn-out the arduousness would be. To begin with, at least, the effect on time perception was the opposite of what I'd experienced at Solesmes. Where, at the abbey, it had become increasingly difficult to keep track of time, here you were agonisingly aware of it, of each passing second, progressing to the next with a sort of viscous unwillingness. From behind a hedge, or round the corner of the dharma hall, a foot would appear, gradually lower itself to the ground, and only as it rolled forward from heel to ball would it be followed by its owner, inching in to view as if in the grip of some debilitating virus. It was like a scene from an experimental zombie movie. Horrifying, but low on drama.

It was warm, unseasonably if not alarmingly so for the north of England in late spring, and the impression of bone-deep languor was only increased by the appearance of the main building, across the car park from the dharma hall, a suburban Edwardian villa whose painted surface, peeling off in glistening strips, gave it an incongruously subtropical look, as if the Burmese family who ran the place had brought the climate with them. Further off, towards the city, the pinnacles of a gloomy, disused Gothic Revival church peered over the garden fence, curious, having lost its congregation, what the pagan neighbours were up to. Walking, drinking, brushing your teeth: for the next ten days life was to be lived in slow motion, giving us the chance, so the teachings went, to notice not only every sensation but all its component parts, the sequence of millimetric shifts that went into each footstep, the tiny discrepancies in depth and duration between one breath and the next.

Buddhism splits into either two or three schools, depending on who you consult. Theravada is most prevalent in Sri Lanka and continental south-east Asia, including Myanmar, where the style of meditation we were practising originated. The largest school, Mahayana ('the Great Vehicle') is dominant in China, Japan, Indonesia, Malaysia, Vietnam and elsewhere; Vajrayana, the set of esoteric traditions sometimes referred to as 'Tantric Buddhism', is variously treated as a subdivision of Mahayana or as a school in its own right. Theravada shares with Orthodox Christianity an adherence to its origins. It is the older of the two main sects, something implicit both in its name – 'Theravāda' is Pali for 'speech of the elders' – and in the inspiration it takes from the *Tipitaka*, or Pali canon, widely held to be the earliest and most complete record of the Buddha's teachings. It is wintry, rule-bound, doctrinally conservative.

Vipassana, which in its modern form constitutes a revival of ancient Theravadan meditative techniques, is an expression of that rigour. Among my friends its reputation as the Iron Man of contemplative practices had gained ground with Phil's adoption of it. Despite deciding against full ordination as a Buddhist monk, he had kept up the meditation practice, topping it up with regular retreats at various vipassana centres around the world. The previous year he had taken leave from his teaching job and spent forty-five consecutive days meditating in a hut in southern Nepal. When I submitted my new applicant's questionnaire to Dhammasoti, Phil's Belgian-born Sayadaw, I got the following reply: 'We have received your answers. There is a huge difference between MBSR and intensive meditation in the Mahasi tradition.' In other words: jog on. I had nowhere near the chops to meditate with the big boys.

That was the point of coming to Salford: to earn my chops. As at Solesmes, there were six of us on retreat. Two had left almost immediately. The first was a pale, dreamy-looking woman in her late thirties, whose unexplained departure on day one had been so quiet that I wasn't entirely sure, in retrospect, whether she had been there in the first place. The second to leave, on day two, was a blond guy in his early twenties who the Sayadaw – our resident monk and meditation master – had caught listening to a voicemail on his mobile phone. It turned out the one exception to Mahasi-style slowness was in its manner of expulsion. Within about fifteen minutes an Uber had pulled up and the blond guy was trundling his suitcase across the car park.

That left me, Corinne, Jason and Greg. (I knew their names from the schedule pinned to the dharma-room door, giving the time-slots for our daily ten-minute interview with the Sayadaw. 'Melissa' and 'Nick' had been crossed out within minutes of their respective departures.) Corinne was a serious young Frenchwoman whose utter stillness, in sitting meditation, I assumed was the result of long experience, but who after the retreat was over told me she'd never meditated before. Jason was from the US, twitchy, overweight, a little cautious or introverted in manner. Greg was from Ruthin in north Wales, even bigger than Jason, six foot four and ostentatiously camp. Corinne was by all appearances a natural, but of the remaining three of us it remained to be seen who would last the full ten days. Vipassana means 'insight' – or, more accurately, as the Burmese meditation master U Pandita teaches us, 'seeing through various modes'. The modern form was developed in the late nineteenth and early twentieth centuries as a means for lay people to gain insight into the three characteristics of existence laid down in the Pali canon: *anicca*, or impermanence, *dukkha*, or unsatisfactoriness, and *anatta*, not-self. That is, nothing lasts, life is pain, and you or I as unchanging, permanent selves do not exist. Cast off the delusions of permanence and abiding self and you become a *sotapanna*: a stream-enterer, having attained the first of the four stages of enlightenment.

The style of insight meditation taught by the Burmese monk Mahasi Sayadaw differed from the methods taught by other influential vipassana teachers like S.N. Goenka in focusing on the rising and falling of the abdomen – as opposed, for instance, to the passage of breath through the nostrils – and on the finely detailed noting enabled by slowing everything down to a crawl. Opposite the Saraniya Centre was a low-rise housing estate, and during walking meditations the same group of drinkers, a thin young woman and two blokes in grey hoodies – often accompanied by a slender grey cat, slinking between their legs or jumping up onto the wall to be stroked – would loiter on the patchy grass up front, clutching their cans and staring, impassively, as we enacted our own weird ritual of elective incapacitation. 'During an intensive retreat,' writes U Pandita, 'a yogi should act like a hospital patient: frail and sick.'

For frail hospital patients, the schedule was pretty strenuous. Up at 4 a.m. for an hour's sitting meditation at 4.45 a.m. Then alternate, hour-long walking and sitting meditations until the final sit ended at 10 p.m. Lay yogis observed the Eight Precepts – to the monks' 227 – including abstention from sex, killing, telling lies, listening to music, and, most pressingly – given that opportunities for sex and killing people were limited – eating after midday. Breakfast was at six, lunch at eleven, meaning that the only other breaks in the meditative round were the early-afternoon interview with the monk, and a recorded, witheringly puritanical 'dharma talk' between seven and eight in the evening, given by an American nun who sounded like Marilynne Robinson shorn of all the warmth and humanity. Example: how anyone who failed to keep the Five Precepts – including the ban on intoxicants – was 'no longer a true human'. Dinner was to be avoided as 'a meal that often leads to other indulgences'. The advice for young yogis struggling under the burden of lust was to visualise the object of their desires dissected into thirty-two pieces, and reflect on their repulsiveness. You could imagine a better night out with Abba Ammonius and his red-hot iron.

It was an eighteen-hour day, in other words, at least fifteen hours of which were spent in formal meditation. Not that the remaining three hours amounted to time off. You practised *satipatthana*, mindfulness, without let-up, taking note of every movement and intention to move as you ate, drank, showered and tied your shoelaces with excruciating slowness. It was, at least for the beginner, an exercise in Olympic (or sectionable) pedantry, Knausgaardian attention to minutiae, Warholian immersion in tedium. In the dharma hall, we sat facing the Sayadaw, U Tarraka, plump in his saffron robes, his wire-rim spectacles perched above an expression of unwavering sternness. Behind him, on a dais, a golden Buddha watched over the hall, his head at the centre of a light display that flashed red, blue, green and white in concentric circles, radiating a distinctly disco-oriented lovingkindness. Alongside the Buddha, on the hour, a speaking clock announced the time and room temperature in a weirdly prepubescent synthesised voice, zero-seven-hundred-hours, nineteen-point-eight-degrees, which meant, at the beginning of each meditation, the secondary mental object it was my task to label then let pass without judgement was invariably Gil Gerard's robot sidekick Twiki from *Buck Rogers in the 25th Century*.

In their seminal study, *The Science of Meditation*, the Harvard psychologists Daniel Goleman and Richie Davidson posit four levels of meditative intensity. Levels 1 and 2 constitute the 'deep path': 1, the intense practice of Theravadan and Tibetan renunciates, and 2, practices in the same lineage but removed from their monastic or ascetic contexts. Levels 3 and 4 are the 'wide path': 3, the deracinated, secularised and ultimately far less exacting forms of mindfulness I had studied under Vanessa, and 4, the sort of watered-down (and therefore most accessible) mindfulness you might encounter in apps like Headspace and Calm.

Sitting with the Sayadaw definitely felt like Level 2. Dhammasoti was right. There *was* a huge difference between MBSR and intensive meditation in the Mahasi tradition. Every time I tried to focus on my belly my mind would slip off, my mental fingers too weak to grip the climbing hold, a failure that would have been instantly forgiven in a mindfulness class, even treated as a positive learning experience, but here, under the iron invigilation of the monk, disinterred the miseries of childhood PE, shivering in my gym shorts as I tried to understand how anyone could be physically capable of climbing a rope. And like childhood PE, it *hurt*. After twenty minutes of sitting, even in a loose quarter-lotus, my hips would begin to ache, so much so in the following ten or fifteen minutes that I would begin to shift on my cushion, chased around in fidgety little circles by a pain I could never escape. Once this began to happen – particularly if I looked up to check if any of the other three were having the same problem – the loss of concentration was invariably terminal.

'What should I do?' I asked in my after-lunch interview. These took place upstairs from the dharma hall in the office, Bhante Tarraka in an armchair, Tin, the centre's general admin guy and translator, sitting beside me on the floor. There was no specific instruction to keep my head bowed – nor, I had been repeatedly assured, was this any sort of interrogation or exam – but combined with Bhante's implacable expression the seating arrangements kind of dictated I keep my eyes on his feet. 'The pain,' I said. 'It's so distracting.'

Bhante breathed in with a grimace before saying something in Burmese.

'Then look at it more closely,' translated Tin. 'Use the pain as a focus.'

Sara Lazar would agree. Sara was the Harvard Medical School researcher whose 2005 study had indicated that long-term vipassana meditation could alter the brain at the anatomical level. I visited Sara a few months before my vipassana retreat at her office in the Boston Navy Yard. Vast fragments of ice were drifting in the Mystic River, and the snow lay pushed in grubby mounds against the old warehouse buildings. We know from the work of Giuseppe Pagnoni and others that meditation has the effect of switching our cognitive resources from our 'priors' – the internal models we've built of the world, based on our past experience of it – to observable reality. It wakes us up to the present moment. By stimulating the production of brain chemicals like BDNF, Interleukin-10 and GABA, and redressing the balance between our sympathetic and parasympathetic nervous systems, meditation (and meditative practices like yoga) can also inhibit neuronal excitability, that is, calm us down.

To understand in more detail how meditation promotes attentional focus – precisely what I would have such trouble achieving, sitting in the dharma hall in Salford – I asked Sara to explain her work on the 'salience network', the disparate group of brain regions that regulates what we pay attention to, and when.

'So, right now you're not paying much attention to what your elbow feels like, right?' Lithe, with a cascade of greying curls, Sara was sitting on a swivel chair with her bare feet tucked underneath her. Following her train of thought took a degree of meditative focus: she spoke at the speed that her mind worked, with the result that whole clauses were apt to meld into single, German-style compounds. 'But if something suddenly hit your elbow, and it hurt, you'd pay attention to your elbow. But, of course, information is coming from your elbow twenty-four/seven.' The salience network preserves cognitive resources by selecting only the stimuli it deems worthy of attention. 'So it's sort of directing traffic.'

Current research suggests that meditation promotes increased activity in the salience network – in other words, that it helps us to direct our attentional traffic more effectively. The impression I would form in Salford, that the pain of sitting in the lotus position was causing me to lose focus, was the wrong way round. It was my failure to focus that was causing the pain – or, rather, making the pain harder to put up with. 'If pain arises during meditation,' writes U Pandita, 'a yogi should summon all of his or her courage and energy simply to look it in the face.' Focus on the pain and the pain becomes more bearable: it is the wandering mind that makes it less so. Basic MBSR shows us that meditation can help switch off the wandering mind and focus our attention on a certain stimulus – be that pain, or the spot on the floor five feet in front of our noses. What Sara's work demonstrates are the neural structures underlying this transfer of attentional engagement – the brain mechanisms that bring phenomena into focus.

'There are two parts of the salience network that come up over and over again in studies on the effects of meditation,' she told me. 'The insula and the amygdala. Oh, and the PCC.' The PCC is the posterior cingulate cortex, a central node in the default mode network that brain-imaging studies have shown to be activated during self-related cognitive processing – that is, when we're thinking about ourselves.

'So the PCC is all about the self,' said Sara. 'And it becomes deactivated during meditation – but also more connected. And that's a long-term change. It becomes more connected long-term.'

Greater connectivity between the PCC and other control networks in the brain is a marker of its reactivity: it helps it switch on and off quickly, where, conversely, the failure of the default mode network and its component regions to deactivate when necessary is a correlate of impaired cognitive function, excessive mind wandering and so on. Meditation both assists in switching off our sense of self and in enhancing the neural network that makes sure our sense of self is switched on and off at appropriate times. It is both the switch and the switch-maker. Being lost in thought is inherently constitutive of self: you are temporarily oblivious to your surroundings, caught up in your head. As Sara told me, 'the default mode network is like: the chatter is all about me. And so most of the time we're not paying attention to the sensory. What happens with meditation is, you're flipping it. The chatty mind gets shut off and the sensory gets paid attention to.'

In a meditative state, a lessened sense of self and increased attentional focus are two sides of the same coin. Quite how the insula and amygdala interact with the PCC is something neurobiologists are yet to understand fully. Nonetheless, the function of the network is clear: constantly to monitor which stimuli deserve our attention. What meditation appears to promote is the timely switching from self-directed, wandering thought patterns to intense attentional focus.

As with Giuseppe Pagnoni, Sara's academic speciality grew out of a personal interest. A keen runner, she was training for the Boston marathon when 'a bunch of knee and back injuries' led her to try yoga. What she had initially understood as purely physical therapy soon revealed other possibilities. 'I'd been a runner for a long time, I'd always stretched. But this wasn't stretching. It wasn't exercise. It was something else.' Sara's specialism at the time was bacteriology. So taken was she by the meditative elements of yoga that she not only started practising vipassana but decided to make it her academic field.

'It was like, okay, I have to switch. And here I am.'

Sara's 2005 study built on earlier findings in neuroplasticity. It had long been established that activities like juggling, or, famously, acquiring the Knowledge, the network of routes

London cabbies are required to memorise, could induce changes in grey matter. Sara's research suggested that meditation could similarly alter the brain at the anatomical level.

'It's well known that the front part of the brain shrinks with age,' she said. 'In our study, there were a couple of regions where fifty-year-old meditators had just as much grey matter as the twenty-five-year-olds.' Long-term meditation guarded against age-related cognitive decline by thickening the areas prone to shrinkage. In the meditators, greater cortical thickness was detected in the anterior insula and parts of the prefrontal cortex, regions implicated in attentional focus and interoception, our ability to monitor the internal state of our bodies – our somatic self-awareness, in other words.

A number of subsequent brain-imaging studies seemed to corroborate Sara's findings. Goleman and Davidson urge caution, however. While a meta-analysis conducted at Stanford, taking in Sara's study and twenty of the neuroimaging studies that followed it, lent further weight to the idea of brain growth as a function of long-term meditation, it conflated a number of different traditions and techniques, from vipassana to Zen and kundalini yoga, each of which can involve sharply distinct forms of mental activity, relating in turn to different brain areas. It was impossible to tell if the results pertained to meditation in general, or were skewed by certain techniques that had a disproportionate effect. More significantly, attempts at Davidson's lab, at the University of Wisconsin, to reproduce Sara's findings on cortical thickening met with failure.

None of which is to say that the 'hints of neural rewiring' undergirding meditative trait effects are anything other than credible. It's just a question, as so often in these fields, of reaching a critical mass of data. Sat Bir Singh Khalsa is confident the research will soon become incontrovertible. 'I'm already there myself,' he told me. 'And I think a lot of scientists already pretty much accept that these practices can lead to these sorts of neurobiological changes.' Neurotheology, or 'contemplative-sciences research', as it's sometimes called, is still in its infancy. 'In the

1950s, there were scientists doing studies on smoking causing cancer,' he said. 'And the critics were saying, oh, the evidence is weak, there's just not enough there. The fact that the evidence was weak doesn't mean that smoking doesn't cause cancer, it's just that we weren't there yet. So I think we're in the same area with contemplative-sciences research. It's really a new area.'

Sara's second major study was into the effects of long-term vipassana meditation on fluid intelligence – that is, our ability to use information to solve novel problems, irrespective of experience, training or pre-existing knowledge. The IQ test is the classic example, throwing us back on our faculties of logic, reasoning and pattern recognition. Ordinarily, fluid intelligence is another ability that declines with age. ('Crystallised intelligence', on the other hand, drawing on the knowledge that we accumulate over time, tends by its very nature to increase as we get older, at least until age-related memory impairment kicks in). One of the cortical regions that seemed to be preserved in the long-term meditators is implicated in the neural basis of fluid intelligence.

'So we gave them the standard IQ test,' said Sara. 'Because again, it's well known that that goes down with age normally. But in the long-term meditators it was more or less preserved. Not a hundred per cent preserved, it went down slightly, but nowhere near as much as in the non-meditators.'

Fluid intelligence as a response to the uncontextualised present: again, there seems – with all Goleman and Davidson's caveats – to be a neural basis for meditation as a means of tipping the cognitive scales in favour of immediacy, the world as it is in the moment. And the more intensive the practice, the stronger the results. Retreat, thinks Sara, is not just a respite from unmindfulness. It's an opportunity to accelerate the structural changes to your brain. 'I feel a week on retreat is equivalent easily to a year or two of regular practice.' Although Sara still took a yoga class once or twice a week, vipassana was her one true path. She did a regular silent retreat at the Insight Meditation Society, sixty miles west of Boston in Barre,

Massachusetts, where Joseph Goldstein, Jack Kornfield and Sharon Salzberg had laid the groundwork for the American vipassana movement, reconciling the strict Theravadan teachings with a more pliable, integrative approach.

'I think I've done nine there,' said Sara. 'They rock my world.'

I drove from Sara's office to Barre after three days of heavy snowfall. That morning it had rained and iced over, before breaking out in sunshine, turning the fields and front lawns either side of Route 122 into sheets of celestial brilliance, as if all of New England had been paved in mirrors, or I had fallen asleep on the Massachusetts Turnpike and woken up in the dazzling afterlife of an Emily Dickinson poem. In Barre, I left my rented Chevy in the parking lot off Pleasant Street and picked my way through the snow to the rather grand, columned portico of the Insight Meditation Society. Inside I was met by Steve McGee, a veteran meditation teacher with a neatly trimmed beard and a nervy smile that sprang back the moment it formed, as if his cheekbones were electrified. How had he originally come to Buddhist meditation, I asked?

'Like most people come to the dharma practice,' he said. 'Suffering. Life was not going the way I wanted it to. I was looking for some reasons why, etcetera, etcetera. Yeah?'

We went on to discuss *upadana*, clinging, and how overcoming it, practising non-attachment, was perfectly compatible with the intense attachment you might feel, for instance, to your children. In 'relative reality', you loved your kids. In 'more absolute reality', there were no kids there to love, and no you there to love them. Still, even in relative reality, detachment had its points. Steve used to be an avid sports fan. Now he watched less, because he couldn't take the anxiety. 'There's never rest,' he said. 'You can't rest.'

'But isn't this the same as loving your kids?' I said. 'The anxiety is the price you pay for loving your ...'

'What I'm saying is certain things we do let go, because it isn't worth it. We do detach. Yeah?'

It was hard to escape the feeling that I was getting on Steve's nerves. I wondered if I was encountering the same problem I'd run into with Sister Nectaria – that my questions, by their very nature, their very constitution in words, disqualified me from participation in the numinous – that my effort to understand was an act of bad faith when the domain of enquiry was beyond human comprehension. Either that, or Steve belonged to the same class of spiritual gatekeeper as Phil's forbidding Sayadaw Dhammasoti. The suspicion that the wisdom tradition was overseen by grouches who had ascended to a higher plane then pulled up the ladder was something that I was keen not to let harden into an internal model. I had often asked myself if the real impetus for Phil's long retreats in Rangoon and Nepal was not the clarity of mind they offered but the distance they put between him and the rest of us. To subject himself to arguably the hardest of all meditative disciplines, for that long, in forty-degree heat – might that not have been at least a semi-conscious attempt to leave us all behind, to rationalise the gap he felt between himself and others by making it un-bridgeable? That was certainly the way it felt with Steve, that snowbound afternoon at the IMS, at least until I mentioned that I was booked in for a ten-day silent meditation retreat at a Mahasi centre back home in England.

'They're going to push you hard,' Steve said. We were in the vestibule now, retreatants in sweatpants and snood scarves footing past in their socks. In the time we'd been upstairs in Steve's office it had started snowing again. Through the glass walls of the dharma hall the view had turned grainy, as if observable reality's aerial had snapped in the storm. 'One of the pitfalls of Mahasi – and it's not inherent in the system, it's what we bring to it – is striving. You've got to really stay relaxed.' They were going to push me hard, Steve was saying, not to push myself too hard. 'Practise the form intently, but do it with a relaxed attitude. Yeah?'

*

Pretty much every retreat I'd been on – save the solo ones, of course – had a non-joiner or two, a misfit, a rebel or insurrectionist. It was an inevitable consequence of the group dynamic. Someone was going to chafe against it. It's one of the main pointers in Benedict's Rule: how to deal with monks who won't fall into line. In Salford, we were evenly split between obedience and insurrection: Corinne and I on the path to righteousness, Jason and Greg in the naughty corner. Jason's non-compliance was by omission. I would learn, over the coming days, that he had extensive knowledge of the suttas but almost no interest in, or patience for, the practice. Greg was a different matter. Shaven-headed, a giant by nature and habit, Greg had been a worry from day one, when I caught sight of him after breakfast, twisting and untwisting a hand towel around his enormous fists. His facial expressions alternated between loose-lipped scowls of barely contained psychic pressure, and, when he knew someone was looking, the mock-scandalised pouts of a pantomime dame. He was like Private Pyle in *Full Metal Jacket*. I seriously feared he was going to murder us all.

There may have been only two meals a day, but they were plentiful, huge stockpots and steamers of delicious Burmese stir-fries, curries and stews. Greg would take full advantage, loading his plate with two types of curry, rice, noodles, stir-fried vegetables, anything that was going, then balancing five or six samosas on top. Then going up for seconds. On the first day, I had been assigned the seat opposite him, and we were expected to sit in the same place at every meal. Hypersensitised to sound, now no talking was allowed, it was as much as I could do to keep my own food down, listening to Greg slurp and crunch bones and audibly swallow, finishing off his breakfast with a large slice of chocolate cake and a rhubarb Activia scarfed down in two spoonfuls.

The proper conditions for mindfulness are laid out in the *Anapanasati Sutta*, the most detailed of the Buddha's discourses on awareness of the breath as a basis for meditation. The monk should go 'to the wilderness, to the shade of a tree, or to an empty building'. In the *Bhagavad Gita*, Krishna instructs the yogi to 'practise the harmony of soul: in a secret place, in deep solitude'. True wisdom comes of 'retiring to solitary places, and avoiding the noisy multitudes'. Steering clear of distraction is a *sine qua non* across the contemplative traditions. 'When thou prayest,' Jesus tells us in the Gospel of Matthew, 'enter into thy closet, and when thou hast shut thy door, pray to thy Father which is in secret.'

And yet the meditation masters warn against a common temptation: getting wound up when the conditions are less than ideal. Even the great U Pandita, student of Mahasi Sayadaw, admits to having felt irritation during his early experiences, meditating under the venerable master at Mahasi Sasana Yeiktha in Rangoon. The lay meditators 'seemed to communicate and move about in an uncivilised, impolite manner'. He soon realised his error. He was there to practise the dharma, not to criticise others. Joseph Goldstein, founder of the IMS and luminary of American insight meditation, describes the irony of reacting to unmindfulness in others: you can only do it by being unmindful yourself. The trick was to note, without judgement, the sound of Greg swallowing a huge clump of incompletely chewed rice and mutton curry, and move on.

Perhaps, it struck me, Greg had been sent as a test. I thought of Catherine of Siena, the fourteenth-century Italian mystic admired by Sara Maitland, who, as a 'tertiary' or lay associate of her local Dominican order, lived in near-complete silence and solitude at home – a home she shared with her twenty-four siblings, roughly half of whom survived beyond infancy. 'Build a cell inside your mind, from which you can never flee,' she told her friend and spiritual director, Raymond of Capua. Could I do likewise, even as Greg, passing me on the stairs as I walked up to my interview with the monk, turned his large, sweatpant-clad rear end toward me, and twerked like Miley Cyrus? After lunch on day three, as I filled a plastic cup from the water cooler outside the dharma hall, Greg caught my eye.

'Bored yet?' he whispered. 'I'm bored out my fucking mind.'

I put a finger to my lips. But the next day he did it again – outside, round the back of the dharma hall, as our paths crossed during a walking meditation. 'I'm so fucking *bored.*' This time I wrote him a note – something along the lines of, sorry, I'd like to observe the silence, let's have a chat when the ten days are up – handing it to him with a mix of indignation and embarrassment, that he'd put me in the position of being the class swot, the pious square. Because I couldn't imagine surviving ten days of silent meditation without submitting to its strictures. It was a question of immersion, like diving into a Norwegian fjord. Unbearable if you tiptoed in, painful but ultimately okay – exhilarating, maybe – if you took the plunge. Not that I was meant to be doing anything other than noting Greg's unmindfulness, but it seemed, to my own unmindful mind, as if he was bored out of his precisely because he wasn't accepting the boredom, plunging into it, working through it to the other side. Without this, ten days at Saraniya would indeed be an exceptionally bleak and unstimulating way to spend your Easter break.

It was bleak, anyway, certainly for those first few days, the constant failure, the lack of mental purchase, together with a dawning recognition of the truth in Steve McGee's words – that trying harder, marshalling all your reserves of will and analytical firepower as you might with an intellectual problem, simply wouldn't work. There is much talk of 'penetration' in the meditation literature – penetrating the object of observation, penetrating into the true nature of phenomena. What I was experiencing was a form of meditative impotence. The harder I willed it, the more flaccid my retreating brain became. Sara Lazar had spoken of her tendency to plan during sitting meditations.

'I don't know about you,' she had said. 'But I have planned entire people's lives while I was on retreat.'

I did the same, except in place of other people's lives, I planned my own, my forthcoming trip to the Arctic Circle to meet the solo adventurer Randi Skaug, the lazy pleasure of itineraries, packing lists, possible interview questions, until *ah*, the sudden pang of awareness, planning planning, and the absolute determination not to let it happen again, until it did, about five seconds later.

'What did you notice about the primary object?'

This was Tin again, translating for the Sayadaw in my after-lunch interview. The 'primary object' was the rising and falling of my abdomen, what I was meant to be focusing my attention on.

'I noticed it wasn't always smooth,' I said. 'Sometimes my stomach seemed to expand a little jerkily.'

A rapid nod before Bhante spoke again.

'Any problems?' translated Tin.

'My mind keeps going out. My grasp feels so weak.'

Bhante took a deep breath, then spoke for what seemed like about two minutes. The only word I recognised was 'yogi', presumably referring to me, and recurring so often that I could only assume I was being given a detailed and scrupulously made-to-measure bollocking. I felt like the Ndembu chief-elect, steeling himself for his ritual humiliation.

'This is good,' said Tin. 'It shows your concentration is getting better.' I dared a glance at Bhante, to check if there had been some translation error. But Bhante just sat there, nose nobly elevated, interlaced fingers resting on the bunched robe above his belly. The gist of the argument was that to notice my grasp was weak was a sign, paradoxically, of its increasing strength, of my growing ability to notice subtle changes in my mind. I was still getting used to the drift of these interviews. I knew that a level of *koan*-like cryptography was common to many contemplative traditions; on the train back from Mount Saint Bernard Abbey I had met an elderly man who told me, somewhat mysteriously, that his life had been saved by a riddle. The riddle with Bhante's interviews, for their part, was in their apparent simplicity: there seemed, on the basis of the four I'd had so far, to be a slightly formulaic tendency to contrariness or expectation-reversal in play. Any time I reported progress,

I'd get a 'hmm' or a 'You have to look more closely.' Reports of difficulty, on the other hand, would be met with broad approval. This topsy-turvyism did, I supposed, accord with the principle of non-attachment, not getting too pleased with success, or down about failure. It was just hard to suppress a lifetime's desire to please teacher, to present the shiny apple in the expectation of praise.

Tin produced a spotless paper hankie from the pocket of his jeans. 'This is your mind,' he said. It wasn't clear if he was continuing to translate or had gone off on his own tangent. 'Imagine you spill a drop of coffee or curry on it. If it was dirty, you wouldn't see the stain.'

The self is what stains our hankies. There is a widespread and entirely mistaken claim that the Western notion of the self – as defined as our essential identity, whatever it is in us that remains the same throughout (and for the faithful, beyond) our bodily lives – is a relatively recent invention, not properly articulated until the Renaissance, and the development of realistic, volumetrically modelled self-portraiture, as in Masaccio and Filippino Lippi's frescoes in the Brancacci Chapel in Florence. Others date the evolution of the unified self to the time of Descartes, and his conclusion that for a thought to exist, there must be a 'thinking entity' – that is, a self – to think it.

A closer look at the history of Western thought reveals that ideas corresponding to selfhood and subjectivity date back much further, to late antiquity – if not to the classical period, when, in the dialogue known as the *Phaedo*, Plato has Socrates define his *psyche* or soul as his true self. Not only does the soul survive the body, but it passes the test posed by later theorists of self by remaining unchanged while the individual is still alive. To speak in this way of 'the self' in an ancient or medieval context might be anachronistic, but by the definitions offered by Plato, St Augustine and others, it's fair to read a notion of a unified, immaterial, and moreover continuous self into what classical and Christian thinkers referred to as 'the soul'.

The early Christian Church picked up and extended this principle of selfhood both through the doctrine of God's love – that He loves us all, equally, but as distinct individuals – and by asserting that it's up to us, as *sinful* individuals, to make ourselves worthy of that love. Early Christian thinkers differed as to the precise nature of personal immortality, but thanks largely to the influence of Augustine, the view prevailed that after bodily death a person retained the same immaterial soul and material body as they had possessed in life. The point, for our purposes, is this: continuity. Our essential selves are unique to each one of us, and continue unchanged, even after death.

With Descartes's equation of mind and self, and later, the English philosopher John Locke's view that it was the individual's consciousness that accounted for his personal identity, came the gradual dethroning of the soul in favour of a 'self' produced by mental processes. 'For since consciousness always accompanies thinking,' wrote Locke in his *Essay Concerning Human Understanding*, 'and it is that that makes everyone to be what he calls *self*, and thereby distinguishes himself from all other thinking things: in this alone consists *personal identity*, i.e. the sameness of a rational being.' We are 'ourselves' from the moment that this consciousness begins. In the early nineteenth century, the German philosopher Georg W.F. Hegel proposed that our consciousness of self arises from our interaction with others. By recognising person B as a self-conscious being, we infer that they must recognise the same in ourselves. We become conscious of our own selves by seeing ourselves as others see us – a theory that does, of course, have profound implications for isolated retreat, and its effect on the retreatant's self-consciousness. In the twentieth century, the Hegelian idea that we depend on others for our sense of self can be traced, via the existentialist phenomenology of Martin Heidegger and Jean-Paul Sartre, in the existential and humanistic psychology which was to have such influence on Fritz Perls, and thus on

Gestalt, Esalen and the subsequent world-conquering notion that there is, in all of us, deep down, under the deadening accretions of normality, a 'true' or 'authentic' self it is in our interests to uncover.

All of which, of course, runs directly counter to Eastern modes of thought. According to the Buddhist doctrine of *anatta* ('not-self'), the unchanging, permanent self is an illusion. It does not exist. Clinging to the delusional idea that it does is a major source of *dukkha*, or suffering. There is, in truth, a strain in Western thought that maintains much the same thing. The Scottish philosopher David Hume proposed that the self was a fiction, an idea picked up and extended by Friedrich Nietzsche: we merely experience successive states, undergirded by a unity entirely of our own invention. These views are outliers, however. Christians speak of kenosis, the 'self-emptying' submission to the will of God – although without, as Sara Maitland reminds us, 'losing specific personality'. The self is still there, for all that we might loosen our grip on it. Post-war developments in analytic philosophy, postmodernism, and, in more recent years, gender and critical race theory have done much to undermine the notion of a unified self – replacing it, you might say, with a pick-and-mix infinity of social, political and sexual identities – without, nonetheless, disputing the self's reality. With the exception of thinkers like Hume and Nietzsche – and certain neuroscientific accounts of the self as an illusion created by the brain – in Western culture the notion of the self as a non-illusory site of individual personhood, the place where our 'I' resides, has proved remarkably tenacious. The self exists, even if in a pile of incoherent fragments, where in Buddhist metaphysics it is nothing but a mirage.

Which points to a contradiction in Westernised meditation, especially as practised in commercial wellness centres. How can a tradition founded, in the case of Buddhist meditation, on the illusoriness of the self be placed at the service of self-improvement? We know from the work of Richie Davidson, Sat Bir Singh Khalsa and others that the transcendent state reported by experienced meditators corresponds to the deactivation of brain areas implicated in 'self-related cognitive processing', that is, in thinking about ourselves. Switch the self off and we feel closer to eternity. The neurotheologist Dr Andrew Newberg cites recent research that found patients with tumours affecting the parietal lobes – again, brain areas involved in the building of our sense of self – were more likely to 'express spiritual feelings' than the control. The transcendent state and the sense of self are not only incompatible. They're directly opposed to one another.

Or perhaps it's not such a contradiction, or needn't be. The American psychologist and founding member of the Insight Meditation Society, Jack Engler, speaks of the 'particular vulnerability' of two types of individual often seen at Buddhist retreats – young adults emerging from adolescence, and those 'entering or passing through the mid-life transition'. Engler characterises these individuals as having 'a borderline level of ego organisation'. Among them, Engler thinks, there is a tendency to misinterpret the doctrine of not-self as a free pass to self-neglect, an excuse to duck out of the 'essential psychosocial task' of identity formation. If the self doesn't exist, these borderline types calculate, then I needn't bother figuring out who I am. Engler sees this as a profound mistake. It's a bit like that Picasso quote about it taking him four years to paint like Raphael, but a lifetime to paint like a child. You need to learn the rules before you start breaking them – that is, to establish a strong sense of self before you accept its illusoriness. 'Put very simply,' Engler writes, 'you have to be somebody before you can be nobody.'

The breakthrough came on day five. The other side of the fence behind the dharma hall was a ginnel, the kind of cobbled back alley common in northern towns but exotic to a Londoner. The street's retreat. Often on my walking meditations a grey cat – possibly the one I'd seen with the drinkers outside the council block – would squeeze through the locked metal gate that gave onto the ginnel and pad mindfully past, before slinking back out again, or leaping up to lick its paws at the top of the fence. On this occasion it had stopped, and, ears pricked, was observing me closely – noting noting – as I paced the paving stones, lifting my foot, lifting lifting, moving it forward, moving moving, then dropping the heel to the ground. At the fence I would stop, note my intention to turn, then turn, in five treacly stages, turning turning, before setting off in the opposite direction.

And then without quite noticing the transition I had *entered* the walk, as it were, begun to notice not only the three stages of each footstep but the limitless tiny sensations each stage comprised, and which differed, minutely, with each step: a tension in my left arch as it flattened, a greater pressure at the base of my right little toe, a scarcely perceptible click between the tendons attached to my left big toe and its neighbour.

Tedious as it sounds, it was anything but: I was a toddler again, transfixed by first principles, forcibly down-regulating my priors until the present moment opened up to reveal its infinity. The last time I remembered experiencing anything vaguely comparable was in about 1998, taking magic mushrooms and staring at a flattened patch of chewing gum on Clapham High Street, for what Phil later told me was more than an hour, fascinated by the fractal immeasurability of its coastline. Here, however, the experience was clean, clear, without any of the oh-Christ-I'm-fucked, juddery self-awareness of the psyche-delic high. Just a succession of sensations, noted the instant they occurred, still like film frames run to give the illusion of continuity. The next time I looked up the cat had gone, and it was time go inside for the sitting meditation.

Twiki announced the hour and I closed my eyes. And the same thing happened: very soon, after the first few rises and falls of the abdomen, I began to notice the ever-changing small-print of each rise and fall, how, on one rise, the left side of the right side of my abdomen seemed to dilate more than the rest of it, or how, on another, the mild twinge between the second and third ribs on my right side seemed connected, at maximum dilation, to a tension below my right shoulder blade. Again, in retrospect I was reminded of Karl Ove Knausgaard, describing the irregular perimeters of his cornflakes in volume three of *My Struggle*, just as I had been transfixed by the patch of gum on Clapham High Street. My salience network had been hijacked: I couldn't *not* pay attention. It was both an exhilarating and disconcerting feeling, the extreme focus that was at once a partial loss of control, like the first uncertain circuits of an ice rink. Still, the effect on my experience of pain was remarkable.

Formerly, like I say, I couldn't sit still for more than half an hour without succumbing to the discomfort in my hips. Now, the minute attention I was paying to the rise and fall of my abdomen seemed to encompass my sensation of pain, particularising it, splitting it into its component parts, a heat that might be a pressure, a pinch of something colder or more needling, a throb whose texture started out soft and became grainy, like the sand underfoot in the Ganges, with the result that the pain became more an impersonal object of interest than a cause of offence. There wasn't less pain. I just didn't mind it any more.

The Four Noble Truths of Buddhism go like this: that life is *dukkha* or suffering, that craving or attachment is the cause of suffering, that suffering can be ended with the elimination of all attachments, and that the Noble Eightfold Path shows us the way to bring an end to suffering. In the *Sallatha Sutta*, the Buddha teaches us that ignorance of the Four Noble Truths can lead to unnecessary suffering. Being struck by an arrow causes pain, no doubt about it. Worrying about *why* you were struck by the arrow, getting angry or upset about it, wishing you weren't in pain or punishing yourself for feeling it in the first place is to be struck by a second arrow. The 'two arrows paradigm' has become something of a Buddhist platitude, an old saw to embroider on a bookmark or hang above the cistern.

'Pain is inevitable, suffering optional.' Nonetheless, my experience post-breakthrough demonstrated the truth of the teaching pretty irrefutably. To sit and observe the arrow quivering in my hip was to understand, in a comprehensively practical way, that the unbearable part was not the pain but my reaction to it.

Professor Christopher Eccleston sees the application of this understanding to chronic pain. Chris is a medical psychologist at the University of Bath, where he directs the Centre for Pain Research, with a special focus on the psychology of 'neglected' senses like proprioception and interoception. We spoke by phone a few months after my Salford retreat. Chris's voice is an analgesic in itself, soothing, measured, calm: ibuprofen for the ears. The psychological function of acute pain, he told me, is 'to promote an awareness of potential harm in your environment'. Attending to it is appropriate, a natural protective response. 'To not attend to a signal of harm is a bit like sitting in a building while the fire alarm is going off.'

The problem comes when the pain is both long-lasting and with no immediate or localised cause. Generally speaking, our willingness to accept that pain is an unreliable signifier of harm depends on the place and duration of that pain. 'Most of us tend to understand that if you have a headache it doesn't mean you have some serious disease. We just think we've evolved this odd tendency to have irrelevant pain.'

Applying this insight to more intractable conditions like back pain is notoriously difficult. 'Most people [with back pain] find it very hard not to believe that they've damaged themselves,' said Chris. The great value in meditative practices is in forcibly 'breaking the cultural pact that pain means harm'. Pain is intrinsically egocentric. 'It's an alarm that tells you, now. Stop everything you're doing.' Attend to yourself. Again, in the case of acute pain, this is beneficial. Burn your wrist on the grill pan and your temporary egocentrism is excusable: you need to stop everything and run it under the cold tap. By contrast, in cases where pain is unlikely to indicate harm in your environment, as with my aching hips, or in chronic physical and mental conditions like back pain and depression, to lessen the egocentric element – to take the 'I' out of pain – is to demonstrate that pain is only another phenomenon, impersonal, independent, and subject to the same law of impermanence as everything else. It arises and so must pass away.

If pain arises, summon all your courage and look it in the face. Pain is the great teacher, our ever-reliable, in-house propagandist for the three characteristics. Nothing lasts. Life is suffering. And our ego only stands in the way, arms folded, the cauliflower-eared bouncer at the gates of truth.

Meanwhile the retreat was falling apart. In vipassana, the increasing absorption of the meditator is described in terms of 'jhanic factors'. In the Pali texts, there are four *jhanas*, each relating to an ever-deeper state of meditative consciousness, but we'll concern ourselves only with the first, itself divided into the five factors the meditator must attain to develop insight and wisdom. (The Five Jhanic Factors, The Noble Eightfold Path, The Seven Antidotes to Drowsiness: Buddhist bingo callers have a lot to work with.) The first two factors, *vitakka* and *vicara*, relate to the processes of directing your mind at the meditative object, and keeping it there, rubbing away at the object to perceive its true nature. Once these factors have manifested themselves, the mind enters *viveka*, or 'seclusion', secluded in that it has drawn back from the Five Hindrances (those numbers again) of desire, aversion, sloth, restlessness and doubt. This, in turn, leads to the third factor, *piti*, or rapture, the kind of euphoric rush or tingle I had felt driving past Stonehenge, and the fourth, *sukha*, happiness.

A danger arises here, and one that can forestall the fifth factor, *samadhi*, or concentration. Practise sincerely, U Pandita says, and you can overcome the *kilesas*, or defilements, of immoral action or thought. There is, however, a special category of defilement, the *vipassana kilesas*, comparable to the monastic vice of spiritual pride in that they often entail excessive self-regard: if I feel this great practising meditation, I must be pretty good at it.

I'd been guilty of this *kilesa* even before my breakthrough on the walking meditation. It was implicit in my irritation with Greg. Now, though, it was threatening to get out of hand. Once I'd got on top of the pain my *vitakka* and *vicara* went through the roof. The wall clock in the dharma hall was set fifteen seconds ahead of the speaking Twiki-clock; I would get so absorbed, especially in the early-morning meditations, that when the minute hand struck twelve, with a sprung little metallic sound it only made on the hour, I'd come to with a jerk, as if roused from a sleep that was actually a deeper wakefulness. Random thoughts still arose, but much less frequently. There was also a marked shift from the verbal to the visual, the drifts of interior monologue giving way to a succession of sharp apparitions – many of them, for some reason, featuring Sean Connery as the middle-aged Robin Hood in *Robin and Marian* – that arose and dematerialised with a serenity that was itself an aid to concentration. Sometimes I wondered if I could perceive a mental chatter just beyond the reach of comprehension, like a conversation in another room I was only aware of now a hush had descended at closer quarters.

'Good,' said Tin, when I mentioned this at my next interview. 'Your concentration is getting better. So you can hear more things.'

The possibility that my new-found powers of concentration were going to my head was a topic never directly addressed in these interviews, although it could arguably be inferred from the Sayadaw's general air of indifference. No matter how encouraging the words coming out of Tin's mouth, the Sayadaw's expression was a reminder not to get too encouraged by them, as if the simple act of translation had falsified his meaning by softening it. The better gauge was my attitude to the other retreatants. Jason and Greg were now in open revolt. Most often Jason could be found sunning himself round the back of the dharma hall, or, on rainy days, sitting in the vestibule flicking his Adam's apple or perusing the bookcase sparsely stocked with pamphlets in Pali and Burmese. Greg had stopped observing the silence altogether. He wasn't even trying to speak in an undertone. The zero-tolerance policy that had seen poor Nick kicked out on day two had been replaced, it seemed, now the retreat was drawing to a close, with a demob-happy free-for-all. Even serious Corinne had succumbed. She and Greg had developed the habit, at the top and tail of sitting meditations, of exchanging little Oliver-Hardy-ish tinkle-fingered air-hellos. Late in the afternoon of our penultimate day, at the end of a sitting meditation, Greg rose from his cushions and gave me a quizzical look.

'Are you a friend of Dorothy's?' he said.

Discipline had broken down to the extent that I couldn't be bothered not to answer. 'Who's Dorothy?'

'Well,' said Greg. 'If you don't know, there's no point in me asking.'

'Oh, I see.' It had clicked: he was asking if I was gay. 'No, I'm not.'

Was that really the first thing he wanted to ask after eight and a half days of silence? And why should I mind? The *kilesas* are also known as 'The Ten Armies of Mara'. Mara is derived from the Sanskrit for death. He is the personification of all that kills virtue. His Tenth Army is self-exultation: getting on your high meditative horse, thinking that just because you'd achieved a basic level of concentration, and a hyperactive but essentially amiable misfit was incapable of keeping his mouth shut for ten seconds, that you deserved preferment, a star-of-the-week sticker from the Sayadaw. (The next morning, at breakfast, when the ban on talking was lifted, it turned out that Greg was deeply versed in Tibetan Buddhism. All the fidgeting and rule breaking, by his account, had been because he found Theravadan practice so joyless by comparison.) Of all Mara's armies, the tenth is the most dangerous. Devadatta, the Buddha's cousin and brother-in-law, grew so admiring of his own powers of concentration that he tried to have the Buddha killed. Forgive. Recognise your own imperfections. And so I was getting to my feet, very slowly, noting Greg's failings but struggling not to exult in them, when I realised for the first time that the Buddha's disco lights were no longer radiating lovingkindness. He was just sitting there, noting my presence.

Strive not to strive. In Barre, briefly before I left the IMS, Steve and I had looked out on the intensifying snowstorm.

'Don't worry,' he had said. 'It won't settle.'

I drove back towards the 122 along Pleasant Street, the bare branches of the trees rimed in hoar frost and touching overhead to form a nave of fine white tracery that extended as far as I could see. After a couple of miles Pleasant Street began to descend, gently, to an intersection with the main road. I squeezed on the brakes. Nothing. I squeezed a little harder. The Chevy's back wheels began to slide out behind me. Ahead on the 122, to my left, maybe fifty yards away and closing, was a truck, an eighteen-wheeler with a dark-red, snub-nosed cab and a trailer adorned with a leaping German Shepherd and the legend VICTOR: A TRUSTED NAME IN PET NUTRITION.

I remember, as I glided over the stop line into the path of the truck, perceiving the grain in the Chevy's black-plastic dashboard with a fully sensuous clarity, the calfskin reticulation of it, and feeling, in the frictionlessness, in the immaculate attentional focus, in the nearness of death, the same weird kind of deranged exhilaration, or freedom, as I would feel a few months later, travelling back on the train from Salford. In the latter case I can remember exactly where I felt it: just over a mile outside Congleton. I knew this, although I'd never been to Congleton, because the feeling was so strong that I wanted to record where I'd had it, and so I opened up Google Maps on my phone. The blue dot representing my location was moving a little fitfully down the black line representing the railway track. From my window seat I could see a kink of grey river emerge from rolling folds of green. The window itself was bubble-wrapped in rain. And then it happened again: a wave of euphoria, like the Stonehenge tingle but more powerful, longer-lasting, as if the highs I had experienced sitting with the Sayadaw were merely a prelude to a delayed but more intense response, a loss of control that was as frightening as it was rapturous, the same mad time-dilated helplessness as I felt sliding in front of a freight truck and missing it by the wail of its horn.

6.

Benedictines of the Actual

Yaddo was born in bereavement. Christina, the second child of Spencer and Katrina Trask, founders of the artists' colony, came up with the name aged four, after her older brother Alanson had succumbed to meningitis. 'Call it Yaddo, Mamma,' she said. 'It makes poetry – Yaddo, shadow, shadow – Yaddo ...' Within eight years Christina and her two younger siblings would be dead, too, Christina and Spencer Jr. from diphtheria, the fourth and last, Katrina, within two weeks of her birth in 1889.

The storm had hardly subsided in the three-hour drive from Barre to upstate New York. By the time I pulled off the main road from Saratoga Springs, the wooded hill that forms the better part of the Yaddo estate was knee-deep in snow. The steep lane uphill to the mansion had been freshly snowploughed but looked about as navigable as a luge track. After my close call in Barre, I had listened twice to the 'Sigur Rós Sound Bath Experience' on my Calm app, piped through the Chevy's speakers, so that by the time I hit the I-91 I had arrived at something resembling a resting heart rate. Either side of the lane to the mansion was a lake named after one of the Trasks' dead children. I crept forward with a Mahasi-style slowness the Chevy's speedometer was unable to register, mindful, with every yard, that my wheels could spin and I'd begin and end my visit upended in Lake Alan.

The mansion sat on the hilltop hidden in huge evergreens. Spencer Trask had made his fortune on Wall Street, largely from financing the expansion of the railroads. The Trasks' determination to turn the spoils of that success, their 400-acre country estate near the fashionable spa town of Saratoga Springs, into an artists' retreat, arose in part from the aching void of bereavement. Now Christina and her siblings were gone, the artists would be their children. Even today, after nearly a century at the heart of American cultural life – to date, Yaddo alumni have seventy-seven Pulitzer Prizes, thirty-one MacArthur Fellowships, sixty-nine National Book Awards and a Nobel Prize (Saul Bellow) between them – there is a sense of Yaddo as a fissure, a hermitage or secular monastery that artists would disappear into, only to emerge, six or eight weeks later, with a manuscript or string quartet they had carried in with them as fragments, a feeling, an itch in the brain.

Maybe it was just the weather, but in the low light the house looked more mausoleum than monastery, with its sombre grey stone and vaguely medieval rows of leaded windows. Mario Puzo stayed at Yaddo three times in the fifties and sixties, and as I walked to reception I was reminded of the Corleone compound in the first *Godfather* film, under doomy skies and the low piano chords that invariably presaged an execution. It would be a few months until I upped my own contemplative practice at the vipassana centre in Salford. In the meantime, I wanted to consider how places of secular retreat, like Yaddo and the many artists' colonies it inspired, owed their guiding principles to the religious traditions that pre-dated them. Was there anything substantive in common between the contemplative practices of a Catholic monk, say, and the deep concentration available to residents at an artists' retreat? Were writers really monkish? Elaina Richardson, Yaddo's Scots-born president, certainly suggested as much: she saw her role as akin to an 'abbot or Mother Superior'.

'In the beginning,' she told me, 'I was probably of the instantly modernising sort of bent.' Elaina carried a trace of

Glaswegian in her accent like a half-remembered tune. She took on the Yaddo job in 2000, after four years as editor-in-chief at *Elle* magazine. 'The quiet hours, for instance. Because I'd been a journalist for so long, I knew you could focus in a room filled with forty other people, all typing away. So it took me a while to understand the simplicity of the mission at Yaddo.'

'And what do you think that was?'

'Again, it goes back to monasticism. The rules of an order turn out to be the things that shape it. I think for Yaddo that combination of an insistence on solitude and an insistence on community is a remarkably simple thing that just worked.'

In 1909, in a tragic stroke of irony for a railroad investor, Spencer Trask was killed in a train crash en route to New York. Katrina lived on until 1922. The first artists took up residency four years later. Apart from commemorating their children, the Trasks had founded Yaddo out of a more generalised philanthropic zeal, typical in a rapidly industrialising America where the civic generosity of self-made magnates like Andrew Carnegie and John D. Rockefeller was to fill the gap left by weak state and federal government. Katrina had written of her bewilderment at 'the wretched inequality of life' and her hopes for a new social order.

At the same time, the distinctions between high and low culture were becoming more rigorously enforced. In mid-nineteenth-century America, Shakespeare was considered popular entertainment. By the turn of the century his plays had been appropriated by a well-to-do audience that considered itself sufficiently cultivated to appreciate them. What emerged, significantly for places like Yaddo and its equally prestigious rival, MacDowell in New Hampshire, was the notion of an élite culture that needed insulation from supply and demand, through the patronage of a philanthropist class that owed its wealth to precisely those forces. Rather as medieval aristocrats donated land and money to monasteries in exchange for intercessory prayer, so, for the Trasks, Yaddo was payback, or propitiation, a haven from the very vulgarities that had made it possible.

Ever since, residents have observed a routine that in its tidal throb of solitude and community invites comparison with the more eremitical Catholic orders like the Camaldolese. Cabins in the woods. Communal meals. Quiet hours from 9 a.m. to 4 p.m. and again after 10 p.m. The secular contemplative life, given just enough structure to keep it from falling apart.

Literature and Western monasticism are, of course, intimately related. It's an irony of Christian iconography that St Jerome, the great early Doctor of the Church, should so often be depicted in paintings as an emaciated hermit, lion at his side, when his spell in the desert had been such a conspicuous failure. Jerome lived out his years as a scholar near Bethlehem, and in his argument – most notably laid out in his preface to the Book of Job – that translating Biblical texts was just as hardcore a form of self-mortification as anything the desert anchorites got up to, he cleared the way for his scholarly successors to view book work as respectably ascetic. We owe the monastic transmission of classical knowledge in large part to the example set by Jerome.

Before the establishment of cathedral schools and universities, monasteries had an effective monopoly on literary production. In the ninth century, under the sponsorship of Charlemagne, monks across the Latin West were engaged in a vast, systematised project to preserve those classical texts that had survived the cultural desecrations of the Dark Ages. Without the work done in monastic scriptoria, hand copying ancient Greek and Roman manuscripts onto less perishable parchment codices, the classical revivalists of the Renaissance would have had a lot less to go on. As the literary historian Stephen Greenblatt has shown, the discovery, in the fifteenth century, probably in the Benedictine Abbey of Fulda in present-day west-central Germany, of a ninth-century manuscript copy of Lucretius' *De rerum natura* ('On the Nature of Things'), was to have an incalculable influence on Renaissance artists and thinkers.

Ironically, given the debt owed to the monks for its preservation, among the many radical ideas the poem proposes are that the universe consists exclusively of elementary particles in an infinite void, that God is indifferent to human activity, and that the afterlife doesn't exist.

Thus the monasteries contributed to a revolution in human thought that would undermine the very basis of organised religion. In the twelfth century, Bernard of Clairvaux, not the founder of the Cistercian order but the abbot who oversaw its first ascendancy, was renowned both for the intensity of his contemplative practice and for a level of literary productivity that might seem antithetical to it, words pouring out of the silence. On the basis of his mystical writings, most famously the *De diligendo Dei* ('On Loving God') and the eighty-six *Sermons on the Song of Songs*, Bernard is considered one of the founders of the French moral tradition that would culminate in the stridently anti-clerical novels of Émile Zola.

That the monasteries were crucial to the preservation and generation of the written word is beyond doubt. It is, perhaps, no accident that literary culture should have flourished in circumstances conducive both to quiet reflection and a detachment from worldly concerns. Writing is often a cloistral activity. (Although not always: against the mass of Kafka-like isolates, we might oppose Karl Marx, or D.H. Lawrence, the writers who, like Mozart, or Schubert, or Sara Maitland's favourite Catherine of Siena, could concentrate any time, anywhere, in the racket of the reedbeds.) Of all the retreats I've experienced researching this book, by far the longest, and arguably the most intense, has been the one I'm on now, sitting at home, with the door closed, six months into a writing process that, even before the virus, had dramatically streamlined my social life. More than that, it's hard to escape the suspicion that writing itself is a distancing measure, an effort to keep reality at one remove by encasing it in words – the opposite, in effect, of the impetus of apophatic prayer, gesturing at the Divine by recognising the futility of describing it.

It's arguable that literary productivity not only requires a level of monastic seclusion but is a rationale for seeking it – that writing alone in a room might be an adaptive way for the natural retreatant to manage the hand they've been dealt. Emily Dickinson, Thomas Pynchon, Edgar Allen Poe: all writers whose talent was inseparable from their determination to hide it from view. Working on *In Search of Lost Time*, for three years Marcel Proust scarcely left his apartment on the Boulevard Haussmann, sleeping during the day in a bedroom soundproofed with cork, and writing all night in his gloomy studio, the windows firmly shut for the sake of his asthma. 'He looked like a man who no longer lives outdoors or by day,' recalled his friend, the poet Léon-Paul Fargue. 'A hermit who hasn't emerged from his oak tree for a long time.' Following his brief spell of literary recognition after the Second World War, the Scottish poet W.S. Graham retreated to Penwith, the very south-western nib of England, and sank so far into obscurity that by the 1960s his London publishers assumed that he had died. 'Very gently struck / the quay night bell': as with Sara Maitland, or the chanting at Solesmes, the engagement with silence in Graham's work, the silence his spare, essential poetry holds at bay, is both response to and reason for his isolation.

The conflation of monastic and writerly vocations has form. Such was the austerity of Balzac's work ethic that Henry James called him 'a Benedictine of the actual'. As the literary critic John Carey argues, the notion of the artist as separate from mainstream society is, in essence, a reaction against the advance of mass culture in the late nineteenth century, a wish on the artists' part to distinguish themselves from the philistine majority, rather as the early ascetics supercharged their self-sacrifice in reaction to the spread of Christianity. The idea has cast a long shadow in twentieth-century culture. In his 1931 essay, 'Foreheads Villainous Low', Aldous Huxley, who was to have such a direct influence on Esalen's founders, made the case against universal education on the basis that 'for the great majority of men and women, there obviously *is* nothing in culture. Nothing at all – neither spiritual satisfactions, nor social rewards.' Culture was for the elect, with the natural corollary that to be a bona fide producer of that culture, the artist must withdraw, be separate, monasticise himself.

This idea found its convenient counterpart in the urge of philanthropists like Spencer Trask to absolve themselves of a money-grubbing lack of refinement. Philanthropist and artist could conspire in the massaging of the artist's ego to the benefit of both. It's telling that Yaddo's period of maximum influence on American culture coincided with the era of the hard-drinking, hypermasculine, hypercompetitive artist, the mid-century, Cheever–Mailer heyday of the writer-as-prize-fighter.

It's tempting to view the contemporary popularity of artists' retreats as a sublimated impulse to return to that golden age of artistic egoism. They can't get anyone to join the monasteries, but artists' residencies are turning them away. Between 1965 and 2018 the number of Catholic brothers in the US declined by more than 65 per cent, from 11,326 to 3,897. Compare that to the rise in the number of known artists' residencies in the US: from sixty in 1990 to five hundred in 2012, an increase of more than 730 per cent. Might the urge to go on artistic retreat not be a more or less secretly aversive response to the contemporary participatory mode of the arts, the flattening of the reader–writer hierarchy – now that the barriers to at least some form of publication are low to non-existent – and the consequent diminishment of the artist's separateness or prestige? You go to Yaddo or MacDowell or the Arvon Foundation in Devon to restore a simulacrum of separateness that no longer applies in the real world. It is surely to service a fantasy of the artist as aristocrat that so many artists' retreats should be held in mansions or castles: Yaddo is a case in point.

The artist is the *inverse* of the monk. Freud conceived of the artist as someone who 'turns away from reality because he cannot come to terms with the renunciation which it at first demands, and who allows his erotic and ambitious wishes full play in the life of phantasy'. That is, artists are overgrown kids, refusing to relinquish the capacity for wonder that adult responsibilities are apt to suppress. There's an echo here of Sara Maitland's refusal to characterise her solitude as renunciatory. Where the artist and hermit coincide is in rejecting everyday bourgeois existence, the compromises involved in fitting in. In Anthony Storr's view, what marks the artist out is his or her capacity for 'personal development in isolation', where the rest of us mature, psychologically, 'primarily through inter-action with others'. Artists need retreat like the rest of us need company. Where they differ from religious solitaries is in the purpose of that retreat. 'Writing is a terrific ego-activity,' Sara told me. 'Prayer is a de-ego-ing.' To be an artist is to assert your right to ego fulfilment, to embrace the *kilesa*, the Tenth Army of self-regard. As Sara argues in *A Book of Silence*, the Romantic poets sought solitude not to empty themselves, like the desert hermits, but to discover 'their own individual voices'. Artists' retreats are like their religious counterparts, repurposed to opposite ends: ego monasteries.

Or are they? There's no doubt that a residency at a top-notch retreat like Yaddo carries a good deal of cachet. The accept-ance rate for fiction writers runs at between 5 and 7 per cent. It's a facelift for your résumé: Yaddo fellow. Communal feeling among the artists is not uncontaminated by rivalry. When Elaina Richardson first started as president, she told me, cell phones were still banned. 'There were two pay phones,' she recalled, one near the dining hall. 'It was like being in LA. At dinnertime, you would be called to the phone, which people loved. It sig-nalled how important they were.'

Still, among the residents I met, there seemed an equal and opposite impulse to self-effacement, together with the convic-tion that artists' retreats like Yaddo were uniquely equipped to encourage it. 'It's all about ego,' said Dominic Finocchiaro, a playwright from Brooklyn. 'The more you can push that aside, the more you can let the process be the process.' I met Dominic at MacDowell, in rural New Hampshire, a mile outside the picturesque small town of Peterborough.

Edward MacDowell was a composer, perhaps America's first of real note, who, in 1904, aged forty-four – in an eerie portent of Spencer Trask's death – was hit by a hansom cab on Broadway. He never recovered. His premature decline prompted his wife, Marian, to convert the farm they used as a summer retreat into an artists' colony. Edward died in 1908, a year after the first artists arrived. Until her retirement in 1946, aged eighty-nine, Marian MacDowell presided over an ever-expanding sanctuary for artists of all kinds, an interdisciplinary utopia where, for example, James Baldwin could work on *Giovanni's Room*, Leonard Bernstein on his *Mass*, and the painter Milton Avery on his quietly harmonious semi-abstractions.

Each artist works (and in some cases sleeps) in one of thirty-two stand-alone studios distributed over 450 acres of woodland and open pasture. Breakfast and dinner are taken communally, in Nevins Hall, the magnificent, white, converted clapboard barn that greets you on entrance. Lunch comes in a woven ashwood basket, discreetly left on your porch by an amiable old fellow called Blake, who seems as permanent as the trees. The tradition dates back to pre-colony days, when Marian was reluctant to disturb Edward as he composed in the log cabin that served as his studio. As at Yaddo, freedom is underwritten by structure. Respectable New England widow that she was, Marian MacDowell had a reputation for strictness verging on puritanical fervour, often turning up at artists' studios, on the pretext of delivering firewood, to check if they were up to anything the good townsfolk of Peterborough might consider unseemly.

If the current regime is liberal by comparison, there is still an air of sobriety about MacDowell, the sense that all impediments to sustained concentration have been discreetly removed. The one sacrosanct rule is that no-one is allowed to visit an artist's studio without express permission. 'If you want to work, come

to MacDowell,' said Kia, a novelist and playwright, when I met
her after dinner. 'If you want to get laid, go to Yaddo.' Kia said
this with such impish good humour that I took it, I suppose,
as the prelude to an hour or two of fun, post-prandial mix-
ing, until, very suddenly, everyone disappeared, back to their
studios, leaving me alone with Julian Maynard Smith, the sole
other Brit in residence, hanging for a drink.

The result was an intense hush, further intensified by the
snow. The woods were like a vast recording booth, the sound
of each footstep and drip of thawing ice crisply self-identical,
without echo or reverberation. 'When I go to MacDowell, I
always apply for winter time,' said Žibuoklė Martinaitytė, a
New York-based composer originally from Lithuania. Žibuoklė
spoke with a cheerful clarity to match her outfit: bright blue
jumper, cat's-eye glasses with aquarium-blue frames. 'The silence. I want to capture it, you know?'

For Dominic and Žibuoklė alike, the ego was there to be
defeated. Another corrective to excessive self-satisfaction was
the 'tombstone', a wooden board, often leaning on the studio
mantelpiece, that each resident signed and dated before they
left. It was aptly named, as the most powerful impression given
by the lists of residents, some going back to the early twentieth
century, was that you'd heard of hardly any of them. For every
Baldwin or Bernstein there were dozens if not hundreds of
names as heartbreakingly particular, and forgotten, as the list
of long-dead captains on an honours board.

Mostly, though, it was the silence, and the opportunity to
work without distraction. 'In our lives,' said Žibuoklė, 'we make
such a complex web of everything.'

'And so the point of the residency is to simplify your life?'

'Exactly,' said Žibuoklė. 'The concentration gets so high that
I really forget myself. There is no "me" in the picture. It's like
meditation, because you just focus on something outside you
instead of focusing on yourself.'

*

Between 1952 and 1957 Saul Bellow spent four residencies at Yaddo. It was during a stay in 1956, as he wrote to his editor Pat Covici, that he did 'more and better work' on *Henderson the Rain King* than ever before. With a novel under way Bellow could be formidably focused. Of *Henderson*, he told an interviewer, 'I wrote it in a kind of frenzy.' In Zachary Leader's biography the depiction of Bellow conforms to that Yaddo-ish, mid-century myth of the pugilistic egoist. Bellow would start his day's work with a towel slung Sonny Liston-style around his neck, emerging at lunchtime drenched in sweat. For him concentration was a fully physical matter. And yet, as Bellow himself observed of Mozart, the fruits of this concentration were not won through effort, precisely.

'Easily or not at all,' he writes, 'that is the truth about art. Concentration without effort is at the heart of the thing.'

Strive not to strive. What mattered was to make yourself receptive to inspiration, and then let it come, much as Christian contemplatives prepare themselves, through silence and prayer, to receive the Spirit. 'Will and desire are silenced (as many mystics have understood), and work is transformed into play.'

It's just as Žibuoklė described. The loss of will, together with much distinction between the actor and the act, the composer and the composition: the artist becoming their art. Psychologists call this the 'flow state', the pleasurable feeling of complete concentrative absorption that can characterise anything from high-level sporting activity to baking a cake. Action and awareness of that action merge. The sense of self diminishes or disappears: no 'me' in the picture. Time dilates, so that an afternoon spent in an absorbing activity might seem to pass in a few minutes. It's sometimes referred to as a 'moving meditation', like vinyasa yoga, qi gong or tai chi. In the case of creative flow, particularly if it involves language, the tenor of attentional focus differs from, say, vipassana meditation in that discursive thought is of course actively encouraged, rather than noted and allowed to pass. But the fundamental principle is the same. You engage your entire body-mind on a single activity. Mind wandering diminishes along with reflective self-consciousness. From a neural perspective, activity in areas of the default mode network is temporarily reduced. Neurochemically, the system is flooded with noradrenaline, anandamide, dopamine, endorphins and seratonin, promoting focus and lateral thinking, and, crucially, activating the brain's reward centre.

Žibuoklė believed that she got into the flow state from her very first experience of composing at the age of fifteen. 'I didn't know what it was,' she said. 'But I knew that it was so wonderful that I wanted it again and again.'

'And when you weren't in it?'

Žibuoklė laughed. 'It's like a drug user. If they don't get the drug, they're miserable. And I become really, really miserable if I don't work. My parents knew that from a very young age. They said, "Well, if you haven't worked for a week, it's impossible to deal with you."'

Nice as recognition undoubtedly was, the payback for the artist was in the neurochemical fix of concentration, the wages of staying awake. Just as for the monk, obscurity was not a disadvantage, as long as there was food on the table. The real joy came in isolation, and was as powerful a pull away from friends, family, or social contact as any addictive high.

For Giuseppe Pagnoni, like other forms of meditative absorption, the flow state is paradoxical. 'It is relaxed, but it's kind of an active relaxation. It should become effortless, but you are completely engaged.' And this engagement depends in turn on the physical element, even if that entails nothing more than typing on a keyboard or writing in longhand.

'Your awareness of sensory perception is very tight, very much in real time, and at the same time unusually devoid of conceptual elaboration,' said Giuseppe. 'When you are completely immersed in the flow of writing, you're still immersed in a kind of action.' It's hard to enter the flow state if you're just staring out of the window. Absorption feeds off its physical correlate. 'There needs to be this sort of connection with the body – the active circulation between perception and action needs to be very alive.'

Work is what distinguishes the Trappists from other Catholic monks. The Trappists are a branch of the Cistercians, themselves an offshoot of the Benedictine order. Trappists are officially known as 'the Order of Cistercians of the Strict Observance'. As strictness of observance was, in turn, the founding principle of Cistercianism, you might conceive of the Trappists as the strictest of the strict. The Cistercian order was formed in 1098, when twenty monks under Robert of Molesme broke away from Molesme Abbey, a Benedictine foundation in Burgundy, feeling that in its dealings with the secular world the order had compromised the spirit of the Rule.

The new house they established was in a marshy wilderness called Cîteaux – 'Cistercium' in Latin – laying the ground for the defining Cistercian principle of founding monasteries outside the busy population centres where Benedictine houses tended to be built. As Dr Max Sternberg, the expert on monastic architecture, told me, the Cistercian monastery had a possible precedent in the Roman villa. Both lay in the *rus*, the rural area beyond the city walls, and were agriculturally self-sufficient. The key consideration was remoteness. In later years, the Cistercians were not beyond razing entire villages in order to *create* the appropriate wilderness. If you can't retreat from the material world, there's always the option of forcing it to retreat from you.

'The founders of Cîteaux wanted to live differently,' said Dom Erik Varden, until recently the abbot of the last remaining Trappist monastery in England, Mount Saint Bernard Abbey, in Charnwood Forest, Leicestershire. Mention Dom Erik in Catholic circles and the reaction ranges from sober admiration to a barely suppressed squeal of hero-worship. (Since we met at Mount Saint Bernard, Dom Erik has left to become Bishop-Prelate of Trondheim, in his native Norway). Dom Erik was slight, younger than his forty-five years, and as precise in his enunciation as he was in his gestures, often reaching out with a pinched thumb and forefinger to tap out his syllables, like the bouncing ball in an on-screen singalong. 'The founders were very strict that they were not to live as landed gentry, they were not to live off rents. They were to live by the work of their hands.'

The stress on work was of a piece with the physical separation of the Cistercian houses. It was an assertion of independence. For the monks to provide for themselves was to retreat, economically, from reliance on the outside world. This quickly proved as problematic as it had been for my parents. Self-sufficiency is time-consuming. For the rebel renunciates of Cîteaux, the tension between the need for financial independence and time spent in scriptural study demanded urgent resolution.

'They saw from the beginning that they couldn't really do both,' explained Dom Erik. 'And so the Cistercians came up with something fairly radical. They instituted the lay brothers, who were entrusted with the upkeep of the monastery and the administration, largely, of the property, and who weren't committed to the liturgical duties. They therefore had hours at their disposal – the sort of hours you need for agriculture, which was their main work.'

The other Western monastic orders soon followed Cîteaux's lead in transferring manual duties to a brotherhood of almost-monks generally, but not always, drawn from the peasantry. To conceive of the lay brothers as a lower class within the social structure of the monastery would be to miss the radic-alism of the idea, enabling, as it did, the participation in the religious life of those who would otherwise, on account of their illiteracy, poverty, or both, have been excluded from it. Their function was as facilitators, relieving the choir monks of any duties that might get in the way of scholarship, prayer or liturgical observance. Cistercians have been farmers since the secession of Robert of Molesme. In the thirteenth century, they were crucial to the development of commercial sheep farming in England. One reason the call for reform – for a return to proper strictness – was so strong in later centuries was that the Cistercians had become rich on the proceeds of their estates. The order had fallen prey to the worldliness it had been founded to repudiate. By the mid-seventeenth century, pockets of reform had begun across mainland Europe, most notably under Armand-Jean le Bouthillier de Rancé, abbot of La Grande Trappe in north-western France. The Trappists, as they came to be known, were renowned for the extreme austerity of their observance, placing particular emphasis on hard manual labour at the expense of study. The idea was to return to the rigour of the Rule, with an extra helping of penitence, a furious self-abasement to atone for the layabout monks that had preceded them.

In the twentieth century, the penitential severity of Trappist observance began to give way to a more forgiving interpretation of the original reform. In *The Shattering of Loneliness*, his brilliant meditation on Christian communion, Dom Erik frames the monk's vocation in aspirational terms, as an 'option for what is good, not *against* what is thought bad', a willing embrace of silence and simplicity rather than the rejection of its opposite. The distinction between lay brothers and choir monks was effectively abolished in the 1960s. There is still plenty of practical work to be done, however: buildings and grounds to be maintained, bees to be kept, guests to be greeted, elderly monks to be cared for. Dairy farming no longer being financially viable, the monks have switched to brewing beer. Demand for 'Tynt Meadow', the first and only Trappist ale made in England, now outstrips supply. For the monks, work is prayer, a simple, direct means both of supporting the community and of enacting their vow of obedience. It is also a means of separation, a guarantor of their autonomy, a shared assumption of the practicalities so that the higher work of contemplation and liturgical prayer might take place.

*

It was much the same deal at the Marble House: we pooled responsibilities so we could get on with our work. The main building was built around 1820, from marble cut from its own quarry, one of the most productive in this part of Vermont until it closed in the 1870s. In 2012, the current owners, Danielle and Dina, began work on restoring the mansion and grounds, by then in a state of semi-dereliction. From April till November, artists of all disciplines could apply for a three-week residency, working in their own studios, sleeping in the mansion, and coming together in the evenings to cook and eat communally, often using produce from the kitchen garden bordering the quarry.

Where the Marble House differs from Yaddo and MacDowell – apart from being new, and small, its capacity limited to eight artists per session – is in offering a family-friendly residency, for two weeks every July, where the residents can bring their partners and children. My wife is also a writer, and so the residency solved two problems at once, how to get any work done over the summer, on the one hand, and on the other, how to go on retreat without abandoning your family. (Incidentally, when I told Sara Maitland what my wife did for a living, she looked appalled. 'I could never fuck anyone who did the same thing as me,' she said.)

From 9 a.m. to 3 p.m. the kids were on summer camp, feeding the chickens, picking blueberries, building cardboard robots or swimming in the spring-fed quarry pool, supervised, the summer we were there, by Morgan and Sarah, art-therapy students from Brooklyn seemingly put on earth to charm and encourage young children. When the bell went at three the grown-ups would emerge from their studios and gather with their families in the pool, or walk up to the quarry proper, the huge, grey rectangular blocks left where they were at the time production stopped, stacked beside the cuts, now filled with spring water, the blocks furred with moss and lichen and encroached on by the woodland that separated the quarry from the rest of the grounds. Beyond, to the east, the Green

Mountains quivered in the summer heat. It was a vision of freedom and communal good cheer which was hard, eight months later, locked down in London with the death-ticker rising whenever you looked online, to imagine as only distant in time. It seemed like a different reality.

'I've just realised something,' said my wife, breezing into my studio halfway through our second morning. 'I'm a workaholic!'

'Is that right?' I said. 'What are you doing here, then?'

'Just getting a drink.' And she was off, via the communal fridge, back up the stairs to her studio. Compared to the wood-panelled comforts of the main house, the studios, it was true, were a little closer to the monastic ideal: foldable chairs, desks improvised from whitewashed plywood doors, white fibre-board walls, riddled with hundreds of tiny holes where previous residents had pinned up their work. Having my wife work directly above me meant that I could monitor her workaholism. When the pacing about on the floorboards stopped, I knew she had got down to it. And it was true – there hadn't been a lot of pacing. We were, in truth, well aware of this tendency in each other. It was possibly the reason our marriage had survived fifteen years of us both working from home. We had a similar arrangement there – I worked in the spare bedroom downstairs, my wife in the kitchen directly above it, so, as at the Marble House, I could hear her moving about until a hush descended with the beginning of the working day. In any case, once it had, the immersion in work – or rather, the need to be immersed in it – was so complete that we might as well have kissed on the front step and headed off with our briefcases to the office.

'See you at lunch,' I'd call up.

'Maybe. Depends how I get on.'

And the doors would close. It had taken the Marble House experience, however, to demonstrate just how reliant on, or addicted to, work we had become, what a psychological safe haven it had come to represent. The residency had done this, I supposed, by extending the purview of work beyond normal working hours, or even the occasional weekend, to cover the family holiday. Not just the odd stolen morning on the laptop, while the kids watched TV or ran screaming through the lawn sprinkler, but the whole thing, an entire two weeks designed specifically to fill those long, hot hours with exactly the activity whose absence made the ordinary vacation intolerable: work. If my wife was right, and we were workaholics, then the Marble House was the world's worst rehab centre, an AA meeting in a cocktail bar. During happy hour.

In a sense an artists' retreat is the inverse of the restorative kind: not a respite from your everyday circumstances but an intensification of them. You go to MacDowell or the Marble House to enter more deeply into what you're probably spending most of your time doing anyway. A closer comparison would be with the periods of temporarily intensified seclusion undergone by some types of monk. A Tibetan *trapa*, for example, will spend time away from the monastery meditating or writing in a hermitage. It is his customary practice, turned up a few notches. A retreat centre like Vajrasana, near Walsham-le-Willows in Suffolk, includes a regular working retreat on its programme, whereby in return for a reduced fee, visitors complement their meditation practice with three hours a day of gardening, cleaning and maintenance.

This is work as respite, however, a therapeutic spell outdoors for the ordinarily office-bound. Here, work was work. You could see how self-perpetuating this dynamic might be. Several of the residents I had met at Yaddo and MacDowell had spoken of a sort of peer effect of intellectual industry. It was like the communal hermitry of the Camaldolese or Carthusians: you worked alone, but conscious that others were doing the same, your solitude given shape by the group. My wife's footsteps going silent on the floorboards. At Yaddo I had met a novelist from Rhode Island called James Scott. 'As monastic as Yaddo is,' said James, 'I feel like I would be a good monk if I was with other good monks. Knowing people are working really hard makes me work harder.'

This went some way to addressing an obvious objection to artists' residencies in general. If it's peace and quiet you're after, why not rent a bedsit in Basingstoke? Answer: because of the immanent sense of shared purpose offered by communal retreat. The corollary of the collective work ethic was the stigma attached to anyone who failed to sign up for it. A few weeks before visiting Yaddo, I had lunch with a friend who had written his debut novel there, in two-month stints over a year and a half. 'You can tell the people who've done a lot of work on that day,' he recalled. 'Their heads are somewhere else. And the ones who haven't – typically, in a group of, say, twenty there'll be one or two people like this – will be the ones trying to engineer evening activities.'

This may have been more of a problem at a place like Yaddo than it was at a family residency. Again, the regime at Yaddo encouraged withdrawal from the communal, or familial, dynamic of ordinary life in the name of concentration. The idea at the Marble House was not to hive off but to integrate the two sides of your life, work and family, withdrawal and participation.

At three you'd call it a day, a little grudgingly, not wanting to stop, but wanting to stop, and emerge into the sunshine to meet Morgan and Sarah leading the kids down the slope from the barn, spend the rest of the afternoon hunting for salamanders or toasting s'mores or pushing the kids around the pool on the inflatable lemon slice. In the run-up to the residency, my wife and I had harboured some start-of-term anxieties about fitting in, that the gap between British and American cultural expectations, senses of humour, tolerances for irony or its absence could only be magnified in the hermetic setting of retreat. That we would be visitors from Babylon in a houseful of true pilgrims. As it turned out everyone was really nice. Amanda and Jeremy, a novelist and screenwriter from LA, were laid-back and clever and funny in that American way that made you wonder why anyone would envy us Brits for our supposed articulacy. That we all got on so well may have been down to the fact that the obstacles we ordinarily faced, juggling childcare with working from home, were being removed, temporarily but very effectively, with the result that everyone was in a good mood for the same reason, a mood whose source went deep into the circumstances of our lives. That summer really felt like summer. Evening activities didn't need engineering. They just happened, by the pool, round the fire pit, in the living room after the kids had gone to bed, with such ease and regularity that the only hitch in our happiness was the suspicion, mostly suppressed, that it was all a bit indulgent, that we were falling for the fantasy of the artist apart, that to an outsider we might seem a little self-satisfied.

If there was a misfit, a Marble House Gianni or Greg, it was Rob, the 'culinary artist'. Rob was from Seattle, pale, sinewy, with a birdlike and slightly mischievous alertness. 'You're pretty wedded to routine, aren't you?' he said to me at one point. 'For an easy-going person.'

He was right, and went about everything with such twitchy energy that you forgave him the personal remark. He was also an extremely good cook, spurred on, it seemed, by the group's long list of intolerances and dietary restrictions to make soups, salads and especially frozen desserts that were more delicious, you felt, than if everyone had been a lactose-tolerating carnivore. The problem was in the definition of his role. Officially the culinary artist was meant to be on a par with the other residents, spending the day developing recipes in the kitchen studio, helping out with the evening meal only when the resident whose turn it was to cook lacked the culinary competence. In reality it didn't quite work out like that. For one reason and another Rob found himself cooking every night, the rest of us demoted to kitchen assistants in the preparation of a meal so elaborate the planning and pre-prep began to eat into Rob's studio time, with the result that he felt increasingly resentful about the impact on his own work, and the secondary status that implied. Without meaning to he had ended up as lay brother to our sacramental band of choir monks.

Matters came to a head at supper on day six.

'Listen,' said Rob, rising to his feet and tinking a water glass with his fork. 'I love cooking for you guys. But every evening? It's too much. So as of tomorrow, we're going to be transitioning to a rota system. I really hope that works for everyone.'

It did. It was also weird, being made to feel guilty for a turn of events that hadn't really been willed, had just happened, mainly out of inertia and Rob's natural tendency to take charge of an activity he was better at than everyone else. We already *had* a rota system. It's just that no-one, Rob included, had been sticking to it. Maybe the awkwardness arose from an incongruity – that Rob's plea for help had a whiff of sharing about it, the sort of attentiveness to the self you'd expect at a wellness centre like Esalen, not at a working retreat where the conversation, more often than not, dwelled on pretty much anything but our emotional well-being.

There were other things to talk about. Brian Harnetty's new project, as it happened, coincided to a considerable extent with mine. Brian was a composer and sound artist from Columbus, Ohio, who set archive voice recordings to dulcimer, banjo and piano. Six-six, with a monkish buzzcut and a long, greying beard that wouldn't have looked out of place on Mount Athos, Brian had a gentle, considered manner that was also explosively humorous and insightful, like an ember you weren't expecting to spit flame. Everyone loved him. The archive recordings he was now setting to music were of the Trappist monk and mystic Thomas Merton. In 1941, Merton entered the Abbey of Gethsemani in Kentucky, later describing his retreat into the 'order of grace' in *The Seven Storey Mountain*, a book which has encouraged generations of Americans to take orders themselves. Merton was a one-man monastic revival. From 1965 until his death four years later – electrocuted in the shower during an interfaith lecture tour of Thailand – Merton lived in a hermitage in the grounds of the Abbey. In 1967, he was given a reel-to-reel tape recorder.

'And immediately he starts reading his own poetry, he's doing these meditations over jazz records,' said Brian. The recordings preserve the texture of Merton's retreat: the contemplative thinking out loud to himself. 'He's diving into Beckett and Foucault and the Sufi poets, and all along talking about the tape recorder as a medium between what it is to be human and searching for God.'

Brian was brought up in a devout Catholic family. His mother was a lay Carmelite contemplative. 'Merton for me as a teenager was material for arguing,' he said, laughing. 'Because he was the lefty part of the church, and open to other mystic traditions and religions.' Later, and particularly after the Catholic sex-abuse scandals began to emerge in the late 1980s, Brian grew disaffected. It wasn't until he had completed his PhD, in 2014, that he found himself drifting back to the material. The tapes were a way for Brian to revisit the contemplative side of his former faith without submitting to its dogma: a secular return to the sacred. Merton's metaphysics provided a route not back towards faith but to Brian's artistic practice, the numinous divested of God. 'I just felt that the contemplative part lined up far more with the artistic part than does the analytical, academic part,' he said. 'That was the yearning – to get back to that.'

On the penultimate evening of the residency Rob cleared his throat and made another announcement. We were sitting around in the living room after supper. The atmosphere, as usual, was relaxed, diffuse, a little merry. Rob didn't drink, and so had sat there, quietly, a little at a remove, while the rest of us talked.

'Guys,' he said. No glass-tinking this time, but it was clear that our undivided attention was required. 'I have to share this with you. I'm feeling a little excluded?'

The complaint seemed to be that although Rob was grateful to have been relieved of his nightly cooking duties, we had left it at that – failed to do the remedial work necessary to integrate him into the group.

'So I have a suggestion.'

Over the course of the residency a few of us had used the after-dinner get-together to present some work in progress, get some constructive feedback from the group. Jeremy had shown a few scenes from his new film about the destruction of his childhood neighbourhood in Detroit. I had read a passage from this book. Rob's plan for gaining bona-fide group membership, late in the day as it might be, was to present some of his non-culinary work, thereby establishing artistic credentials independent of the talents that, impressive as they were, had led to his feelings of exclusion.

'Some of you may not know this,' he said, laying a hand on his breastbone. 'But I have a history of self-harm.'

A silence like the moments before Mass. 'And the way I've processed that is to write about it. Specifically, in the form of the slam.'

Rob stood, closed his eyes and began.

They were long, the three slams he read, delivered with scarcely a pause in between, ardently, flow sustained with shoulder-rolls and his right hand slicing horizontally at the air. And then they stopped. And still there was nothing to say, no allowable opinion on content or form, no white lie excusable given the starkness of the subject matter. At Esalen, Rob's slams would probably have been met with a round of applause and a group hug. Maybe that would have been better, the more human response, but here, when everyone was just gathered for a drink, for some time off from themselves, the incongruity was so dumbfounding that it couldn't help but look – for all that we told ourselves that Rob's fears were unfounded, that he was hammering at the wall when the door was wide open – as if we *were* excluding him, or rather, failing to stop him excluding himself.

An unlit corridor led to a space I was only dimly aware was larger, a black box or chamber. Without the handrail I'd probably have turned back. It was like needing a pee and not knowing where the light switch was: groping forward, the blackness at your throat, every step a potential collision or precipice. Eventually my shin found the edge of a hard object a hesitant frisk identified as a chair. So I sat. And waited. And waited, and waited, and waited some more, for a form or an outline or a point of light to stop the horrible sliding feeling and remind me where and who I was.

Of course I knew where I was in one respect: at MASS MoCA, a contemporary art museum in North Adams, Massachusetts, just over the state line from Vermont. We had stopped there on the drive back to New York from the Marble House. The next morning, at JFK, my wife and kids would be catching a flight home to London, while I flew on to South America. So we were making a day of it, taking the drive slowly, buying the kids' consent to the museum visit with a roadside-diner lunch of waffles and quesadillas and sundaes the size of their heads. At the museum, the others made straight for the VR exhibition while I ventured alone into *Hind Sight*, the James Turrell light installation that so far appeared not to involve any light whatsoever. It was a Ganzfeld chamber, essentially, a place of perceptual deprivation like a flotation tank. Such was the totality of the blackout that, even as my pupils dilated, the forms that I might have expected to reveal themselves, the edges or contours of objects not previously perceptible, stubbornly refused to, save in the fleeting, hallucinatory form of objects that weren't actually there. My priors had taken over: starved of reliable sensory evidence, my perceptual faculty instead fell back on its internal models. I began to see my memories of what it might be like to sit in a darkened room.

At some point I recalled that Turrell had flown rescue missions out of Tibet, liberating Buddhist monks after the Chinese occupation; some have speculated that he was working for the CIA. (Turrell just says that he found some 'beautiful places to fly'.) And then, slowly, only just perceptibly, after maybe fifteen minutes, when my pupils had reached their maximum dilation, something did begin to reveal itself, or seemed to, a smear or hazy patch of greyish light whose precise position, proximity and, indeed, reality proved impossible to determine. The more I focused my attention on it, the more I got the feeling that the object of that attention was not in fact a smear of light but my attempt to perceive it, my perceptual apparatus perceived from the outside. And the longer that went on, the longer I had the slightly nauseating feeling that my perception was somehow exterior to itself, the more I wondered who, in that case, was doing the perceiving, and whether this was how Rob must have felt that last evening at the Marble House, freefalling, skating on black ice, no longer being sure he was there.

7.

The Urge to Be Alone

Solvitur ambulando, wrote St Augustine. It is solved by walking – but then he'd never been on an airport travelator. Did it mean I'd solve my dilemma twice as fast? I had been invited to join Phil and some friends of his on a plant-medicine retreat in the Peruvian rainforest. These sorts of retreat were all the rage. Claims were being made for the benefits of ayahuasca, and other naturally occurring hallucinogens like huachuma, as a 'treatment modality' for refractory depression, PTSD and addiction disorder. They were also a good way of deep-frying your brain. Until I kissed my wife and kids goodbye I suppose I'd been behaving as I usually did: suppressing the question of how much I actually wanted to go until I had forced my own hand and was strapped into my plane seat. Now all the reasons I shouldn't go were pushing against me with the full force of their indisputability. Foremost among these was the suspicion that the main drawback of group retreats – the queasy feeling that you were being coerced – could only be multiplied, many times over, when everyone was off their tits on the world's most powerful hallucinogen. In a sense the group element of the aya-huasca retreat had served its purpose by shedding light on a form of withdrawal I was yet to examine at close quarters. Its main effect on me – now, at least, when my flight to Lima left in less than two hours – was to instil the contrary and unignorable urge to be alone.

It was true that I'd been a bit slack with my preparations. A week before arriving at the Marble House I'd received an email from Carolina, the organiser of the ayahuasca retreat, with details of what to bring to Peru (headlamp, bug spray, reading material as long as it wasn't 'merely entertaining') and a list of things I was advised to forgo: red meat, cheese, alcohol and chocolate, all of which contained an amino acid that could interact, apparently, with the psychoactive compounds in ayahuasca to cause headaches and high blood pressure. Either this was sound neurochemistry, or – as I half-suspected, given that sex and TV were also off-limits – the familiar path-seeker's prohibition of anything nice. In any case I'd spent my evenings at the Marble House gorging on bourbon and Vermont cheddar. Apart from that, I felt quite ready. Together with the local *curandera*, or folk healer, who owned the retreat centre, it was Carolina's job to lead the nightly medicine ceremonies, guiding the group in the *icaros*, the traditional songs used to ward off evil spirits and help deepen and lend shape to our ayahuasca experience. As a way of tethering ourselves to reality, in the event that the hallucinations took us alarmingly far from it, Carolina had recommended single-pointed meditation; I had upped my daily practice accordingly, and felt reasonably insured against the possibility of total psychic disintegration in a forest six thousand miles from home.

And then the doubts massed like dogs at the end of the travelator: that I was a father, ill-advised to toy with a drug that had sent Nasreen, my apparently calm and well-adjusted friend from Vanessa's mindfulness class, into what she described as a panicky, depersonalised state that lasted nearly a year; that the simply backwoodsy remoteness Carolina so prized in the retreat centre was also what would make it stupidly dangerous if anything went wrong; that for all their hippie-ish benevolence Carolina's emails had an unmistakable whiff of cultishness about them. Taking ayahuasca in the rainforest now seemed like deliberately impairing my judgement to submit to a group dynamic that I would recoil from in non-narcotised circumstances. Wasn't it out of a horror of such submission that contemplatives like Sara Maitland were moved to go it alone? By the time I stepped off the travelator I had made up my mind – or rather my mind had made itself up, probably some time ago. I didn't feel ready at all, and most likely never would.

Hang on a second, though. *My mind had made itself up.* Wasn't this my internal models talking? Would I be typing the Peru trip like this if I'd experienced it at first hand? The longer I looked at retreat the more I realised how delusional I had been to think of myself as open-minded, how riddled with received opinion I was, how my self-conception as open to experience was itself an internal model, an increasingly stale idea resistant to external evidence. Because didn't I harbour the prejudice, really, if I was honest with myself, that half the people who went on retreat, who were into yoga and meditation and other Eastern-influenced practices, were also, of all my friends and acquaintances, the most depressed, the angriest, the most aggrieved at what the West had done to them, the drugs it had addicted them to, the mess it had made of their parents' marriages, and had turned to the East as a sullen teen might turn her back on her father? That these were damaged people repelled by and yearning for daddy? That they went on retreat not to get better but to be amongst others of their kind, to seek validation through shared experience? That the respite and rehabilitation on offer were, underneath it all, nothing but the age-old, holy-roller's urge to righteousness, to purity, to us-against-them, tendencies that had led humanity into the deadliest of its many dead ends, away from art, complexity, negative capability, having a fucking drink? See how *righteous* we are. Wasn't righteousness the urge, the addiction substituted for the alcoholism or screen fixation or obsessive negativity that had preceded it? Being right, the headiest and most addictive intoxicant of them all?

I loved my kids in relative reality, Steve McGee had told me. The implication being, I loved them in a reality inferior to the absolute, that my love was 'samsaric', just another turn in the endless cycle of illusory pleasures. Well, how about this? To quote Christopher Hitchens? *Fuck off*. How dare you say my reality is inferior? Maybe it just seems that way because you're so maladjusted. The very fact that I could, after a few moments' reflection, get so worked up about the groupthink and tribal pieties my internal models were telling me I'd encounter in Peru, seemed, after a few more moments' reflection, to be a very good reason to go to Peru. To find out what it was actually like, not to yield to preconceptions that only amounted to a reluctance to see, to give the sensory its due, to resist the slow, asphyxiating comfort of the already known. It was clear. I should go. In Departures I bought a coffee and took out my phone to message Phil.

'How's Lima?'

'All good. You at airport?'

'Yep.'

'So listen.'

'I don't think I can come.'

When her niece, Martha, visited Emily Dickinson at 280 Main Street, Amherst, Massachusetts – the poet's home for all but fifteen of her fifty-five years – Dickinson showed Martha up to the sunlit corner bedroom where she wrote most of her poems, mimed locking the door, and turning, said, 'Matty: here's freedom.'

The myth of Dickinson rests on retreat. When, in 1855, her family moved back to The Homestead, the house on Main Street they had vacated fifteen years earlier for financial reasons, Dickinson, then twenty-four, was given the corner bedroom Martha was to visit later. For the first time she had a room of her own in the sense Virginia Woolf was to make famous seventy-four years later. Unattached, with the burden of household duties largely shouldered by her younger sister Lavinia – Emily was in charge of the baking, and was a keen gardener

– Dickinson began writing in her corner room late into the night, on the tiny, square-topped cherrywood desk by the window that overlooked Main Street. Little by little, she withdrew into what posterity has recorded as a timid, spinsterish reclusiveness, terrified of the world beyond The Homestead's front porch. For the final twenty years of her life, she scarcely left her room.

The idea that the artist requires periods of solitude for his or her genius to find full expression is, of course, an invention of the Romantic movement. As Sara Maitland argues, it's a sort of inversion of the religious ideal of retreat. The hermit withdraws to the desert, or cell, in the name of a kenotic emptying of the self, the more humbly to receive God's grace. The ego is annihilated. The poet sits on his Alpine crag for the opposite reason: to find his authentic self. If the Romantics sought silence, it was only so that they might hear themselves more clearly. 'They certainly did not want to be silenced,' writes Sara. 'They wanted to use silence as a way to finding their own individual voices.'

In the early 1860s, her period of greatest productivity, Dickinson did nothing if not find her individual voice, the volcanic, syntactically complex, death-suffused, exquisitely paradoxical voice of 'My Life had stood—a Loaded Gun' or 'Four Trees—upon a solitary Acre'. But her solitariness was very far from the windswept sublimity of Shelley's on Mont Blanc. Hers was a withdrawal into an apparently sedate, domesticated seclusion that afforded her complete intellectual and artistic independence from a society – corseted, Calvinist, patriarchal New England – ill equipped to accommodate her. It's reminiscent of Gustave Flaubert's famous advice for artists: 'Be regular and orderly in your life, like a bourgeois, so that you may be violent and original in your work.' Dickinson's withdrawal was a means of reducing externalities – stripping her worldly self down, like a Carmelite contemplative – to the point that she could manage them, be regular and ordinary, leaving her free to be as unrestrained, as psychologically extreme, as she could be in her poetry.

Dickinson's seclusion, some say, was the result of an unhappy affair. Others have speculated that her health was to blame, that certain passages in the poetry suggest that she suffered from epilepsy, accounting both for her social detachment and the transcendent, hallucinatory states that marked her poems. It seems equally likely that she withdrew because that was what her gift demanded, an inoffensive hoarding thrown up to conceal the deeper, dirtier work behind, to give voice to an authentic self capable of emotional and intellectual intensities nineteenth-century New England would neither understand nor tolerate. Like John Donne, Dickinson was an apophatic poet, in receipt of revelations so obliterating they could only be addressed obliquely, as the sun is observed through a pinhole projector. In her corner room, Dickinson was free to be as powerful, even as dangerous, as she felt.

'I HAD A STRONG INSTINCTIVE FEELING THAT CHUCKING EVERYTHING OVERBOARD WAS THE CORRECT THING TO DO.'

I was due to meet Arran at his two-man tent in the woods. Then coronavirus happened. Arran had no postal address, never mind a phone or internet access, so we needed to come up with a plan. In the end it worked out like this: I sent a letter containing my questions, along, by way of a thank-you, with a copy of *The Peregrine* by J.A. Baker and some cash in an envelope, to Gill, an acquaintance of my wife's who lived near Arran's patch of woodland, bordering the beach a few miles outside Axmouth in East Devon.

On the morning walk he was allowed under lockdown restrictions, Gill left the package at Arran's designated dead drop, a hedge, returning to the same spot a few days later to collect Arran's answers. Gill then mailed these on to me. Much as I'd been looking forward to meeting Arran face to face, our old-fashioned method of communication was strangely satisfying. I loved receiving Arran's envelope, a little water damaged from its spell in the hedge, and containing eight sheets of reporter's-style notebook paper, filled with Arran's reflections on his life as a hermit in black biro. Transcribing these, at first I typed them out as they were, in block capitals, but reading them back realised that this was to falsify a quality of the originals. Even in upper case Arran's handwriting was fluent, almost cursive, and so had the oddly inverse effect to the transcript of my conversation with Sara Maitland. It read as quiet. So forgive the switch to lower case: it's as close as I can get to the man.

Arran was in his late forties, strikingly blond, or so I'd heard, with a straggly beard and the kind of saddle-grade tan that came of living outdoors. His tent was in a small clearing in the woods. 'Candle light, cook on wood fire. Sleeping bags, a few mats,' he wrote. 'At home I am comfortable.' He had lived there for eight years. Originally from a small town in West Yorkshire, in the early nineties Arran worked in a record shop in Huddersfield until he was forced to leave in short order. 'There is something about me which has provoked frequent verbal and physical attacks from fellow inmates.'

By 'inmates' I don't think Arran was being literal. He just thought of the world as a prison. He moved to London. Years of nothing much followed. 'Music, books, cannabis, LSD, walking, laying in the sun.' A bit of painting and photography. A flirtation with heroin. For a while in the late nineties he hoped he might have a viable career as a musician. Then the doubts set in. He decided instead to expend his creative energy on himself, on making his life into a work of art, a socio-economic experiment, a radical eco-statement. 'How to get with as little effort as possible as much as I can from what little there is.'

Moving out west to live in the woods was both a departure and a return to something deep seated. 'Twenty years ago it would have seemed improbable, but 40 years ago less unlikely.' As a child Arran only felt free playing in the fields or lying in bed with a cold. The chance to read, to think, to find things out for himself. To remain open, alive to the unknown. 'When

I began to live as I do now it was soon clear that it was a natural extension of the ideas I had as a child for ways of living as an adult without doing things you don't wanna do.'

Arran made a little money selling driftwood and the edible plants he found on the beach. Sometimes the more kindly disposed local residents would donate food, clothes, boots, cash. What staples he could afford to buy – rice, tinned beans, nuts, dried fruit – he supplemented by foraging. He ate a lot of sea kale. He had just discovered that when peeled the thick stalks were a bit like watermelon. The mystical element in Arran's disposition – 'I am open minded about all the paranormal subject matter, have experienced frequent telepathic, precog, OBE, messages from the disembodied' – seemed, as so often, inseparable from the reclusiveness. ('OBEs' are 'out-of-body experiences'.)

'I wanna be left alone to dream. All I ever did want.'

Reading and rereading Arran's letter I found it exceptionally hard to weigh his idealism against his disenchantment, how much his desire for freedom tempered the disgust he felt for the society he had left behind. Even the solipsistic daydream he could sometimes sustain – that he was the sole survivor of a species that had consumed itself into extinction – was snuffed out whenever he looked upwards. 'The atmosphere over me and from horizon to horizon is saturated with a substance that has been placed there by machines (aeroplanes).' The world destroyed by our refusal to live in it as he did, to confront reality.

'All those people doing what they call living whilst never really being.' Everyone, Arran felt, could benefit from a few months eating sea kale in the woods. But that wasn't going to happen. And so he wasn't going anywhere. 'After eight years in the jungle I don't see a way out other than death.'

Returning to society would involve such compromise, such disruption to his dream state, that the hardships of getting by on sea kale and donated rice paled by comparison. There was a quote Arran liked by Charles Fort, the American researcher into anomalous or 'Fortean' phenomena.

'He said that everyone appeared to be looking for a needle that isn't lost, in a haystack that never was,' Arran wrote. 'I stopped looking for the needle, sidestepped the entire charade, found myself in paradise, with a twist. The sky will be hellish. I haven't fully escaped. There are military evils too, the sound of machine guns, bombs exploding, lo-frequency pulses. Unpleasant stuff for me and the planet, the birds, the whales, everything.'

Hell on earth. Arran's was a contemporary version of an impulse codified in late antiquity. *Fuga mundi* was the desire to escape from the world, to be separated from it. *Contemptus mundi* – contempt for the world and its concerns – was the reason the desire for *fuga mundi* took hold in the first place. The theme of *contemptus mundi*, drawing on earlier, pagan ideas of the superiority of spirit over matter, was most fully developed by the sixth-century Roman statesman Boethius in his *Consolation of Philosophy*. Humans were despicable sinners bound by the pursuit of 'false felicity', the illusory pleasures of the sublunary world. Their only hope lay in God's mercy.

This perspective, with its roots in secular classical philosophy, converged with the Christian tradition of self-discipline exemplified by the Desert Fathers, to form a major strain in medieval thought. *Hora novissima*. The last days are upon us. This is laid out, for example, in Bernard of Cluny's twelfth-century *De contemptu mundi*, a 3,000-verse satire excoriating everyone from his fellow Benedictine monks to the papacy itself. Society and church alike were irredeemably corrupt.

Contemptus mundi is the pall hanging over medieval literature and art from *The Reeve's Tale* to the apocalyptic visions of Hieronymus Bosch. With the first stirrings of humanism in the late fourteenth century, the punitive gloom of the medieval world view began to lift, although as an artistic and literary motif *contemptus mundi* persisted in the *vanitas*. Smoke, rotting fruit, hourglasses and skulls all reminded the viewer of the brevity of life and the futility of material pleasure. In Shakespeare's *Timon of Athens*, Timon, the Athenian nobleman, incensed when his so-called friends fail to return his famous generosity, withdraws to a cave in the woods, to plot the destruction of the city he now loathes to the point of insanity.

'Is man so hateful to thee / That art thyself a man?' asks Alcibiades, the rebel soldier whose attack on Athens Timon will shortly agree to finance. 'I am *Misanthropos*,' replies Timon, 'and hate mankind.'

It's essential, however, to distinguish such secular disgust for the world from the true monastic motivation for retreat. As Dom Erik Varden, abbot of Mount Saint Bernard, pointed out to me, a person might choose to enter monastic life out of disappointment or weariness with the world, but to despise it would be to contradict the Scriptures. 'For thou lovest all things that exist,' says Solomon to God in *The Book of Wisdom*, one of the books that make up the Septuagint or Greek Old Testament. 'For thou wouldst not have made anything if thou hadst hated it.' The monk, conscious of his own sinfulness, regards the worldly sinner not with contempt but with compassion. Far from repudiating the world, his retreat into monastic seclusion is done out of love for it, and the desire to see it redeemed. 'There's always the temptation, in any movement, in any élan of renewal, to frame your position in reactive terms,' Dom Erik told me. 'But that's never going to remain a motivating factor in the long run. Your basic motivation has got to be positive and aspirational.'

The monk understands what secular life might teach us less assuredly, that *contemptus mundi* is an unsustainable position. Even Apemantus, the cynical philosopher, chides Timon for his fanaticism, veering from hysterical largesse to all-out misanthropy: 'The middle of humanity thou never knewest, but the extremity of both ends.' It can be hard, for the outsider, not to read contempt for the world into certain monks' accounts of their decision to retreat. Thomas Merton, the Trappist monk whose tape recordings Brian Harnetty was setting to music, published his autobiography, *The Seven Storey Mountain*, in 1948. For the unprepared reader early Merton can be hard to swallow. The case he makes for receiving God's light seems to pale by comparison to his argument for escaping the darkness of secularism, perhaps because the truth and joy of Grace are, to him, self-evident and therefore incommunicable. ('If you did not believe it, you would never understand.')

The foulness of impiety is, on the other hand, condemned with unstinting vigour. You might say that, in the wake of the Second World War, Merton could be forgiven for taking a dim view of the world. Still, such *disgust*: when an advocate for the pure love of Christ writes of the 'rank, savage paganism' of everyday life, the 'futile aestheticism' of all non-devotional music and literature, the 'cheap and petty and disgusting lusts and vanities' in the 'selfish, stupid, idiotic world of men', it's hard not to sense Merton undermining his own argument, exposing the theology of hate behind his piety. Wasn't this just like my yoga friends, the habitual retreatants, their spirituality a means of perfuming their embitterment? Could Merton's vocation be read as anything other than a movement away, rather than towards, a withdrawal from human society inspired, like Timon's, by a fanatical aversion to it, a bitterness it was hard to square with Grace? Dom Erik would say that it could – that Merton's withdrawal from the world was motivated not by contempt for it, but by his growing conviction that only in the light of Christ did the world make any sort of sense. 'This is the center of all the vitality that is in America,' Merton writes, of his first formal retreat at Gethsemani, the abbey in Kentucky he was shortly to enter for life. The world might be a hellhole, but Merton's wish was not to condemn it but to take part in its redemption.

Hermitry is the original monasticism. Antony and the earliest ascetics that followed him withdrew into the Scetis Desert to be alone with their God. With the development of cenobitic monasticism, and its flourishing under St Benedict in the sixth century, however, came the danger of corruption. To live in a monastic community, as opposed to a hut or an anchorage, was to be a step closer to worldliness.

The High Middle Ages saw an attempt to revert to the purity of the eremitic life while retaining some of the advantages of the community. How to be alone amongst others, to maintain the hermit's commitment to solitary prayer in a communal setting? The Carthusian order was founded in 1084 with the express purpose of returning monastic observance to its desert roots. The Carthusians were to live together, but in isolation, each monk occupying a cell – effectively a small terraced cottage off the main cloister – with an adjoining enclosed garden, the *hortus conclusus* that doubled as a private space and a synecdoche for Paradise. The Carthusians owe their name to their mother house, La Grande Chartreuse, in a remote mountain pass in south-eastern France. ('Chartreuse', apart from the green liqueur made by the monks since the eighteenth century, also gives us 'Charterhouse', the English term for a Carthusian monastery.) Communal prayer was restricted to three services a day. Each monk observed the rest of the Liturgy of the Hours alone, in the miniature chapel inside his cell known as the oratory. Conversation was allowed only during the weekly walk in the surrounding countryside.

It was a bit like modern urban life, essentially. The monks lived side by side and had as little as possible to do with one another. Of all the Catholic orders the Carthusians are the most isolated and committed to silence; it's not uncommon for Carthusian novices to be ex-Benedictines or Cistercians grown dissatisfied with the relative leniency of their rule. There is a probably apocryphal story that the fourteenth-century Pope Urban V tried to convince the Carthusians to ease up on their austerities, maybe to eat a little meat now and then, until the monks sent a delegation in protest. What changed Urban's mind was not so much the rudeness of the delegates' health per se, as the fact that the youngest among them was eighty-eight. The oldest was ninety-five. Parkminster, in West Sussex, is the UK's only surviving Carthusian monastery. The Carthusian reputation for longevity was borne out by my host at Parkminster, Father Cyril Pierce, who, at eighty-seven, seemed to be running on some mystical superfuel, all the more remarkable given that only the year before, visiting a recently established Charterhouse in South Korea, he had fallen down some concrete steps, broken his back and been laid up in the care of his non-English-speaking hosts, unable to move or communicate save with hand gestures.

'I was more prepared than most people, no doubt about that,' he said, with a chuckle. Father Cyril was a Dubliner, and spoke with a merry fluency that seemed at odds with his fifty-nine-year commitment to near-total silence, until you remembered what Father Michael at Solesmes had said: these guys were half out of their minds with joy.

'But this was quite different. Here, you're with people you can speak to, but choose not to. There, I just couldn't.' In constant pain, unable to sleep, Father Cyril lay in his cell for two months until he was well enough to fly back to the UK. Extremes of privation were the Carthusians' speciality. In the Chapter House, where the Parkminster monks departed from their habitual silence to hold their annual chapter meeting, Father Cyril showed me a cycle of murals depicting the monks martyred at the London Charterhouse during the Reformation: hangings, decapitations, a monk being quartered with an axe. We stood in silence for a while.

'These were serious men,' said Father Cyril.

For forty years before his appointment as Parkminster's prior, Father Cyril was its novice master, responsible for the formation of prospective monks, the process of detaching them from their worldly concerns in preparation for a life of silence and isolation. 'This sort of vocation, it's not a question of acquiring virtues,' he said. 'It's getting stripped down.'

Formation generally took ten years, and was fraught with setbacks. 'Yourself and God are going to have some pretty bad moments.' Father Cyril sat back in his armchair and laughed. 'It's only bit by bit that you begin to hear Christ. The novices, they would come up to me when they were about six or seven years in, and say, Father, I've got it!' A belly-laugh this time. 'And I'd say, no you haven't!'

I had been introduced to the apparent paradox of communal hermitry on my trip to California. The Camaldolese, an off-shoot of the Benedictines, are the other great Catholic order to combine the eremitic life with elements of the cenobium. 'Sit in your cell as in paradise,' wrote the founder, St Romuald of Ravenna, in his eleventh-century Rule. 'Put the world behind you and forget it.' The Californian branch of the order, the New Camaldoli Hermitage, was founded in 1958, high in the Santa Lucia mountains overlooking the Pacific, ten miles down Highway 1 from Esalen.

If the Camaldolese regime seemed easy going by comparison to the Carthusians, that perhaps had something to do with the setting. The monks still rose before dawn for Vigils; they still spent the majority of their time in silent prayer, alone in their hexagonal, cinder-block cells, coming together only at meal-times and for the Divine Offices. Still, if you were going to be a hermit, there were worse places to do it. The hermitage sat on a plateau between canyons shaded by giant redwoods as old as Christianity. Before Vespers, I would hike further up towards the ridge, where ground fires had burned vast, blackened caverns at the bases of the trees. It was a landscape that invited retreat, the late-afternoon sun giving the present moment the lustre of memory. The monks were gracious if sometimes abstracted hosts. As with so many of the contemplatives I had met, they were at once intensely present and elsewhere. On the morning of my second day, in a ramshackle outhouse by the monks' refectory, I got chatting to Brother Ken, who, at thirty-six, was one of two postulants at the hermitage, candidate monks trying out the life before they were admitted as novices.

Ken's faith was relatively new. His parents had emigrated from Vietnam in the 1980s. 'I was an atheist,' he said, unloading white vestments into a laundry cart. 'A non-practising Buddhist.' Ken had wispy facial hair and an explosive laugh to match his generally precipitous manner. Nobody had said as much but I got the sense that there was a question mark over Ken's suitability. The day before, in the kitchen after lunch, he had hung back before relieving me of the washing up, suddenly, clattering through a pile of catering-size stock pots and roasting trays like it had questioned his commitment to God.

'What were your first impressions of the hermitage?' I asked.

'I fell in love,' said Ken. 'Just the autonomy that one has, being a hermit, to pursue the mystical life of contemplation. It's basically the silence, the solitude, that really sold me.'

Ken burst into slightly manic laughter. In the background, the hermitage bell tolled its solemn invitation to prayer.

As at Solesmes, the hermits' day begins at 5.30 a.m. with Vigils, the ancient custom of sanctifying the hours of darkness with a sequence of chanted psalms. Lauds are sung at 7 a.m., followed by the midday prayer, and Vespers combined with Mass at 5 p.m. By the standards of traditional Benedictine observance, it's a stripped-down liturgical schedule, allowing the monks plenty of time to sit in their cells in prayerful silence or study.

Which is not to say the Camaldolese are exclusively contemplative. The walls here are more permeable than at Parkminster or Solesmes. The element of outreach in the Camaldolese 'charism' – the defining spiritual character of the order – might involve teaching off site, or providing spiritual guidance for the lay people who come here on short-term retreat. To rewrite Romuald: 'Put the world behind you and forget it. But not entirely.'

'So you see what a balance it is,' said Father Cyprian. Cerebral, soft-voiced, authoritative in the most genial way, Cyprian became prior of the New Camaldoli in 2012, having joined the order in 1992. Recently sixty, he seemed twenty years younger as we hiked the steep mountain trail above the hermitage. In its earliest days, explained Cyprian, observance at the hermitage was closer to the Carthusian idea of silence and austerity. Partly as a result of the freedom of Benedictine monasteries from central command, however, the New Camaldoli has gradually adapted to the Californian climate.

'There's a possibility,' said Cyprian, 'that this kind of life, because of its flexibility, may be a harbour for people who are looking for something a little outside of the norm – who still want the monastic life, still want the liturgical spirituality, but don't necessarily want that militaristic model that you so often find in monasteries.' But liberalism had its limits. 'The liturgy, the scripture, the ritual, the tradition, is the container that holds this life together. It's the highest common denominator. You start losing that, it's a free-for-all.'

Back at the hermitage I attended Mass. For the eucharist, we passed into the rotunda, lit a cool, science-fictional blue. The chalice, the pall and the Missal were placed on the altar. It was a little frightening, in truth: the communicants arranged around the perimeter, vaguely cultish or uncanny in a ring; the swinging thurible and its growing pall of incense; the presiding priest, arms outstretched in consecration. One by one the communicants stepped forward to receive the host.

It was hard, witnessing the absorption of the monks in the liturgy, to imagine this pitch of observance ever fading, but as with most Christian monasteries the numbers were discouraging. Of the fifteen monks remaining at the hermitage, twelve were over sixty. Ken aside, new vocations were exceptionally hard to come by. For Brother Bede Healey, the answer lay in greater openness. In 2017 Bede left the hermitage to become Superior of its daughter house, the Incarnation Monastery in Berkeley. 'We have to stop thinking we know what young people need,' he told me. The charism must adapt to its applicants. 'It has to be forward looking. More than that: forward moving.'

Cyprian was more circumspect. 'I'm quite open to experimenting with new ways of belonging,' he said, as long as it 'doesn't do away with the traditional, classical approach.' As it was, the leniency of the regime was controversial in some Catholic quarters. 'The more conservative of our critics call us the hot-tub monks.' It was Cyprian's job to strike a balance between the reformists and the old guard. 'The two guys who are coming in now, the two postulants, they're getting by-the-books monastic history, monastic observance, liturgical spirituality.' It was certainly what Ken seemed to want. Far from seeking recognition for the qualities he could offer the order, his purpose was renunciation, complete withdrawal from the material world. 'I have to crucify everything,' he said, as we walked the concrete path to midday prayers. 'Die to all my desires, my dreams, my aspirations. I have to give it all to the Lord.'

'Do you think you'll make it all the way to solemn vows?' I asked.

'I'm going to be buried here,' he said, erupting in laughter again. 'That's the goal.'

A peculiar upshot of the Camaldolese commitment to outreach was that the hermitage had become home to a looser congregation of seekers, secular hermits taking advantage of their religious counterparts' generosity. In the woods behind the monks' refectory lived a rag-tag bunch of drop-outs and vaguely Thoreauvian eccentrics, drifters who had arrived, one day, usually on foot, and settled in old cabins and decrepit Airstream trailers, squatting on the monks' land in exchange for the odd bit of gardening or maintenance work. It was an entire community of Arrans, a mirror image of the Camaldolese among the laity: a bunch of cranky loners living in each other's laps. At the time of my visit, a legendary figure known as Jack Daniels still lived in a trailer high up among the fire-scarred sequoia, although I never saw him, and there were rumours that he was gravely ill. Wilko, on the other hand, was a common sight, kicking around the premises oiling creaky storm doors or shuttling visitors to and from Monterey and San Francisco in his battered old Suzuki. At one point he ushered me into a storeroom with the air of someone with urgent, if not highly sensitive, information to impart.

'First thing,' he said. 'We both like women, I know that. But I fucking *love* you.'

We had met less than thirty-six hours earlier. Wilko was originally from Brooklyn, although his keyed-up, big-city jitters were cut with something odder and more ancient, the Brooklyn of Whitman not the artisanal donut, the suggestion of pulpit or frontier in his glowering eyes and long salt-and-pepper beard. The second thing he had to tell me was something impenetrably complex about the White House, Wall Street and the Vatican, and how they were conspiring to destroy the hermitage. Not that, in Wilko's opinion, this mattered very much. 'It's the *land*, you get me? It's fucking *sacred*. People will always gather here, monks or no monks.'

There was a pleasing irony, it struck me, in an institution as fundamentally conservative – for all its liberal peculiarities – as a Catholic monastery harbouring what remained of the Californian counterculture. Wilko and the others were the kind of oddballs that might have hung out at Esalen before money turned it into a strange, orderly simulacrum of itself. 'This is Big Sur,' said Cyprian on our hike in the mountains. 'There are so many hippies around, and lots of drifters of various types on the California coast anyway.' The hermitage was a retreat for the spiritually indeterminate too. Tim Quarrie was a New Zealander in his mid-forties based until recently in Colorado. Wilko and Tim didn't get along.

'I'm a pretty reasonable person,' Tim told me. 'He doesn't have to speak to me like I'm a fucking cunt.'

Tim was bunking down in a cabin on the edge of the woods. 'You want to watch out for that guy,' Wilko had warned me. Other than that, he wouldn't be drawn, but I got the sense that, for Wilko, the argument was only a local flare-up of a longer-standing personality clash, Wilko's nervy, mystic charisma versus Tim's quieter and more professorial air, his habit of launching into long if often pretty inventive speculations on human nature, combining evolutionary biology with attachment theory and computational neuroscience. Tim seemed a natural hermit: highly intelligent, a bit fragile, and unable to resist perpetuating his aloneness by rubbing certain people up the wrong way.

One afternoon, promising to catch him later after a particularly intricate lecture on the central nervous system, I retired to one of the hermitage's two libraries, only to find him there, draped on a recliner, as if he existed like a sort of quantum hermit in all places at once. We picked up where we had left off on the effects of stress and toxic urban environments on our basal ganglia. Tim thought of his spell in the woods as a 'neural fast'. Modern life was degrading our nervous systems. 'We're not adapted to live the way we do. We're just not.'

If it wasn't for the hermitage, Tim didn't know where he would go. Earlier that year he had split up with his girlfriend in Denver. Trump seemed like the harbinger of societal collapse. Retreating to the woods no longer seemed like an option but the only sensible course to take. 'It's the quietude that I like, the beautiful scenery.' Did he think the hermitage could survive in its present form? 'I hope so,' he said. 'Because I think places like this can literally save people's lives.'

It seemed safe to conceive of Tim and the other drifters at the hermitage as misfits squeezed out by a capitalist society that had no place for them. They had nowhere else to go. The monks, for their part, had retreated because they believed silence and solitude were their clearest path to Divine encounter. But it would be a mistake to think of the eremitic impulse as limited to drop-outs and religious contemplatives. The idea of hermitry as an ornament or indeed aspiration in comfortable, upper- and middle-class society dates back to at least the eighteenth century. A 'hermitage' was not only a rude hut occupied by a long-bearded eccentric in rags. It might also be a palace. The Hermitage in St Petersburg – the world's second-largest art museum – is an extension of a smaller building called the Petit Hermitage, commissioned in 1764 by Catherine the Great as a retreat from the formality of the Winter Palace next door. Jean-Jacques Rousseau's idea of the natural man was immensely popular among European elites of the time. The Empress was expressing her natural nobility by offering guests a simpler, informal alternative to the mind-curdling ostentation of her official residence. (The informality was relative. At dinner, for example, guests were served by dumb waiter. Such was the aristocratic idea of a return to rustic simplicity: fricassee of tortoise served by pulley.)

The notion of noble withdrawal soon spread. In England, the ideal of 'the natural' had taken hold in the late seventeenth century. As the historian Gordon Campbell notes, by the following century 'The Hermitage' was becoming increasingly popular as a house name, as the convention trickled down from the estate-owning aristocracy to the middle classes. The Arcadian ideal of the untamed wilderness also informed the fashion for garden hermitages, purpose-built grottoes in the grounds of stately homes. These were frequently occupied by a living, ornamental hermit, paid by the landowner to grow their hair long and avoid conversation with any passers-by taking the air. The landscape garden at Painshill Park, near Cobham in Surrey, had a hermitage partly built from the roots of old fir trees. An entry in the *London Evening Post* from 1773 suggests that the owner, the Hon. Charles Hamilton, had advertised successfully for a hermit to occupy it for seven years, on the condition that he was 'not to be shaved, not to cut his nails, nor his hair during the whole time'. (In Tom Stoppard's *Arcadia*, Noakes, gardener of the fictional Sidley Park estate in Derbyshire, suggests to his employer Lady Croom that they place a newspaper advertisement for someone to occupy the hermitage he has built. 'But surely,' objects Lady Croom, 'a hermit who takes a newspaper is not a hermit in whom one can have complete confidence.') Hamilton's hermit at Painshill, a Mr Remington, was apparently paid £500 for his seven-year retreat. Not bad for the mid-eighteenth century, when the average yearly wages of a footman were £7.

Later garden hermitages featured hermit automata. Visitors to Hawkstone Park, in Shropshire, could enter a dimly lit chamber containing a stuffed, bare-footed old mannikin, capable of rising, bowing and reporting his age. Automation was threatening jobs as far back as the early nineteenth century. Campbell sees the ornamental hermit as the precursor of the garden gnome, a sentimental embodiment of a newly fashionable idea, that solitude conferred authenticity, that an individual of means and sensibility would by necessity choose retreat in a natural setting over the company of his fellow men.

The idea endures. 'I want to earn enough money I can get away from everyone,' says the oilman Daniel Plainview in Paul Thomas Anderson's *There Will Be Blood.* It should come as no surprise that Elon Musk's ultimate ambition is to make it to Mars. Supercharged by the tech-driven hyper-individualism of contemporary Western societies, the long association of privilege and withdrawal has hardened into a given: that misanthropy is the default mode of material wealth. Civil society is for those too poor to avoid it. In Greenwich, Connecticut, once a bastion of moderate, Waspish Republicanism, until the first years of the twenty-first century the walls around residents' estates were much as they had always been throughout New England: waist-height, as we assume the dry-stone partition is in Robert Frost's 'Mending Wall'. Now the influx of hedge-fund money has given us the phenomenon of the 'Greenwich wall': nine-foot, mortared-stone perimeters screening the financiers' mansions from view. In Frost's poem, walls represent a division the speaker thinks is unnecessary, unlike his neighbour, who is all for them. '"Good fences make good neighbors."' At nine feet, the debate closes down. What neighbours? I have *neighbours*?

In the phenomenon of the billionaire prepper – Peter Thiel and his fellow tech-libertarians building luxury survival bunkers as a haven from the coming AI apocalypse – there's an echo of Franz Kafka's unfinished short story 'The Burrow'. An unidentified creature has secured the walls of its burrow by ramming its forehead thousands of times into the soil. 'I was happiest when bloodied, because that meant the walls were beginning to acquire firmness.' But the creature lives in fear of attack, driven mad by a constant hissing noise that might be nothing or an animal digging down to invade the burrow and tear the creature to pieces. 'Someone is coming.' In a sense, the story's incompleteness is its masterstroke. The invader never arrives, but the unrelenting expectation that it will means the creature can only carry on securing the burrow, firming up the walls with repeated blows of its brow. Retreat as infinite regress: you just go on retreating, further and further into the abyss of your paranoia.

Two hours' drive north of Wichita, Kansas, the discerning prepper can already invest in the 'Survival Condo Project', a former missile silo converted into a luxury underground apartment complex guarded by snipers and built to withstand nuclear attack. Residents can watch live, HD footage of the prairie above them, streamed to the video screens that stand in for windows. A full-floor, 1,820-square-foot unit will set you back $3 million, although survival training and a 'three-year-per-person food supply' is included in the price.

It's in initiatives like these that the peculiarly American style of eschatological fervour meets something more universal, the misanthropic impulse that stands in perpetual tension with the communal ideal, the sense of shared obligation subjected to near intolerable stress by material inequality. The greater the divide, the more we retreat, into the ideological bunkers represented by Brexit and Trumpism and the scandalised liberalism they defy. It's just that the better off can afford to reify that impulse in bricks and mortar. In Japan, the phenomenon of the *hikikomori* – men between their teens and early forties who lead lives of extreme social isolation, often in their parental homes – applies almost exclusively to the middle and upper-middle classes. Under pressure to succeed academically or professionally, bound by the inflexible hierarchies and conformism of Japanese society, the *hikikomori* absent themselves because they can, retire to their childhood bedrooms to download TikTok videos or play *Metal Gear Solid V* safe in the knowledge that their parents' wealth will keep the outside world at bay.

You retreat because you want to be rid of everyone who isn't you. Citizen Kane in Xanadu: here the withdrawal into reclusiveness constitutes not the annihilation of the ego but the wounded assertion of it. Timon's hatred for mankind is, after all, a bit of an overreaction. The failure of a few friends to return your generosity does not, in the final analysis, justify calling for Alcibiades to 'be as a planetary plague' in his attack on Athens. Timon is throwing his toys out of the pram, with the same inflated self-regard that characterised his generosity. As Aristotle remarks in his *Politics*, any man who lives outside society must either be a god or a beast. The ego is either suppressed or left to grow monstrous. The danger with reclusiveness is that the ego, deprived of an external object for its contempt, has nowhere to turn but on itself. 'Glory and tranquillity cannot dwell in the same lodgings,' Montaigne tells us. This is fundamental to the stress on humility in religious and spiritual hermitry. The ego *must* be suppressed, or the solitude will drive you mad. If you're going to withdraw from all human contact, you had better be cut out for it: a superhuman ego-suppressor. I was reminded of this at Simonopetra, when I asked Diakon Seraphim about the few remaining hermits on Mount Athos. Most started out, he told me, as fully fledged members of their monastic communities. The few judged able to withstand the hardships of total solitude were given special dispensation, by the bishop, to live in a *hesychasterion*, a wooden hut or cave often high up on a cliff face and scarcely accessible even on foot.

'It's not easy,' said Seraphim. 'You have to be a very spiritual man, and very humble. If you are not humble, the Devil will destroy you.'

*

Naustholmen is a tiny island of thirty-three acres, eight hundred miles north of Oslo inside the Norwegian Arctic Circle. Getting there involved flying to Bodø then catching the *hurtigruta*, the fast ferry that navigates the countless uninhabited islands and skerries that litter the coast. Inland the mountains ascended, gradually, until, by the jetty at Nordskot, they loomed like a reckoning over the cluster of cheerful, red and white clapboard buildings that lined the front, where Randi was waiting for me.

The crossing to Naustholmen took less than three minutes by speedboat. Randi is a solo adventurer, the first Norwegian woman to climb Everest, who, since her ascent in 2004, has also completed the Seven Summits, climbing the highest mountain in every continent, from Denali in Alaska to the Vinson Massif in Antarctica. More recently she had kayaked the northern coast of Norway, alone, 1,800 km from Rørvik to the Russian border. At the wheel of her boat, in her trademark slim-fit fleece and hiking trousers, wind finning her white-gold bob, Randi cut a stern figure, which, I was shortly to learn, couldn't have been further from the truth. If there was one quality that had propelled her up Everest and deposited her, aged fifty-five, on her rocky private island in the Arctic, it was cheerfulness, a tenacious, plain-spoken optimism she had turned to her commercial advantage. She was at once a natural solitary and about as far from the contemplative temperament as could be imagined: a kind of corporate hermit.

'What I learned from all my mountain trips and expeditions in nature, especially when I was kayaking the coast, was this: it takes the time that it takes.' Randi and I had walked down to the pebble beach at the island's north-eastern tip, facing the Nordskot jetty across Leinesfjord. It was a perfect, cloudless afternoon, the traverse above Nordskot achingly sharp against the sky, the water between us and the mainland a turquoise so pure you felt it like an absence in your chest, as if the mere sight of it had increased your lung capacity. If the tranquillity of the place was at all undermined it was because

John-Magne and Unni, next door on the island of Grøtøya, were having an extension built onto their boutique hotel, by helicopter, the prefabricated walls suspended by long line and flown over the fjord like the statue of Christ at the beginning of *La Dolce Vita*.

Randi had planned to complete her solo kayak expedition in a year. In the end, it took her three, completing a stage or two then sitting out long spells of injury and bad weather. Psychologically, the first year was harder than expected.

'My head was turned on all the time,' said Randi, raising her voice as the helicopter swatted the air above Naustholmen. '"What's the wind like, are there any ships, how big are the waves?" I didn't have the patience to wait.' It was only gradually, through persistence, that she learned how to turn her head off, to live in the moment. 'It takes the time that it takes.' And this new skill helped Randi defend herself against the cynics who had criticised her slow progress. 'Come on!' she said. 'I don't care what people say. I counted four hundred golden moments that summer. If anyone wants to complain about what I've done, they can count their own golden moments, and see how many *they* got.'

Randi ran Naustholmen as an island-adventure retreat for Oslo executives eager to absorb a measure of her self-reliance. In her dining room, overlooking the fjord, Randi showed me her memoir-cum-self-help book, *Finn Konge-Følelsen*, 'Find the King Feeling,' with a photo on the cover of Randi grinning in a fleece and stripy beanie. Randi's motivational-quote approach to adversity reached its high point on Everest, an ambition of hers since childhood. Aged forty-four, having quit her job in IT, Randi teamed up with three male adventurers, all of whom dropped out during the ascent, the last, a fellow Norwegian called Truls, holding on until 7,900 metres before succumbing to exhaustion. Randi climbed the final thousand metres alone. The way she spoke of it, Randi's decision to leave the rat race and join the great Norwegian lineage of adventurers was less of a departure than it seemed, a chance to apply the skills she had learned in the boardroom, except this time primarily to herself. Everest was a project to be managed, the summit a deliverable.

'I worked on it as if it was a business case,' she told me. 'We had targets, we had a mission, we had values.' Generosity, Respect for the Mountain, Humility. 'I can't remember what the last one was.'

The helicopter was over us again, hovering, impatiently, its section of wall twisting on the line, while the crew on the ground screwed the previous section in place. Randi's grey cat, Gråmann, had joined us, sitting at a congenial distance and sniffing at the air with subliminal twitches of his precise pink nose. 'Ambition!' said Randi, congratulating her powers of recall with a quick tap to the forehead. 'Because you do need to be ambitious.'

Later Randi took me for a kayak on the Vestfjord, the larger expanse separating Naustholmen from the Lofoten archipelago, visible on the horizon as a seemingly endless line of snow-capped peaks. During their stay, retreatants could hike, twitch for sea eagles, go fishing or swim in the fjord, alone or under Randi's invigilation. Out on the Vestfjord, I abruptly lost the ability to steer with the hard-to-reach, stiff little pedals near the nib of the boat, a loss of control that took me straight back to my icy slide across the highway in Barre, and, as I might have predicted, only got worse the more I tried to suppress it.

Randi paddled over. 'You okay?'

'Fine,' I said, but it was no use, she'd heard the tension in my voice.

'Drop your shoulders, take a breath,' Randi said, or some such, I can't remember. Whatever the precise nature of the advice, at an unspoken level it imparted such kindness, such patience – which, being unspoken, couldn't be put in a corporate self-improvement manual – that my feet soon found the pedals and I was off, gliding into a silence my internal chatter had now subsided enough to reveal.

It was the universal dream, Randi's – here on her island, with its endless days, the light in the late evening not failing so much as relinquishing colour, the island whitening, fading, as wisps of low cloud floated over it and the sun teased but never quite touched the sea. The place of the island, and in particular of its sole inhabitant, in the European imagination, connects the Arcadian mania for wild places – *Robinson Crusoe* as much as Rousseau helped to inspire the craze for garden hermits – with the contemporary island fetishisation that led Sheikh Mohammed of Dubai to commission The World, the archipelago of artificial islands two miles off Jumeirah Beach. Brando on Teti'aroa, Branson on Necker: like the luxury bunker, the island is shorthand for wealth so great it needs separation from the rest of us, as literalised in the case of offshore tax havens like Bermuda and the Cayman Islands. And like the Greenwich wall, or the Survival Condo Project, the aspirational status of the island, as a totem of social ascendancy, is inseparable from the impulse it embodies to withdraw. The writer J.G. Ballard coined the term 'inverted Crusoeism' to describe the wish, contrary to Robinson Crusoe's unwilled isolation, to stay marooned, like Robert Maitland, the protagonist of Ballard's novel *Concrete Island*, after he crashes his car onto a patch of waste ground cut off by intersecting motorways and decides that he prefers it there.

At Naustholmen, visitors came, and left better able to achieve their objectives. Out of season, when the endless days became endless nights, it was just Randi and Gråmann. 'No-one wants me!' she said, with too hearty a laugh, when I asked if she was seeing anyone. The sense I had of Randi as a sort of anti-mystic, Sara Maitland's inverse, a non-contemplative hermit – a 'reality-oriented person', as she referred to herself – was strengthened by the distaste she voiced for introspection. Apart from Naustholmen she kept a small cabin in the woods outside Oslo. With work to do there, maintenance, wood chopping, she thrived.

'And without it?'

'Ach, boring,' she said. 'Just to sit inside a hut is nearly impossible.'

Randi's stillness was in movement, her metaphysics strictly physical. 'My best meditation is when my body is active, I have fresh air, and I have nothing to think of.' It was what justified and lent structure to her isolation: keeping busy, cultivating her island garden, her paradise without God. The helicopter had flown back to Nordskot and not returned. All we could hear now was the hiss of the Leinesfjord as it clawed back from the shore. 'I do this island on my own. It's a one-woman project,' said Randi. 'My solitude is in the things I do.'

Phil got back to London about three weeks after I did. His ex, Laura, was in town, and pending their final custody arrangements had agreed to let him see their son on the neutral ground of a friend's house in Clapham. Afterwards I'd picked him up and driven him to the tube at Clapham North. I parked round the corner on Landor Road, in view of a pub that for a while in our twenties functioned as a sort of alcoholic annexe to the flat we shared nearby.

'Quick one?'

'Can't,' said Phil. He looked tired, older, whether as a result of seeing his ex, or in the aftermath of ayahuasca, I didn't know. 'Not much point, anyway.'

'Why's that?'

'Lime and soda at the Landor. I can't think of anything more depressing.'

'How was Peru?'

Phil stared out the windscreen. 'Put it this way,' he said. 'If I've had a more terrifying experience, it was somehow contained in that one.'

'Really? The whole fortnight?'

'No, I just got the dose wrong one evening. Otherwise – well, I won't do justice to it. Momentous is probably the word. But if it's all the same to you I won't say much more. I'm still in the midst of it.'

'You still haven't come down?'

'It's not exactly that. Everything just feels a bit fluid.'

I nodded. 'I'm sorry I bailed.'

'I understand. Forget it. There'll be other times.'

If I could sense Phil pulling away it was not only, I thought, because his ayahuasca experience had been every bit as incommunicable as hesychastic union with God. Looking back on that muddled afternoon at JFK, I wondered if my decision to drop out had not, after all, been a last-minute loss of nerve, but something simpler, deeper, that rather than spend another fortnight on the other side of the world I would rather go home. The only question was whether this came from a timely desire to get on with the book, to begin to make sense of all the travel I'd done, the conversations I'd had – to deal on a fundamental level with the paradox that researching this study of withdrawal had been one of the most richly peopled periods of my life – or whether something else was in play, something that may even have been the reason I'd embarked on the book in the first place – that *it* had started, in earnest, the urge to get away from people, radically foreshorten the social horizon, not an uncommon impulse, I supposed, in middle age but one which, for me, carried a special weight of dread, given my vow not to maroon myself in the way my parents had, and the inkling that this vow was only the propitiation of an indifferent god.

This impulse to withdraw was on my mind as I returned to Thomas Merton. His trajectory had been in the opposite direction – or rather, in both directions at once. In 1965, Merton moved into a hermitage in the grounds of Gethsemani. For years he had longed for greater silence and solitude than life in a Trappist community could provide. But his withdrawal into hermitry coincided with a period of notably greater openness. His later journals betray none of the wintry superbity of *The Seven Storey Mountain*. From its inward-looking contempt for the world his theology had softened, broadened, to embrace a radical commitment to denuclearisation and civil rights, the promotion of peaceful inter-faith dialogue, and a profound engagement with secular music and literature. He loved Bob Dylan, Kansas City jazz, John Coltrane at his most perplexingly experimental. In 1966, two years before he died, Merton fell in love, with Margie Smith, a 25-year-old student nurse at the Louisville hospital where Merton, then aged fifty-one, was recuperating from back surgery. Whether or not the affair remained platonic – the record is ambiguous – Merton's infatuation with Margie was indisputable. 'There is no question, I am in deep,' he wrote in his journal. The deeper his retreat, the greater his exposure to the world.

Much later, a month into lockdown, I dropped Father Cyprian a line at the hermitage. How were the hermits doing, sheltering in place, now doubly insulated from the world? Comfortably enough, said Cyprian, although he prayed safety for me and my family. There was news, however, about Ken, the postulant determined to be buried in the cemetery. The monks had asked him to leave seven months ago.

8.

The Nike of the Mind

In hindsight it was just after he turned fifteen that Luke began withdrawing from the real world. 'I'd leave school as soon as possible, spend all night gaming, then go to school the next day, sleep through my lessons, then go home and the cycle would repeat.' Luke grew up in a suburb of Ipswich with his mum and younger brother. His school was on the borders of a middle-class neighbourhood and what he described as a 'very, very dodgy area'. The mix was not conducive to learning. His class-mates were 'disengaged or trying actively to distract me'. The result was his own disengagement.

Luke's game of choice was *Counter-Strike: Global Offensive*, a multi-player first-person shooter in which players team up online to wipe out their opponents, while completing various other tasks, like defusing bombs and rescuing hostages. In 2016, Luke racked up 1,500 hours of game-play. 'Which isn't so ridiculous,' he said. 'But it's still a lot.' He failed his exams. He let his hair grow to shoulder-length, often wearing it over his face. Contact with family and friends was all but sus-pended. In the space of a few months Luke had gone from being an ordinary, averagely sociable teenager to something close to a secular hermit, spending virtually all his time alone in his bedroom. 'My brother lived in the room next door to mine,' Luke told me. 'I think I talked to him maybe ten times in two years.'

Dr Becky Lockwood is a Consultant Clinical Psychologist at the National Centre for Gaming Disorders in south-west London. Gaming disorder, as defined in the ICD-11, the World Health Organisation's diagnostic manual for the classification of diseases, is characterised by impaired control over gaming, priority given to gaming at the expense of other interests and activities, and 'continuation or escalation of gaming despite the occurrence of negative consequences'. Often these negative consequences either equate or accrue to the gamer's increasing isolation. It's worth noting that gaming disorder as a formal diagnosis is not without its sceptics. Psychologists like Professor Pete Etchells at Bath Spa University are doubtful that the evidence base supports the separation of gaming from behavioural addictions in general. There is broad consensus, however, both that excessive gaming can be a response to life problems, and that, whether or not gaming disorder can be usefully separated from other behavioural addictions, multiplayer video games can be dangerously addictive.

For example, in an MMO, or massively multiplayer online game, like Wargaming's *World of Tanks*, continued play is incentivised not only by regular in-game rewards, in the form of credits, performance badges and equipment upgrades, but by the perpetual stream of 'microfeedback' that sustains the player's impression of agency in the virtual world. Spot an enemy tank and a short beep will sound. Direct your gun at it and, as long as it remains in range, the target will be outlined in red. The constantly reinforced sense that your actions in reality have consequences in the virtual world is only intensified by the knowledge that the virtual world will carry on happily without you: digital FOMO. MMOs take place in a 'persistent state world', evolving independently of any single player's interaction with it. You can't press pause and pick up where you left off. To spend time away from *World of Warcraft* is to miss out on a world your fellow players are continuing not only to experience, but to shape.

More than that, once the player is drawn in, 'open-world' games like *Red Dead Redemption II* and *Horizon Zero Dawn* allow them the free and potentially limitless chance to explore their virtual bounds. In *Abzû*, a deep-sea-adventure game, game-play defers to exploration: you can just swim around, dreamily, enjoying a virtual approximation of James's oceanic bliss, much as players find places in sandbox games like *Minecraft* to sit and chill or go fishing. The space-exploration game *No Man's Sky* has no bounds at all: the planets the player is invited to explore are generated on an ongoing basis, automatically, according to algorithms devised by the programmers. The player need never stop: the solitude available is infinite.

Even so, what's striking is how psychologists like Becky view the addictiveness of video games as secondary in the development of gaming disorder. In people who develop gaming disorder, she explained, the impetus is frequently 'avoidance of reality, or of difficulties that people are having in reality'. To log on to an MMO or multiplayer first-person shooter is to retreat to a more manageable reality. 'For people with social anxiety, it feels much safer gaming, because they can hide behind the mask of their character, or just show what they want of themselves.' Addiction comes later, locking the gamer into a pattern of behaviour prompted in the first instance by their incomplete or incoherent sense of self.

After GCSEs, Luke's withdrawal only intensified. His three-day week at further-education college left considerably more time for gaming. 'At this point I was staying up till four, maybe five in the morning.' Luke's predispositions – his unhappiness at school – had caused his retreat into a virtual world. Now he was hooked. 'Gaming took up all my time.'

At Becky Lockwood's clinic, treatment for gaming disorder involves a mixture of cognitive behavioural therapy, mindfulness, and training in social and communication skills. The aim is to help gamers understand and manage the psychological preconditions of their tendency to withdraw from the real world, and, over twelve weeks, to give them the means of returning to it. In Luke's case, the return happened naturally: he grew out of his habit. His team of Kevlar-vested liquidators had largely gone their separate ways. Luke had spent the summer before his first term at university reacquainting himself with his family.

'We went on holiday a few times, we went out for meals and stuff,' he said. Shortly before term started, Luke finally had his hair cut. When we spoke, he was still glad of the decision. 'It constantly reminds me, oh yeah, I'm at uni now, whereas back then I was young. And not very well socialised.'

The advantage of the FV4004 Conway was that the Damage Per Minute was off the scale for its class. It wasn't a tank you'd pick for down-and-dirty, hand-to-hand combat. Its reload rate was too low. Its camouflage values were risible. Where the Conway came into its own was in support, patrolling near the back of a formation ready to slot a high-energy squash-head into an unsuspecting Spähpanzer or Type 64. Something heavy, a Mäuschen maybe, lumbered over the escarpment, exposing its side armour.

'Oof,' said Pete, as the Mäuschen exploded in flame. 'Got him nicely there.' A green bar hovering over the enemy tank indicated critical damage. 'That was just a straight penetration.'

According to its Belarusian developers, *World of Tanks* has more than 160 million registered players worldwide. Players assume command of a single tank, chosen from the range of mid-twentieth-century models available at their gaming level, and join battle in a realistically rendered, randomly allotted terrain with whichever other players are online at the time. This can either be done solo or as part of a clan.

'I actually roll with a bunch of Syrian tankers,' said Pete. 'A lot of them are squaddies who I think are stuck in barracks, playing this in their downtime or perhaps even as training.'

For Pete, however, the appeal lay less in the virtual camaraderie than in the immersion in a virtual world that was all the more immersive for seeming so real. 'It's a proper virtual environment where the laws of physics apply,' he told me.

Pete was a very different kind of gamer to Luke. For starters, he was forty-five: geriatric in gaming terms (although not, it should be noted, in *World of Tanks*: there were a lot of retired and disabled people playing it, Pete told me). As a self-confessed 'pan-psychist', Pete took the view that machinery – including, in this case, virtual representations of machinery by another machine – had a soul. The individual 'character' of each tank in his fleet mattered a great deal to him. It was as if the social element of gaming had been displaced from his fellow players onto the tanks they were playing with. As Pete took me on a tour of his virtual garage – where, he told me, he could spend up to nine days prepping a tank for combat – it became increasingly apparent that, for him, this world of chokepoints and standard shell penetrations represented an escape from a reality whose borders he had, at times, found difficult to discern.

'When I was playing very heavily,' he told me, 'I got myself into a very weird environment at work, with the strange world of the oligarchs and McMafia and all of that.' Quite what this entailed he wouldn't say, but the implication was that he had been hired as a consultant on a project with links to Russian organised crime. At around the same time, he explained, he had suffered a mental health episode. 'I have a long family history of schizophrenia,' he said. 'And a couple of years ago I had what psychologists call "peak experience", which is like the happy side of schizophrenia, if you like. Grace of God stuff.'

Pete had the sense that his experience was far from unique. 'My perspective is that the mystic experience at the root of every world religion, and the schizophrenic experience, are the same thing. Religion *is* schizophrenia.' Mystico-schizophrenics were merely accessing reality in a different way. Pete shared the physicist Tom Campbell's view that so-called 'physical reality' is a simulation. 'I don't think that everyone realises the extent to which they generate their own reality,' Pete said. 'People assume because they see, touch and feel that they're experiencing something outside themselves. Whereas, in fact, we imagine, virtualise, everything. We get data from outside, but we all of us, schizophrenic or not, live in a virtual environment. As virtual as this game is.'

For Pete, inhabiting a game-world amounted not so much to a retreat from reality, as – given his belief that reality is simulated anyway – to swapping one virtual world for another. *World of Tanks* had the advantage of seeming relatively safe; the loneliness of spending eight hours in a single day, slotting high-explosive squash-heads into unsuspecting Spähpanzers, was preferable to the increasingly frightening alternative. Pete's involvement in organised crime had, he claimed, quickly escalated. 'Supranational intelligence agencies were using me as a conduit to transmit messages to Vladimir Putin, after they'd lost control of him over the Crimea. He's a Western intelligence asset that's gone rogue. So I had a very weird time.' Pete laughed. On screen, the Conway sat in his garage, awaiting customisation. 'This is not paranoid-schizophrenic me, this is *real*.'

It's perhaps helpful to conceive of the kind of retreat into virtual reality experienced by Luke and Pete as a form of *contemptus mundi*. You retreat to your virtual cell because the world seems hostile, terrifying, a hell on earth. Pete in particular seemed to embody the impulse to recoil from contemporary phenomena, sitting as he did at the confluence of religiosity, technology, paranoia both justified and otherwise, pan-psychism and mental illness. Experience had pushed him to the edge of the world, and the temptation to slip off entirely was powerful. In the case of the contemplative traditions, the postulant or *sāmanera*, driven by disappointment or world-weariness into monastic or other spiritual retreat, can expect, in their new life of prayer or contemplation, to perceive a reality beyond the world's horrors once the obstacles to that perception are removed. When I raised the question of contemporary political evils with Father Michael at Solesmes, he responded with a composure you might either consider as quietism or the long view of someone whose interior life was calibrated in infinities. ('Monks have great perspective,' he said. 'It's part of our strength.') For the gamer, there was just more gaming. Their digital form of hermitry was closer to the kind of irredeemable misanthropy, contempt for the world, that could only get deeper the longer they indulged it.

If this was true, it had implications for meditative retreat as it was increasingly experienced by most people: in the form of smartphone-based meditation apps like Headspace and Calm. How could purity of mind possibly be promoted via the world's most notorious mental pollutant? How could you retreat online and be anything other than less alive to the world? I had paid a visit to Calm's HQ in San Francisco after my spells at Esalen and the Camaldolese hermitage earlier in the year. I checked in under an arch of variously sized, hard-plastic bubbles in white and three shades of blue.

'You don't have to be a hard-core meditator to join Calm,' said Casey McKerchie, Vice-President of Operations, as we walked through the open-plan, exposed-brick offices to the in-house café. From the street outside came the disconsolate wail of a fire truck. 'Because at the end of the day, our mission is to make the world a healthier and happier place.'

Calm was founded in 2012 by the British entrepreneurs Michael Acton Smith and Alex Tew. As with its number-one competitor, Headspace, the company's main product is its meditation app, featuring guided and unguided meditation sessions, classical and ambient music, and stories aimed at the sleep-deprived, read by actors with soothing voices like Matthew McConaughey and Eva Green. The main difference between the two market leaders is in the hand they extend to the novice user. Headspace assumes little or no experience of meditation. The interface is bright, friendly, iconic, with blissed-out suns and the kind of minimalistic, unmodelled human and animal figures you might find in a pre-schooler's cartoon. You may not need to be hard-core to join Calm, but its presentation is certainly more grown-up, a visual spa more than a kindergarten: rippling water, misty mountainscapes. Its signature feature is 'The Daily Calm', a ten-minute meditation refreshed every day and written by Tamara Levitt, the Canadian mindfulness instructor and Calm's Head of Content. At the time of writing, the Calm app has two million paid subscribers and had been downloaded more than 50 million times. In February 2019, the company became the world's first mental-health 'unicorn' – a privately held start-up valued at over $1 billion.

Like the thousands of other free and subscription-based meditation and mindfulness apps, Calm offers retreat where it might otherwise be hard to access: in the street, doing the laundry, on the packed evening train. The website promises subscribers reduced stress and anxiety and more restful sleep. Dig a little deeper and you'll find blog entries on the role of meditation in lowering high blood pressure, preventing diabetes, protecting against Alzheimer's and improving immune-system function.

'Our goal is for mental fitness to be another tool in people's toolbox,' Casey told me. 'We want to build the Nike of the mind. It's pretty awesome.'

I had to admit to finding my own mental Nikes a little uncomfortable. That meditation I'd done after the icy car-slide in Barre, for instance. I remember being struck by how calm I felt – until, that is, the app started pestering me with messages like, 'Nice work!' and 'You're amazing!' Set a 'mindfulness reminder' and Calm will prompt you with push notifications like, 'It's time to meditate.' Further, it may be that the inherent isolation of listening to a meditation app via earphones neutralises its benefits. Goleman and Davidson suggest that the sense of community common to traditional meditative cultures is crucial to the development of trait effects. I was reminded of Sara Maitland: 'The mobile phone is a great victory for the devil.' Wasn't increased screen use close to an insane response to stress, poor focus, unmindfulness?

Casey McKerchie trod carefully. 'I think the way that we manage it is, we always go back to, what is our core mission? And I think we could gamify, we could have ads in our app if we wanted to make more money. There's a lot of things we could be doing from a monetisation perspective that probably would work, but it's not aligned with who we are and what we believe.'

This is debatable. Calm *does* gamify, according to any sensible definition of the term. Under your profile, your number of 'Mindful Days' is given in a rotating rosette. Underneath, your 'streak' allows you to keep track of how continuously you use the app. Further rosettes are awarded if you meditate for three, ten, fifteen and thirty days in succession. The implication couldn't be clearer: mindfulness as a means of obsessive self-monitoring, no less addictive, or indeed mindless, than maintaining the streak on your Fitbit.

The case for the defence rests on the resolvability of the paradox. Andy Puddicombe, the co-founder of Headspace, spent five years in Myanmar, studying vipassana meditation in the Mahasi form I had practised in Salford. He was later ordained as a monk in the Tibetan tradition. It was during this period of discernment that he realised the potential in bringing meditation to a wider audience in the West. Headspace was founded in London in 2010. Now, with headquarters in Santa Monica, the app has over two million paid subscribers and has been downloaded more than 62 million times. Puddicombe's Don-Draper-like insight on the meditation mat had proved true. There were big bucks in watered-down vipassana.

'For most of us,' said Puddicombe in a 2017 TV interview, 'the phone is the most stressful thing in our life. I love the paradox in that, the irony. The phone's a piece of plastic, a piece of metal, a piece of glass.' For the app apologists, smartphones can act as a kind of vaccination against their own toxicity. 'I love the idea that the phone can actually serve up something really good, that's good for our health.'

But how good is it? Clearly, the argument that the benefits of meditation outweigh the alienating effects of screen use prevails only if those beneficial effects can be substantiated. The clinical basis for the claims made by the leading meditation apps is thin, to say the least. Like Calm, Headspace cites studies supporting the role of meditation in relieving depression, anxiety and stress-related pain. Comparatively little work, however, has been done to evaluate the effectiveness of meditation and related techniques as delivered specifically via apps and other digital platforms. It's classic sleight of hand, backing up a specific instance with the most general claims. Calm cites three independently commissioned studies into its own product. The second, a randomised controlled trial conducted at Arizona State University in 2019, on the efficacy of Calm in reducing stress among college students, showed some positive results in the short term, but acknowledged the need for further studies. Three papers amid the thousands published on mindfulness is a drop in an ocean of tentative evidence, something Calm itself admits on its website: 'Although there are only three published studies using Calm so far, many other studies have been done on mindfulness meditation.'

Neuroscientists like Dr Judson Brewer, of the School of Medicine at Brown University, have inverted the model of the commercial meditation app – roughly speaking, it's based on tried and tested meditation techniques, so it has to work – by starting with clinical trials and developing apps based on their findings. 'Dr Jud's' three apps, applying mindfulness techniques to binge eating, nicotine addiction and anxiety, are grounded in data gathered during their own development. In the absence of such rigour, the risk with meditation apps is that they deepen the alienation they purport to relieve.

The trade-off is in their accessibility. We know from the studies on mindfulness that even the brief exposure to the techniques offered by the apps may have significant effects on attentional focus. Digital delivery gives millions of people access to a potentially useful methodology they might not otherwise have the time, money, or cultural background to experience at first hand. In some cases, this will lead to the further exploration of the traditions that inform it. Calm can be a gateway practice, a dipped toe in deeper waters. As Steve

McGee told me at the Insight Meditation Society, 'I can't tell you how many times people walk through these doors from the apps or from MBSR.'

It's not only in Buddhist-influenced mindfulness that digital delivery has its uses. On the train back from visiting the monks at Mount Saint Bernard I got talking to Malcolm, a widower in his seventies who had just finished a short retreat at the abbey. A few years back, he told me, as we sipped our acrid coffees from the trolley, his job had become so stressful that he had suffered a nervous breakdown and been unable to leave the house.

'There's no doubt about it,' he said. 'I was saved by a riddle.'

I waited to hear what the riddle was. In the event, it turned out I'd misheard: what Malcolm had been saved by was RIDL, 'Retreat in Daily Life', an acronym he'd assumed I'd understand, given that I'd just spent the night in a Catholic monastery. RIDL is a programme based on the *Spiritual Exercises*, the series of prayers and meditations devised by St Ignatius Loyola in the sixteenth century. 'Ignatius's almost unique contribution was to bring the whole of yourself, including your imagination, to bear on this prayer business,' Sara Maitland had told me. 'The purpose of the *Exercises* is to find out what you're feeling. And the way you do that is by bringing yourself, in your imagination, into a personal relationship, usually with Jesus, although it could be with one of the saints, occasionally with God the Father.'

In practice this involves the kind of interactivity familiar to gamers. A short passage from the Gospels is chosen. The task is then to insert yourself imaginatively into the scene. Visualise Betharaba beyond Jordan. Imagine the palm trees. A heron sipping from the river. The wind in the trees, the Baptist up to his ankles. When Jesus says to his disciples, 'What seek ye?', how do you respond?

The *Exercises* were traditionally undertaken over a thirty-day, silent retreat, led by an experienced spiritual director in a dedicated Ignatian retreat house. As few people, these days, can afford to take an entire month off work or away from the family, RIDL is now the most common way for lay people to perform the *Exercises*, praying at home and consulting regularly with their spiritual director. The online, self-directed version of RIDL is also increasingly popular. It's how Malcolm had done his: living alone, confined to his house and in poor mental health, logging on to the *Exercises* allowed him a solace that would otherwise have been out of reach. 'I spent a very enjoyable day as John the Baptist,' he told me. RIDL online is a sort of spiritual role-playing game in which the boundaries between ordinary life and first-century Galilee, between your kitchen table and the miracle of the loaves, are blurred in the service of devotion.

Digital delivery exposes the structural inequality at the heart of retreat. To meditate or pray in any calming environment, let alone at Esalen or Casa Parvati, is a privilege very few can afford. Even a 'free' retreat at Solesmes, Mount Saint Bernard or Saraniya, which operate on the basis of voluntary donations, assumes either that you are retired, like Malcolm, or have the resources to take time off work or from looking after the kids. The result is that precisely the sector of society that might benefit most from retreat – the overworked, the undervalued, the chronically stressed – are invariably denied it. It was the problem I'd encountered at Esalen. At the Insight Meditation Society, Steve McGee had told me that since the outset the dominant demographic had been older and wealthy. Westernised Buddhism was a perk of prosperity. 'They call it the upper-middle path.'

And an overwhelmingly white one. Krista, the self-confessed workaholic I met at Esalen, was conscious of how anomalous she must seem, as a mixed-race woman taking time out to focus on her mental health. For her white friends, a weekend of holotropic breathwork needed no justification. Her black friends thought she had a screw loose. 'They're like, seriously? You're going to hang out naked with some white hippies? You're going to eat nuts and berries for the weekend?'

All of which, Krista felt, betrayed a deeply ingrained, generational distrust of introspection. 'You go to someplace like this, you've got a parent who maybe remembers the segregated community, and they're like, we worked really hard to get you to college, why do you have to go out and, like, hum at the ocean? We gave you everything, and you're still telling us you're confused? Do you have a right to be confused? You don't. Get it together and help somebody else.'

Self-care is the preserve of those who, consciously or not, have always been able to consider it their right. For Aden Van Noppen, Executive Director of Mobius, an organisation supporting socially responsible tech, based in Berkeley, if people from socially disadvantaged and minority-ethnic backgrounds are to feel welcome in the settings of spiritual and contemplative retreat, then the leaders at those settings need to reflect a comparable diversity. 'There's really interesting work happening around this,' Aden told me. 'For instance, the majority of teachers going through the Spirit Rock and Insight Meditation Society teacher-training programme are people of colour.' The East Bay Meditation Center in Oakland offers courses exclusively for underrepresented communities. But there is clearly a long way to go. In the meantime, meditation apps offer an alternative path to retreat. Perhaps the greatest contribution they make to the accessibility of retreat, apart from their relative affordability, is in the privacy they offer. Not from the businesses harvesting our data, of course, but from each other, from the cultural expectations of retreat – the kind held by Krista's friends, for example – that might otherwise have obstructed our access to it. What's open to question is whether the benefits of that privacy defray its drawbacks, the pull of the digital away from human contact, its siren song of isolation.

If the downside of regular meditation apps is the isolation they encourage, the risk with virtual-reality meditation must surely be greater. An app like 'Guided Meditation' for the Gear

VR, Samsung's virtual-reality headset, would seem to court a contradiction. How can you open your eyes to the world with a plastic lunchbox strapped to your face? In the case of VR, immersive surely equates to escapist. 'Guided Meditation' offers a choice of more than a hundred calming, 360-degree environments, from a Nordic spa lodge to a deserted beach with a spectacular Kao-Phing-Kan-style rock tower. Meanwhile a guided meditation chosen from the menu – Zen, Loving Compassion, Maternity, Depression or Sleep – is piped soothingly over your headphones. Many of the environments have motes of dust, dandelion clocks or magic sparkles floating around in them, the main effect of which is to have you swatting at the air as you try to return your attention to your breath. Again, the plus is in making a calming environment available to the stay-at-home retreatant. The minus is in separating that retreatant from reality when the purpose of meditation is precisely the opposite.

Or *is* the user separated from reality? A VR social platform like VRChat, where players in headsets roam around virtual environments, interacting with each other via motion-mapped avatars of their choosing, certainly suggests as much: this is weaponised escapism, the wholesale abandonment of the real in favour of a potentially inexhaustible fantasy. As the writer and VR pioneer Jaron Lanier argues, however, the eventual effect of immersion in a VR environment is to make the user more, not less, alive to physical reality. 'From the brain's point of view,' he writes in *Dawn of the New Everything*, 'reality is the expectation of what the next moment will be like, but that expectation must constantly be adjusted.' Our internal models, perpetually refined by the accommodation of error. By immersing us so completely, the best-designed VR tricks the brain into treating the virtual simulation as a discrepancy between our internal models and a new reality that must be assimilated. Our expectation that we won't open our eyes and find ourselves between the shimmering blue walls of a crystal ravine has been duly adjusted. So far, so escapist. Where VR departs from other, less immersive digital experiences is in what the totality of that immersion does to our brains once the headset is removed. Our internal models, newly accommodated to the iridescent surface of Planet X, are forced to readjust again, this time to a physical reality experienced by our perceptual apparatus as if for the first time.

VR, as Lanier puts it, is a 'palate cleanser'. It refreshes us, lets us see physical reality anew. This obtains whether the substance of the VR experience is purportedly meditative, as in the Guided Meditation app, or concerns an asteroid-mining mission quintillions of light years away. The effect depends not on any explicit meditative element but on the disparity between the virtual environment and the real one. Further, by stripping away real-world phenomena and replacing them with virtual alternatives, VR helps us understand our perceptual apparatus as separate from the phenomena it perceives. Our 'centre of experience persists' even as the world around us changes. 'Virtual reality', writes Lanier, 'is the technology that exposes you to yourself.' In this sense, far from representing a further step away from the real world, VR is much closer to traditional contemplative retreat, a stepping-away to return in better shape, more awake, less wedded to your preconceptions.

'Please find a comfortable position and take a few moments to become still.' I was doing okay on the stillness, but as to the comfortable position, my relief at finding a seat, right at the back on the upper level, was rapidly being dismantled by my neighbours, a man in chunky noise-cancelling headphones with his legs open at roughly 120 degrees, and a smartly dressed young woman, sitting opposite with a roller suitcase that kept escaping from her, like a poorly trained dog, and nuzzling my knees. I turned up the volume on my phone. The screen showed a slow-moving montage of sequoias in evening sunlight.

'Bring your attention to your eyes,' said the voice. 'Imagine and sense a smile spreading through them.' Outside the Bay had

disappeared and we were passing through low-rise nowheres-
ville, storage depots, scrubby backlots. After my visit to Calm,
I'd taken the Caltrain south from the city, to see how (and
if) the purveyors of digital hyper-stimulation – the kind that,
somewhat paradoxically, Calm claimed to relieve – accommodated retreat. How and if, that is, Silicon Valley ever paused
to catch its breath. The suitcase bumped into my knees again,
and as the young woman retrieved it, I tried my smiling eyes
on her. She looked at me blankly for a moment, then returned
her attention to her phone.

Cisco Systems' global HQ is in San Jose, forty miles from
San Francisco at the southern tip of the Valley. At Cisco's
LifeConnections Health Center, I was greeted by Katelyn
Johnson, Senior Integrated Health Manager for Global Benefits.
After the cardio floor and the spa area we arrived in an underlit
room, furnished with a pile of zafu meditation cushions and
some sort of non-denominational altar-piece, a small black slab
like a domesticated version of the monolith in *2001: A Space
Odyssey*. 'I think those are battery-operated,' said Katelyn, of
the semi-circle of faux plastic candles arranged around the
shrine.

It was Katelyn's job to cultivate the Cisco ideal of the 'corporate athlete': ripped in body and mind, driven but not at
the expense of their wellness. At LifeConnections, employees
are invited to focus on the 'four pillars' of well-being – body,
mind, spirit and heart. Upstairs, Katelyn and I stood in a pool
of polychromatic light.

'We have rainbow prisms in each of the skylights,' she explained, with some pride. 'The rainbows move with the earth
so it changes every minute. When you think of rainbows, you
think of healing.' Katelyn radiated the sort of zeal for well-
being you might more readily associate with a holistic retreat
centre than a leading manufacturer of networking hardware.
'While you're at work we want to make sure you're at your
best,' said Katelyn. 'But to do that you have to have full-
person health.'

Cisco is by no means the exception. Similar programmes are in place across Silicon Valley, each taking the principles of wellness and meditation out of their customary retreat settings and recontextualising them in the workplace. At Cisco, employees are offered a five-week mindfulness and resilience training programme, teaching 'cognitive strategies to help them approach their workday with more intent and purpose'. The aim is a kind of secularised *sati*, a business-oriented version of the clear-sighted awareness I had been taught at the vipassana centre in Salford – as core a competency for the tech executive as it is for the seeker on the Noble Eightfold Path.

'Silicon Valley is a rich but intense environment,' said Katelyn. 'It's extremely fast-paced. So we need this mindfulness meditation to help us survive, frankly, because if you don't bring your full self to work, it's pretty tough to innovate and create and keep moving at the expected pace.'

The big challenge was 'to be present'. Such were the distractions, the updates and emails and iMessages – the instruments of attentional overload for which Silicon Valley, of course, could only blame itself – that 'it was pretty hard in this day and age to be fully engaged'. For Katelyn, and the countless other health managers and HR professionals overseeing wellness in the corporate workplace, mindfulness cleared the clutter and forced an engagement with the here and now, the task in hand, the press of unpostponable reality.

It's only ironic that a practice designed to demonstrate the transience of all material things should be put so squarely at the service of the profit motive – of making employees more effective at precisely the sort of material gain Buddhism holds to be futile. Psychologists use the term 'spiritual bypassing' to describe the use of diluted or decontextualised spiritual practices to sidestep the harder, deeper questions the practice is actually designed to address. We've seen how commercial wellness centres have co-opted a tradition grounded in *anatta*, the non-existence of self, in the name of self-improvement. By assimilating the principles of retreat into its working practices, wellness in Silicon Valley, and the corporate culture in its thrall, have taken the co-option – or rather distortion – a step further. I had to keep an ear out for my own pridefulness – satirising New-Agey corporatese was surely to fall foul of the *kilesas*, especially as I'd been treated with such courtesy – but in the idea of the 'corporate athlete' I could only see selflessness put at the service of selfishness, ego-death at the service of ego, mindfulness as a means to its opposite: the ultimate prideful-ness, the Tenth Army triumphant.

'I suppose if you were a cynic,' said Alan Eagle, Director of Communications at Google, 'you'd say that the utopianism of the sixties has been commandeered by the profit motive, and Google's just a giant profit machine.' Alan and I were sitting by the volleyball court in the central courtyard of the Googleplex, ten miles west of Cisco in Mountain View. Employees ticked by on grab-and-go GBikes, painted in Google blue, red, yellow and green. Over the way, a display of outsize concrete statues commemorated successive versions of Android: a donut, an éclair, a dish of froyo, an ice-cream sandwich. Kindergarten Oldenburg. Much the same faux-naïveté informs the Search Inside Yourself Leadership Institute, Chade-Meng Tan's mind-fulness programme spun off from Google in 2012. SIYLI's website features primary-coloured cartoon characters conjoined at the arm to form a Siamese triplet of sunny connectedness. The acronym is no accident: SIYLI-ness goes to the heart of the brand, as if mindfulness were too dry a proposition, or too close to an admission of weakness, to swallow without a dose of the tech industry's signature beer-pong sense of humour.

Still, SIYLI is a hit, both inside Google and with its thousands of external clients in the tech, financial and non-profit sectors. The appeal is clear. Mindfulness training is a relatively inexpen-sive means of reducing workplace stress and anxiety, thereby improving staff retention and productivity. Apart from Google, Cisco, Apple and Facebook, non-tech multinationals like Nike, Procter & Gamble and General Motors all have wellness and meditation programmes in place. In 2015, a reported 5,500

Goldman Sachs employees underwent a mindfulness-based 're-siliency training' programme similar to Cisco's. A 2017 study by the National Business Group on Health found that 35 per cent of all US companies offered mindfulness classes or training, and that a further 26 per cent were considering introducing them. That's more than 60 per cent of all US employers, either offering mindfulness training or open to doing so.

A significant benefit of mindfulness, of course, is in the inter-iority it encourages. One reason that hesychasm – the mystical tradition of prayer I'd encountered on Hydra – became such a dominant practice in the Eastern Orthodox church was that it kept its adherents quiet. As the Byzantine Empire gradually fell to the Ottomans, between the mid-thirteenth century and the conquest of Constantinople in 1453, it was to the Sultanate's advantage that so much of the Christian population under its command should have been committed to a tradition of prayer centred on silence. Hesychasts made poor insurgents. If, to this day, Mount Athos seems suspended in pre-Ottoman splendour, that is in part a function of its long-held status as the centre of the hesychast movement. The fundamental inwardness of Athonite observance meant that its new Muslim overlords were content to leave it in peace.

Similarly, as the management professor Ronald E. Purser has argued, mindfulness as co-opted by corporations leaves their power structures intact by instilling a level of passivity in the workforce. 'Instead of encouraging radical action,' he writes, mindfulness 'says the causes of suffering are disproportionately inside us, not in the political and economic frameworks that shape how we live.' It's not your employer's fault if you're stressed, anxious or lonely. You just need to sit in a quiet room and focus on your breath. What is a 'resilience training programme' but a means of persuading your staff to accept unreasonable demands on their time and energy? It is retreat in its most toxic sense: a workforce coerced into backing down.

There's little doubt that periods of genuine retreat, of un-illusioned reflection, can help to ease the psychological and physical pressures exerted by contemporary technocapitalism. The problem is in what contemporary technocapitalism deems genuine. Like the famous free meals at the Googleplex, the games rooms and volleyball courts and beanbagged breakout spaces, wellness in the workplace is only another land-grab on our private lives, by a work culture abolishing downtime by aping it.

It was still California, though, still the edge of the world, the last stop before the unanswerable vastness of the ocean. What if you just kept on retreating, I wondered, further and further from reach? One of the last conversations I had in California was with Chip Conley, founder of the Modern Elder Academy, a retreat centre down the coast in Baja California, Mexico, specifically for older employees cut adrift by industries that demanded high 'DQ' – digital intelligence. At fifty-nine, Chip was trim and shaven-headed, with a taste for waistcoats on bare flesh and nu-metalish beard tufts minus the moustache. He was, in other words, well preserved in the manner of the Californian high-net-worth individual offended to the point of non-compliance by his own mortality.

'We're all going to live ten, fifteen years longer than our parents' generation,' he said. 'And yet power in the digital society is moving ten or fifteen years *younger*.'

The Academy was founded to plug the gap. Midlife used to mean forty-five to sixty-five. Now people in the digital industries felt over the hill in their mid-thirties, while the older generation, banking on greater life expectancy, felt obliged to work long past a retirement age that bore little relation to trends in longevity. 'If people are going to work till ninety-five,' said Chip, 'I would say that midlife probably *does* go to seventy-five.'

Chip still had a good fifteen years to go – and thirty-five till retirement. At the Academy's beachfront campus, guests, or 'compadres', as they're called, attend all-inclusive, five- or seven-day retreats, meditating, baking bread, intergenerationally sharing, and, most importantly, navigating Chip's proprietary four-step learning arc – EVOLVE, LEARN, COLLABORATE, COUNSEL – with the aim of 'rewiring, not retiring'.

Chip saw retreat as an opportunity for his compadres to prepare for an unpredictable – and potentially very long – future. Later, sitting on the rocks of Baker Beach, a mile from the Golden Gate Bridge but seeming much further, a wilderness, I watched the fog roll in from the ocean and thought of my father, at eighty, in Chip's terms only five years past his midlife transition. Soon the entire view was fogged in, the city overwhelmed, the horizon gone, the sun a weak orange bruise. If the world was to be run by a technocracy of high-DQ twentysomethings, then the rest of us – my dad, Antonia's, Phil, Greg the meditative mutineer – would have to figure out what to do with ourselves, how to answer the vastness, for a period of post-utility Chip expected to last sixty years, with intermittent fasting and a good cardiologist: half of humanity on permanent (or terminal) retreat.

9.

Unwanted Egocentrism

My mother once wrote to R.D. Laing asking if he'd take her on as a patient. As I understood it, the problem she wanted to address was *her* mother, the kindly old lady I knew from the letters she wrote me on that crackly blue airmail paper that folded up to become its own envelope, and who, before her emigration to Australia, had subjected my mother to decades of narcissistic emotional control. As it turned out, Laing was too busy to take my mother on – this was the mid-sixties, by which time Laing was a countercultural superstar, the most celebrated and controversial shrink on the planet – but for the rest of her life she remained sympathetic to, and comforted by, the Laingian idea that mental illness was not biologically determined but a consequence of family dysfunction.

In 1965, Laing co-founded the Philadelphia Association as a radical riposte to the norms of psychiatric treatment. Part of Laing's insight was to apply to mental health a principle that had long obtained in the treatment of physical disorders: that there were types of pain and disease that responded well to retreat, to stepping back from the social and environmental conditions that either caused or aggravated them.

At the PA's first house, Kingsley Hall, on Powis Road in east London, residents suffering from schizophrenia lived communally, as if in an ordinary house-share, unmedicated, free to come and go as they pleased, on the assumption that psychosis was not so much an illness requiring treatment as a potentially valuable experience to be confronted and worked through in a safe and supportive environment. Instead of being consigned to a psychiatric ward, residents had some agency restored to them, choosing to step back from the world and spend time in a therapeutic setting. The distinctions between 'psychiatrist' and 'patient', well and unwell, were abolished. Everyone was in it together.

Mainstream psychiatric treatment rendered the patient other, extraordinary. At Kingsley Hall, ordinariness was the guiding principle, humdrum, domesticated normality for those who might never have experienced it. Laing's notion of the schizophrenic was of someone 'not at home' in the world, homeless not in a literal way but disarticulated from the sense of human belonging that came of healthy interpersonal relations. The schizophrenic's sense of self was split into a 'false self' (or system of false selves) presented as a front to the world, and a 'true self' contemptuous of the fake persona it used to screen itself from view. Thus the true self was shut in by a wall of its own making, deprived of the interactions with the external world it fell to the false self to undertake. 'For the schizoid individual,' writes Laing in *The Divided Self*, his 1960 study of psychosis, 'direct participation "in" life is felt as being at the constant risk of being destroyed by life, for the self's isolation is ... its effort to preserve itself in the absence of an assured sense of autonomy and integrity.'

The aim of the Philadelphia Association was to restore that sense of belonging, of togetherness, of home, to those denied it by their dysfunctional backgrounds. The idea of asylum was thus detached from its institutional connotations in favour of its original Greek sense of refuge, a place for the persecuted or displaced to retreat into safety. After the lease at Kingsley Hall expired the PA bought two houses in North London. Life at the houses continued even as Laing's reputation plummeted, his theories on the social causes of schizophrenia dismissed as so much fashionable guesswork, deaf to the emerging biomedical and genetic accounts of the condition. He died in 1989, discredited where he hadn't been forgotten.

'For a long time there was no Laing taught on the PA training,' said Jake Osborne, until recently a house therapist at The Grove, a PA house in Finsbury Park. The organisation did what it could to find an identity distinct from its founder. The ban on roles was overturned. House therapists were now called house therapists. It had been an irony of the regime at Kingsley Hall that the emphasis on ordinariness largely had the opposite effect. As with the hippie communes cited by Victor Turner, the lack of hierarchy at Kingsley Hall tended to disempower everyone but the figure at the top.

'Nobody thought Laing was just like one of the others. He was a guru,' Jake told me. 'People would sit at his feet, wait for him to dispense his wisdom.' Laing's fame didn't help, any more than the novelty and uniqueness of Kingsley Hall as a countercultural experiment. Laing's friend Sean Connery had been known to drop round. Everyday normality was in short supply.

'The houses are much more ordinary now,' said Jake. If calm, considered normality was the objective, it was easy to imagine Jake restoring it. He had a monkish quality about him, with his shaved head, wire-rim glasses and air of quiet reflection. The Grove is a Victorian terraced house on a cul-de-sac of the same name. Like the other house in Holloway, it can accommodate seven. Prospective residents come to one house meeting a week for four weeks, after which the existing residents decide whether or not to admit them: a kind of fast-forwarded postulancy. 'So it's kind of democratic,' said Jake.

Residents were encouraged to give their potential housemates the benefit of the doubt. 'People have taken a risk with them, so hopefully they're open to doing that with other people.' In the past, residents could be referred by their GPs or social workers, but these days retreats at either of the community houses were almost exclusively elective. 'Now it's more people that have found us, on the internet or wherever.'

House meetings, held three times a week, gave residents the chance to iron out their differences in a controlled setting. Otherwise they were left pretty much to their own devices. Meals were taken together or in the privacy of the residents' rooms. A lot of energy was expended discussing (and enforcing) the cleaning rota. Again – and in this respect the fundamental principle of the houses remained exactly as it was under Laing – the emphasis was on cultivating common ground.

'It's about living together, working things through, finding ways of dealing with other people and with your own difficulties,' said Jake. The communal was inseparable from the personal. 'Trying to treat somebody in isolation doesn't really make sense. People can't be extracted from their context in that way.'

In the majority of cases, serious mental-health breakdowns were treated as experiences to be confronted, and weathered communally. 'If a resident is really floridly psychotic and can't look after themselves, then we might have to say, actually we can't do this any more, you might have to go into hospital for a bit.' For the most part, however, this sort of crisis was where the community-house dynamic came into its own. 'That's one of the main things that the house therapists hold,' said Jake. 'Managing that belief that you're going to get through it. It can feel hopeless, but people do work through it.'

Laing only ever saw the Kingsley Hall experiment as 'a small-scale strategy', an option amongst many, not 'an alternative way of addressing the whole domain of psychiatry'. It suits some people more than others. 'A lot of people want to have a diagnosis,' said Jake, 'and be given some medication because they know what the problem is, and that it's not their fault, and that this will fix it.' Other residents responded well to the process but found it exceptionally hard to re-enter society, a problem that the increasing unaffordability of accommodation in London had only made worse. Meanwhile, technology was undermining the PA's founding principle. 'The houses have become less communal over time,' Jake said. 'When I started there was a TV in the main room. Now, obviously, everyone has computers and phones in their room. So there's a retreat within the retreat. It means people can avoid people much more.'

Nonetheless, from its position on the margins of psychotherapeutic practice, there was a new sense of the PA's influence, of the mainstream adjusting leftward to accommodate it. 'There's been a big shift in the way that people think about people in mental distress,' explained Jake. 'From the idea of asking what's wrong with you to asking what's *happened* to you. That is basically what Laing was talking about. That these things that seem mad make sense in the context of what's happened to somebody. And I think that idea is having a bit of a resurgence.'

As with the Gestalt taught at Esalen, or vipassana meditation, or the silence that prepares the Christian for divine encounter, the goal was confrontation, the clearing-away of impediments to a clear and unillusioned view. 'From the outside,' said Jake, 'a lot of people might think residents are trying to avoid or go under things. Most people on retreat think, I'm here to go *through* it.' Life in the houses narrowed the opportunities for self-deception. 'By putting yourself in a house with some other people, what it is that you do, and how you perpetuate your own difficulties, stares you in the face. It's not a retreat from real life. It's a retreat *to* real life.'

'Switzerland', wrote Scott Fitzgerald in his short story 'One Trip Abroad', 'is a country where very few things begin, but many things end.'

In June, 1930, two months before the story was written, Fitzgerald's wife Zelda had been admitted to Les Rives de Prangins, a sanatorium on Lake Geneva. Ten years earlier she and Scott had been the toast of New York, gold-hatted, high-bouncing lovers of the Jazz Age. Now Zelda had been diagnosed with 'dementia praecox', an obsolete term used for patients that would now be considered schizophrenic. She was to remain at Prangins, alone, disallowed any visits until her condition had stabilised. The situation was desperate.

'If she were an anti-social person who did not want to face life and pull her own weight that would be one story,' wrote Scott. 'But her passionate love of life and her absolute inability to meet it, seems so tragic that sometimes it is scarcely to be endured.' Zelda's letters from Prangins are vivid records of her isolation, painfully lively accounts of life's absence.

'Dearest, my Darling–' she wrote to Scott in the autumn of 1930. 'Living is cold and technical without you, a death mask of itself. At seven o:clock I had a bath but you were not in the next room to make it a baptisme of all I was thinking...'

The European sanatorium had emerged, in part, from a thermal-spa culture dating back to classical antiquity. Hippocrates thought that all diseases were caused by a disharmony of the humours. The cure was a change of environment, especially if it involved a dip in hot and cold water. The Romans built spas close to their garrisons, both as relaxation retreats for healthy soldiers and as hydrotherapeutic treatment centres for the wounded.

In later antiquity, however, public baths developed the reputation for sexual licentiousness that still applied in 1962, when Michael Murphy evicted the regulars from Slate's Hot Springs. In the Dark and Middle Ages, the association of bathing and low morals led to its suppression across the Christian West. In 1538, Francis I of France ordered all 'stew houses' destroyed; similar steps were taken by Henry VIII in England. Some spas were converted into churches.

In Renaissance Italy, meanwhile, the rediscovery of classical texts on the medical properties of thermal waters led to a revival of bathing culture, if only for certain sectors of society. Just as so much of the modern wellness industry caters exclusively to the better off, so public bathing in sixteenth-century Italy was reserved for the upper classes. In De thermis, a study published in 1571, the physician Andrea Bacci stressed that the curative properties of the waters applied only in quiet, pleasant surroundings, with good food and wine to hand. '*Qui dicit balneum dicit comodum*.' Bathing meant comfort, and was therefore of no concern to the poor.

The spa as a locus of privilege, a place of retreat from the unwashed, spread into northern Europe, slowly at first, then rapidly as the industrialisation of the nineteenth century made urban population centres ever more uncomfortable – and unhealthy – places to live. 'Taking the waters' became a fashionable activity for the robust and gout-ridden alike. In spa towns like Bath, Aix-les-Bains, Vichy and Aachen a tourist infrastructure of grand hotels, casinos and ballrooms was built to service an international *beau monde* newly able to socialise, gamble, commit adultery, forge diplomatic alliances and (most importantly) be seen at a remove from the social and political tumult of real life.

This culture reached its apogee in the Black Forest resort of Baden-Baden, known as 'the summer capital of Europe' by the middle of the nineteenth century. At around the same time, sanatoriums for tuberculosis patients began to appear in the US and Germany, operating on the long-held assumption that rest and fresh air were the most effective treatments. In Switzerland, sanatoriums tended to be marginally more medically inflected versions of the central-European spa, offering fine dining and leisure activities to a moneyed clientele. TB by Champneys: they were fashionable places for the unwell to retreat, their glamour heightened by the peculiar cachet lent by this debilitating and usually fatal condition. TB was the 'romantic disease', the agent of the 'beautiful death'. As Susan Sontag points out in *Illness as Metaphor*, good health was banal. The red lips, the pale skin, the emaciation: the visible symptoms of the 'white plague' were the nineteenth-century equivalent of heroin chic. People *wanted* to die of it.

Like the white martyrdom of the Desert Fathers, the white plague elevated the sufferer: by diminishing the body, it liberated the spirit, a belief lent force by popular accounts of consumptives dying not in agony or distress but in a preternaturally becalmed state of grace. As he lay dying, Henry David Thoreau, who had suffered from TB all his adult life, was asked by his stern Calvinist aunt if he had made his peace with God. 'I did not know we had ever quarrelled,' he replied.

Among the swankier air-cure resorts, Davos – now famous, of course, as a retreat for the global political and business elite, just as Baden-Baden became a major diplomatic centre in the post-Napoleonic era – was known for the suitability of its microclimate for respiratory patients. The discovery, in 1882, by the German physician Robert Koch, that tuberculosis was not hereditary but bacterial, both undermined the credibility of spas and sanatoriums as treatment centres for serious disease, and gave them a late lease of life. Advances in bacteriology by Koch and Louis Pasteur in France were consigning ancient Galenic dogma to the museums of medical history. Spa treatments and mountain air cures began to look like the prescientific quackery they often were. As the historian David Clay Large has shown, a radical shift was taking place from retreat under often questionable clinical oversight to full-scale submission to qualified medical expertise.

The response of the larger spas and sanatoriums was twofold: to medicalise themselves, offering conventional diagnosis and treatment before referring more serious cases on for hospitalisation and, second, to switch emphasis to the more diagnostically fudgeable area of nervous disease or 'neurasthenia'. Wiesbaden, as Large notes, emerged in the early twentieth century as 'crack-up central'. Zelda Fitzgerald's sanatorium at Prangins was founded shortly before she arrived in 1930. With the development of the antibiotic streptomycin in 1946, many of the TB-oriented spas and sanatoriums closed for good, or, as with their mental-health counterparts, completed their medicalisation by becoming mainstream hospitals or clinics. ('Les Rives de Prangins' is now known as 'L'Hôpital de Prangins'.) It's only in recent years, with the exponential growth of the wellness industry – and the corresponding distrust for medicalised models of care – that the idea of stepping back to let yourself heal, to resist Westernised, allopathic, evidence-based intervention in favour of taking your health into your own hands, under minimal (or spurious) supervision, in a tranquil and/or naturally beautiful setting removed from a modernity construed as pathogenic, has staged such an unexpected comeback.

You could retreat to make yourself better. Or retreat could make you unwell, set off a cycle of isolation and illness. In my mid-teens my parents had relocated from Wales to East Anglia, partly to be near some old London friends who had moved there a few years before. If anything, this gesture at sociability had the opposite to intended effect. One of the qualities I most love in my father is his candour. He has weak internal models: he sees things as they are. It's what makes him such a good painter. It also makes him a natural solitary. Artists need retreat like the rest of us need company. When their admittedly rather overbearing neighbour Frieda came round for tea and made the mistake of talking over him, my father lifted up his chair – a hefty wing-back recliner, with folding footrest – turned it around, and began a conversation with the wall. It seemed, much as life in our little family unit remained loving and harmonious, like Dad was compelled to dismantle any relationships outside it, withdraw from the world before it withdrew from him, something his increasing complaints of ill health helped simultaneously to rationalise and perpetuate.

My abiding memory from that time is of sitting in the living room, back home for a few days, listening to the collared doves nesting in the chimney pots, their repeated call, coo-*cooo*-coo, echoing down the chimney, and resounding, a little muffled, behind the plywood square my father had painted with a trompe-l'oeil stack of logs and fitted over the fireplace as a draught excluder. I can't hear that call without thinking of my parents and the quiet of those late afternoons. There's a nest somewhere outside my window in London. I can hear it right now, as I write. Coo-*cooo*-coo. For Dad, what had begun as occasional and unspecified unwellness had evolved into constant but no less undiagnosable pain, concentrated in his lower back. It's worth recalling Chris Eccleston's notion of chronic pain as an alarm that can't be shut off. The effects go beyond the individual to the people around them. 'If you get an alarm,' said Chris, 'then you alarm other conspecifics in your environment that there's potential harm.' Over time the consequence of this is isolation. 'They're chronically telling other people that there's danger in their environments. They're talking about their pain.' At the animal level, the message is unambiguous. Leave. Within a few years, my father's back pain would consign him pretty much round the clock to the recliner he'd once had the strength to turn to the wall.

The idea that retreat, far from being beneficial, might be unsuitable or even harmful to certain individuals has an intriguing precursor in early Christian monasticism. *Acedia*, or sloth, was the eighth of the deadly sins before Pope Gregory I collapsed it into *tristitia*, melancholy, to make seven. The Desert Fathers called it the *daemon meridianus*, the noonday demon, in reference to Psalm 91: 'Thou shalt not be afraid ... for the pestilence that walketh in darkness; nor for the destruction that wasteth at noonday.'

For Scott Fitzgerald, 3 a.m. was the dark hour of the soul. I'm with the Desert Fathers: the bleakness that sets in around lunchtime. In early monasticism, *acedia* was considered the fiercest of all the threats to piety, in particular for the hermit. 'Sloth' is a mistranslation, really. *Acedia* is more accurately rendered as 'lack of care', spiritual apathy, an inner emptiness it's tempting if anachronistic to diagnose as depression. Sloth was more of a symptom than the condition itself. In Gregory's view, the sin gave rise to 'slothfulness in fulfilling the commands, and a wandering of the mind on unlawful objects', an admonition the Buddhist masters might have recognised.

Acedia might be understood as a logical if impermissible response to the monastic austerities, to the lack of comfort and companionship, the months and years that might pass with no sense of spiritual progress. Once it had taken hold, the monk was vulnerable to all the other temptations, the gluttony and avarice that blighted late-medieval monasticism and gave rise to reforming orders like the Cistercians. It was the gateway sin to the abandonment of the religious life altogether.

It was the notion that *acedia* or sloth was constitutional, an innate characteristic in certain individuals, that suggested, in turn, that those individuals might be inherently ill-suited to contemplative retreat. In pre-Christian antiquity, the sort of melancholic disposition associated (and later conflated) with *acedia* was ascribed to humoral imbalance, specifically an excess of the black bile secreted by the spleen. The American sociologist Stanford Lyman writes that humoral accounts of sloth have alternated, over the centuries, with its representation as a sin, the implication of the former being that the slothful person was relieved of some or all responsibility for his conduct. 'I can't help it. I was born lazy.' Susan Sontag notes some early-modern instances of idleness or sloth being metaphorically equated with disease. In 1564, the English author Thomas Palfreyman wrote of 'that pestilent and most infectious canker, idlenesse'. (Until around 1700, 'canker' and 'cancer' were used interchangeably.) Literally and figuratively, sloth has long been presented as an affliction rather than a moral failing.

The idea that a disinclination to engage in the rigours of contemplative withdrawal might be constitutional – that, again, retreat might simply be a bad idea for some people – has its counterpart in modern neuropsychiatry. Studies by Dr Willoughby Britton at Brown University have shown that in some individuals with pre-existing mental-health conditions, meditation can cause psychosis, seizures, depersonalisation, suicidal ideation and mania requiring hospitalisation. But the risk of adverse effects is not limited to those with clear-cut disorders. Mark Edwards is a professor of neurology at

St George's, University College London, whose special area of interest is the diagnosis and treatment of functional neurological disorders – symptoms like chronic pain or weakness that appear to be neurological in origin but have no demonstrable basis in disease. Functional disorders are distinct from 'factitious' disorders like Munchausen Syndrome – where people feign illnesses they don't really have – in that to the best of clinical understanding the patient has no conscious control over their symptoms. Essentially, the problem lies not so much in the messages the patients' bodies are sending them, as in their brains' ability to interpret them accurately – to introspect.

'The human capacity for introspection is a massive evolutionary advantage,' said Mark when I met him for coffee near his home in north London. Mark has a round face fringed with a halo of soft, close-cropped blond hair, like a less comical Cheshire Cat: were he to disappear, bit by bit, we'd be left not with a grin but a frown of intense contemplation. 'Instead of having to learn just by raw experience – let's see if the food is good over there – you can play out the scenario in your head. You can model it, basically.' But these meta-cognitive abilities come at a cost. Humans are notoriously bad at assessing the significance of their own internal states – 'interoceptive' stimuli like pain and fatigue.

'You have to remember that all symptoms are filtered through the brain,' Mark told me. 'Lots of studies have been done on people with common illnesses like heart disease and respiratory problems, trying to correlate symptom reports with disease measures like lung-function tests. And the correlation is universally rubbish.' We are not very good at knowing how ill – or well – we are. In people with functional neurological disorder, the discrepancy between the objective reality of their disease state – that none exists, at least to any serious extent – and their subjective perception that something has gone seriously wrong *is itself* enough to produce significant physical symptoms. It's a self-fulfilling prophecy, that is, a means of becoming genuinely ill via the brain's subconscious insistence, against all empirical evidence, that you are. And just as the misinterpretation of internal stimuli is essentially introspective – is an error of introspection – so introspection makes it worse. As Mark said, 'I have seen several patients whose symptoms have deteriorated or indeed been triggered in the setting of introspectional retreat.'

Pain is intrinsically egocentric, Chris Eccleston had reminded me. 'The unwanted egocentrism that fundamentally drags you back in onto yourself.' The problem, as for Mark Edwards's patients, as for my father, came in chronic pain where the link between pain and harm had been broken. The alarm went off and couldn't be stopped. Conscious as you might be that the pain was not indicative of damage, was a false alarm, the brain's pain centres continued to respond as if the danger were real.

'If you are chronically being alarmed,' Chris told me, 'you are chronically interrupted by the painful threat of harm, you are chronically prompted to take action, and you are chronically vigilant for further signals of danger.'

The benefit of meditation in addressing chronic pain is in demonstrating the illusoriness of its source, the ego. U Pandita: 'If pain arises during meditation, simply look it in the face.' If it has arisen, so it must pass away. What Willoughby Britton and Mark Edwards's work demonstrates is the danger of assuming the universality of this benefit, when the introspection inherent in meditation can, in some people, exacerbate or even cause the symptoms it is intended to relieve. For people with functional neurological disorder, rehabilitation often involves tricking the brain into favouring external stimuli over the erroneous internal model. In the case of physical symptoms like weakness, for example, patients might be asked to exercise in front of a full-length mirror. 'That way you're controlling the body in the mirror, not the internal model of your body,' said Mark. 'So you begin to understand that the leg that couldn't move actually *can* move.' Again, where the risk is in excessive attentional focus on the self, the potential treatment is in redirecting that focus outward.

Crucially, Mark suspects that the risks of introspection may extend beyond his functional-disorder patients to the broader population. Recall the notion of the human brain as a prediction machine. The reflective, introspective parts of it build predictive models of the environment, so that when we encounter a new stimulus, a tasty-looking mushroom, for example, we are able to infer its qualities from the model we have built based on previous experience, and minimise the odds of expiring in frothy convulsions on the forest floor. Prediction errors, that is, discrepancies between the internal model and reality – assuming they haven't killed us – are labelled by the brain as important pieces of information, worthy of assimilation into the internal model. Thus the model is continually refined, and the chances of surprise minimised.

It's significant that in people with schizophrenia, these predictive models are weak or absent, so that the stream of sensory input is received without any contextualising expectation. For Pete Gilchrist during his peak-experience, Grace of God episode, everything was a surprise. R.D. Laing reports the case of a schizophrenic patient who, out walking in the park one evening, felt a 'tremendous oneness' with the world, and found it not transcendent but terrifying: the unitive state as a threat to a sense of self whose loss the schizophrenic dreads. It's what lay behind the emphasis on ordinariness at the Philadelphia Association houses: the acknowledgement that, for the sufferer, life on the outside is not ordinary but constantly, terrifyingly surprising.

Psychedelic drugs work in the same way. They switch off our top-down, predictive ability, which is why we can stare at a patch of chewing gum on the pavement and find it revelatory. Given that predictive ability – our faculty for building and refining accurate models of the environment – must have normal distribution in the population, it follows that some of us, without suffering from schizophrenia or being off our heads on ayahuasca, will be less effective at minimising surprise, with all the wonderment and potential for mental distress that entails. For these individuals, removing the props of everyday life, the reassuring context of family and friends and ordinary environment – i.e. precisely what happens on many retreats – runs the risk of both exposing them to excessive surprise and forcing them back on a set of weak internal models that will only get weaker the longer they ruminate on them. The results can be seriously destabilising, and even, as Mark explained, productive of physical symptoms like pain, weakness or seizures. 'It's no exaggeration to say that for certain people, who in the general scheme of things appear to be functioning well, introspective retreat can be dangerous.'

A couple of years before her formal diagnosis my mother began a series of pencil studies of dappled shade. Sometimes she'd work off photos she'd taken in Tunstall Forest or the mixed-growth woods that border the salt marsh between Dunwich and Walberswick. At other times she'd set up her box easel in the garden and draw the soft silhouettes cast by the plum tree. It was a challenge she both thrived on and found frustrating – in particular the technical difficulty of rendering or indeed seeing the feathered edges where light gave way to shadow, of perceiving the point where perception begins to dim.

When, after eighteen months of hesitant all-clears and falsely reassuring cognitive assessment tests, her gerontologist made up his mind – Parkinsonism with Lewy Body dementia – the temptation was to view her forest-floor drawings as an instinctual apprehension of the shadows dappling her consciousness, the dark spots on the brain scan she would never have. Or maybe it was just a good subject to draw. It was only a little suspicious that as the condition progressed – imperceptibly, at first – she turned her attention from dappled to near-total shadow, painting, in delicately controlled watercolour, still life after still life of the black pansies she would snip from the garden and arrange in a tiny, hexagonal, green-glass ink bottle that lived on the mantelpiece above the trompe-l'oeil firewood, where the collared doves cooed. In each case the ground was painted in such a dark shade of green that it was only in certain lights that you could make out the flower. I have one framed in my living room, and at a distance it looks like a hole in the wall. Only when your breath is blooming on the glass can you see how beautiful it is.

When it came the decline was abrupt. If I'd heard someone else comparing dementia to demonic possession, I'd have dismissed it as melodramatic, a cliché – but it *was* as if she were being controlled by a consciousness other than her own, as if the proteins clogging her cortex were not shadows but conscious entities themselves. At one point she brandished her walking stick at me – my gentle, loving mother, who I couldn't until that point recall so much as raising her voice in anger. If only she had meditated, I found myself thinking. Would that have worked? Slowed the ageing of her brain, built up her cognitive reserve, arrested the progress from mild impairment to full-blown dementia? Within a few days the delirium had got so out of control that she was taken to hospital, where it was decided that she could no longer live at home. A place was found at a nursing home ten miles or so from Dad's. It was full circle. Aged six, my mother had been sent to a boarding school in Sussex, by her account grim even by the standards of the time, while my naval-captain grandfather toured the Mediterranean and my grandmother hopped from port to port in his wake. And now, at the other end of life, another oubliette, just as drab if less exclusive, where she could tap out her remaining days on the arm of her vinyl recliner, alone, bewildered, an inconvenience.

And then something miraculous happened. She came round. In hospital she had been floridly delirious, adamant that she was not in a geriatric ward in the suburbs of Ipswich but in a five-star hotel room with a view of the Empire State Building. It was as if the pages of her autobiography had been dropped and reassembled in the wrong order. And yet within three or four days of arriving at the nursing home, quite as if someone had snapped their fingers or wafted smelling salts under her nose, she was sitting up and chatting lucidly, content if completely unable to recall the three months since she had last known where or who she was. In retrospect I wondered if her delirium had been a necessary correction, my mother's subconscious plea to turn inward, the organism, weakening, sensing its end, insisting on retreat, isolating itself for protection. Over the next few months she spent her time drawing the flowers that visitors would bring her, roadside posies of cowslips and forget-me-nots arranged in a vase and left on the windowsill. My father had bought her a set of those colouring pens with brush-like tips, so she could work in bed without fear of spilling paint on the sheets, and by comparison to the dappled-shade and black-pansy pictures the results were vivid with colour, bursts of bright yellow, red and green like the last late-flowering display before winter sets in.

We did our grieving in advance, Dad and I, so that when the end came, three years later, it was – for me at least – like swimming out into the Leinesfjord and realising that I could, after all, let my breath out. As she had done: those last breaths, the in-breaths much louder than the out, the organism still bent on survival, gorging on air, with such vigour it seemed as if it would never stop. And then it stopped. Rising, falling. And then nothing. A few weeks before she lost speech my mother had told me she wasn't afraid of dying, but that she would miss me. The selflessness was generational, perhaps, the way people died when my mother was young. Acceptingly, self-effacingly. In any case, it was typical of her. As if dying weren't enough, she wanted to take on the burden of grief, to relieve me of it, to protect me one last time.

Which I suppose she had, in a sense. For my father the crucial difference, of course, was that he was already alone, and had been for three years, his mobility problems making visits to the nursing home increasingly difficult. Whether or not this had prepared Dad for widowerhood, trained him in what was now an abiding silence, I couldn't be sure. He had been hard of hearing for years, but when I called home in the months following Mum's death he began to have such difficulty making out a word I was saying, however carefully I enunciated, that we wondered if there might be something wrong either with his phone or mine, a theory that was tentatively laid to rest when he put me on speakerphone so his carer Hayley could hear how muffled and crackly I sounded.

'He sounds fine,' said Hayley. 'Clear as a bell.'

'Perhaps it's your hearing aid,' I suggested.

'Don't think so,' said Dad. 'I've just changed the batteries.'

And he could hear the doctor perfectly well when he spoke to *him*. And so it went on, for months, for years – is *still* going on – our every other conversation a meta-conversation about our inability to have one. It remains a mystery, although I have sometimes wondered if his was an elective loss of hearing, that however much on one level we desperately wanted to speak to each other, on another we could both sense me inheriting his reclusiveness, becoming him, and wanted to get off the phone before we were forced to admit it, that his deafness was a defence against the withdrawal he could sense in me.

10

The House at the End of the World

She hadn't wanted me to go. In the end my wife and I decided it would, on balance, be okay, that the cases in India were low and almost non-existent in Nepal, that both Tenzin Palmo and Dhammasoti had all the proper precautions in place. That if this was going to be my final trip I had better take it now. In truth, looking back on it, my matter-of-fact argument for not cancelling might have been a front for a less rational consideration: that, having bailed on the Peru trip, I didn't want to do it again, especially as I was due to meet Phil for a couple of days' hiking between my visit to the nunnery and the meditation hut. But I wasn't going to own up to that.

I had thought of Dongyu Ghatsal Ling as the end of the road, or at least a final staging post, where retreat crossed the line into unimaginable extremity and self-mortification. I was here, on the edge of the Himalayas, to see Tenzin Palmo, the nunnery's London-born, seventy-seven-year-old director famous for spending twelve years meditating alone in a Himalayan cave. The nunnery backed onto a sparsely settled lane between the main Dharamshala–Baijnath road and a rocky stream called Awa Khadd. From the lane you got the sense of a grand building turning its back: a tower, bright yellow at its lower storeys, purple above, and topped with an ornate, gilded pagoda-style roof I didn't really get to see until I'd passed beyond the ten-foot wall that encircled the compound.

Tenzin Palmo met me in the courtyard. It had been sunny when I'd hailed the cab at Dharamshala. Now a bank of purplish cloud had rolled in from the mountains, giving the scene, Tenzin Palmo's maroon off-the-shoulder robe and buttercup undershirt, the temple with its carved floral motifs in red, yellow and turquoise, an aspect of good cheer against the odds. Tenzin Palmo held a hand out flat and looked up. 'The crazy weather this year,' she said. 'It should be hot sunshine now. Every day we've had storms. It's very, very hard for the poor farmers.'

She gestured at the barley fields beyond the nunnery wall, and further off, in the direction of the Khampagar Monastery at Tashi Jong, re-established seat of the ninth Khamtrul Rinpoche, spiritual head of Tenzin Palmo's lineage. 'We're about six kilometres from our monastery,' she said, with a sudden smile. 'Which is good. We're a little apart.'

Tenzin Palmo was born Diane Perry, brought up above a Bethnal Green fish shop owned by her father, who died when she was two. In 1961, aged eighteen, she converted to Buddhism. It was the Tibetan form that attracted her, so much more romantic and fantastical than the furrow-browed Theravadan school that Greg in Salford had found so oppressive. It was barely two years since the Dalai Lama had fled Tibet for northern India. In 1964, Perry travelled to Dalhousie, seventy-five miles north-west of the Dalai Lama's government-in-exile at Dharamshala. Within three months she had met her 'root lama', or guru, the eighth Khamtrul Rinpoche, reincarnated leader of the Drukpa Kagyu school of Tibetan Buddhism.

The decision to become a nun was next to instantaneous. She shaved her head and broke off her engagement with her Japanese boyfriend. Taking the name 'Drubgyu Tenzin Palmo' – roughly speaking, 'Glorious Lady who Upholds the Doctrine of the Practice Succession' – she became only the second Western

woman ever to be ordained in the Tibetan Vajrayana tradition, and the only nun among a hundred monks at Khamtrul
Rinpoche's makeshift monastic community at Dalhousie.

It was a miserable experience. For almost a thousand years
young Tibetan monks had been schooled in logic, philosophy,
cosmology, meditation and – when they were intellectually
and spiritually mature enough – the esoteric teachings of the
tantra, 'the secret way', establishing a tradition of scholarly
monasticism that was at once formidable and completely closed
off to women. The view was that the female body was not a
fit vessel for enlightenment. Tenzin Palmo was twenty-one. To
have renounced her family, her fiancé, her native culture, for a
religious community obliged by patriarchal dogma to hold her
at arm's length was close to unbearably alienating. 'I would
cry every night, I was so unhappy,' she has said.

Still, she stuck it out for six years. It was Khamtrul Rinpoche's
suggestion that she leave the monastery for the greater isolation
of Lahaul, a valley high up in the Himalayas cut off for eight
months a year by snow and ice. Even here, however, in this
secluded Buddhist enclave, Tenzin Palmo yearned to go further,
deeper into silence and solitude, just as Sister Nectaria and Sara
Maitland had retreated further into theirs. In 1976, after six
years living among her pious, yak-herding Lahauli neighbours,
Tenzin Palmo was off again, higher into the mountains, until
she found the cave, 13,200 feet above sea level, that was to be
her home from the age of thirty-three to forty-five.

It was scarcely more than a dent in the rockface, ten feet
wide by six deep. To make it basically habitable Tenzin Palmo
had a team of Lahauli labourers build a brick wall around the
entrance, providing shelter from outdoor temperatures that
regularly dropped below minus 35 but further reducing the
living space to six feet square. She installed a wood-burning
stove, her dharma texts wrapped in yellow cloth, an altar,
pictures of the Buddhist deities and a bucket for a washbasin.
No bed. She slept, as tradition demanded, sitting upright in a

meditation box, two and a half feet square with a gap underneath to insulate against rising damp.

And there she stayed, absorbed in single-pointed meditation for twelve hours a day, sleeping for three. The rest of her time she spent reading the texts, painting portraits of the Buddhas and Bodhisattvas, accepting visitors now and then, but for the most part seeing no-one but the occasional yak-herder or shepherd. For food she relied on the turnips she grew in the vegetable bed below the lip of the cave. The final three years she spent in complete, silent, solitary retreat. In his famous cave on the 'Mountain of Solitude', Jetsun Milarepa, the eleventh-century Tibetan yogi, reformed black magician and murderer, was said to have reached such a height of meditative intensity that he could generate 'tumo', the mystic heat that protected hermits, who often prayed naked, from the extremes of cold at high altitudes. According to oral tradition he had also learned to fly.

Asking Tenzin Palmo what it was like to meditate for that long, at that level of intensity, would, I suspected, be like asking Sister Nectaria to give a direct account of her God. It would fall somewhere on the gaffe continuum between overfamiliarity and missing the point. ('It was so long ago, I hardly remember any of it,' she said, warmly but firmly, when I began to push in that direction.)

'Still,' I said. 'It was a superhuman effort, wasn't it? You have to admit that.'

'Not superhuman at all. At the time it seemed very ordinary. Really, I kept going because I enjoyed it.' We had settled in Tenzin Palmo's office. Outside the gale had set the courtyard flags snapping. Rain had begun striping the windows. I'd heard about Tenzin Palmo's smile, that it 'reached from ear to ear', and found, in this instance, that the cliché had something going for it, the corners of her mouth penetrating so deeply into her dimples it seemed her entire face might hinge open at the cheekbone. This was her manner, it soon became clear, a quietly infectious serenity interrupted at unpredictable moments by seizures of manic energy to match the blue intensities of her eyes.

'I wanted a quiet place in which to do practice,' she said.

'And the cave was that place.'

'I couldn't think of anywhere better to be, so yes, I settled there. And that was it. People don't believe me, they think I'm being modest, but truthfully, even now, looking back, this was just ordinary life, nothing special.'

Nothing special. I wondered if there came a point where another year in a cave made little difference: a sort of inflationary principle of personal austerity. In late eighteenth-century Japan, Sunada Tetsu, a well-digger with a reputation as a hothead, murdered a samurai after a dispute over the favours of a local prostitute. In Japan at that time, entering the priesthood offered immunity from prosecution, and converting to Shingon, the esoteric branch of Vajrayana closer to Tibetan Buddhism than the other Japanese schools, Tetsu joined the seminary at Churenji, on Mount Yudono in the north-eastern Yamagata Prefecture. Tetsu the irascible well-digger became Tetsumonkai the wandering holy man.

He soon gained a new reputation: for heroic – if not to say certifiable – selflessness. Visiting Edo, as Tokyo was then called, his response to a local epidemic of eye disease was to gouge out his own left eye and throw it in the Sumida River. Later, so one version has it, the prostitute he'd killed the samurai for tried to convince him to leave his life of self-sacrifice and come away with her. By way of a no, thanks, he left the room, sliced off his testicles and returned with them neatly tied up in brown paper.

Aged seventy-one, after four decades of extreme privation, Tetsumonkai went a step further and entered *dochu nyujo*, a practice that differed from other forms of advanced meditation in that it involved entombing yourself underground. The preparation for this included a practice called *mokujiki-gyo*, the 'tree-eating austerities', whereby the ascetic would gradually replace his ordinary diet of rice, millet and so on with nuts and roots foraged from the mountainside, decreasing the body's proportion of fat and muscle and thereby making it less attractive to bacteria. To further inhibit bacterial growth, the ascetic would drink a tea made from the bark of a tree closely related to poison sumac. The goal was self-mummification, achieved while the subject was still alive.

Thus prepared, Tetsumonkai was lowered in a wooden coffin into a pit three feet deep and roughly four-and-a-half tatami mats wide. Charcoal was then packed around the coffin, to reduce humidity, and the pit sealed, burying Tetsumonkai alive. A pair of bamboo tubes supplied him with air and water. There, in the blackness, Tetsumonkai entered into a state of deep contemplation, occasionally ringing a bell to signal that he was still alive. When the bell stopped ringing, the bamboo tubes were removed, and the corpse left for a thousand days, in the hope that the long *mokujiki-gyo* process would have prevented it from decomposing. If it had, the body would be disinterred and enshrined as a *sokushinbutsu*, a 'living Buddha', believed to have cheated death in the name of eternal meditation.

The tendency to self-torture in Shingon Buddhism may bear some relation to Shugendo, the sixth-century mashup of ancient mountain worship, esoteric Buddhism, Shinto and Taoism also practised in the Mount Yudono region. Followers of Shugendo were traditionally known as Shugenja or Yamabushi ('he who prostrates himself on the mountain'), and shared with Shingon zealots like Tetsumonkai a craving for purity through self-mortification: fasting, sleep deprivation, meditation in icy waterfalls, walking on hot coals, arduous mountain hikes in split-toed shoes. These days few Yamabushi are ordained as monks. Shugendo practice survives mainly as a system of part-time austerities observed by middle-aged businessmen, retreating to the mountains every now and again to subject themselves to the hardships missing from their everyday lives.

Spirituality as endurance sport. It was, I suppose, part of the reason I was headed to Nepal to meditate under Dhammasoti – the feeling that I would have no real experience of retreat until I'd had a genuinely terrible time. The ego whipped into submission, scolded and pummelled and crowned with burning shit. Part of Tenzin Palmo's ambition for Dongyu Gatsal Ling was to give girls and young women from northern India, Tibet, Nepal and Bhutan access to the education she had been denied at the outset of her religious career. Another ambition was to revive an ancient lineage of female yoginis, the Togdenma. Their male counterparts, the Togden, are renowned to this day as the special-forces unit of Tibetan Buddhist monasticism, if you can imagine a Navy SEALs squadron recruited exclusively from Rastafarian mendicants. The Togden wear ragged white robes and their hair piled up in enormous, matted dreadlocks like wire-wool anacondas. Boys deemed to have potential are separated from the other novices and subjected to the years of rigorous training needed to attain enlightenment in one lifetime. The female lineage was thought to have been wiped out during the Cultural Revolution. Although there are rumours of a revival taking place in remote areas of eastern Tibet, for fear of the tradition being lost the leaders of the Drukpa Kagyu school had given Tenzin Palmo their blessing to oversee its reintroduction in India. Aspiring Togdenma are expected to observe fifteen to twenty years of solitary retreat. Myths of mystic superheroism attach to both the male and female lineages. One Togden is said to have meditated with such intensity that he dematerialised not only his own mortal form but sixty-two of his family members and animals. And why stop there, I wondered? 'There was another Togden did 117.' Why not thousands? Why not the whole world?

The answer was in the moderation Tenzin Palmo had achieved – a moderation achieved *in extremis*. And that the extremity in question was not the cold or the isolation she had experienced, nor the meditative stamina, but the equanimity, the extreme stillness of soul, that had allowed her not only to withstand these hardships but to enjoy them. Tenzin Palmo's egolessness was not the hard-won result of retreat but the means of making it possible.

Dom Erik Varden had written of awareness of God as 'an operating system installed, waiting to be launched'. Similarly, what Tenzin Palmo suggested about stillness was that it was always there, for all of us, if only we opened ourselves to it. Buddhists believe that in any great effort to deepen your spiritual practice, be it twelve years in a cave or twenty at the nunnery, the overriding impulse should be to help others, to gain wisdom primarily in order to pass it on. This is *bodhichitta*: compassion for all sentient beings.

And the wisdom is in how to relate to our minds. 'The prime interest of Buddhism is on taming, and training, and transforming, and ultimately transcending the mind,' she said. 'Whether we're in retreat or in the middle of Oxford Street, we have the mind. The mind-heart. Not just the intellectual side but also the emotional side. And that has to be tamed, and trained, and how we set about it – well, the point is that it *has to be done*.'

Above the courtyard the sky had turned black and the gutters were cascading with rainwater. 'Goodness, it's really coming down now.' Tenzin Palmo laughed. 'Look. If the dharma has any validity it has to be something which can help us in everyday life. Otherwise, what use is it? If you can only practise when you're on top of a mountain then it's irrelevant.'

And suppose I wasn't on top of a mountain but at home, on retreat like the rest of humanity, that I'd listened to my wife and cancelled the trip and that instead of face-to-face Tenzin Palmo and I had in fact met over Zoom, the storm causing the sound to flicker in and out over her unreliable wi-fi. I had only been going to Nepal to test myself, to up the ante, to bury myself with a bamboo stick for a breathing tube. To be *in extremis*.

Integrate the dharma into the everyday, Tenzin Palmo had told me. Well, now I had the best and worst of both worlds, when the everyday *was* extremity, when sitting at home watching the leaf-shadows blur on the kitchen wall was, at once, the non-event it always had been and part of the most extraordinary event of my life, of everyone's lives, both the internal model and its disruption, the prior and the surprise.

It wasn't a retreat for everybody, that was clear. Not for the doctors, the nurses, the paramedics, the bus drivers and social workers and cleaners and carers now wearing surgical masks and disposable plastic aprons to prepare my father's lunchtime crackers and cheese. For Jake Osborne, ex of the Philadelphia Association, home-working was the opposite of retreat. 'I'm quite an introvert, I need time on my own, and I don't really get any at the moment.' Pre-lockdown Jake had treasured his two-hour commute, the withdrawal into professionalism his hospital work represented. Now he was constantly worried about his two-year-old cracking her head open on the stair gate.

For many of us, though, the weird deviations from what had until recently constituted normality were so precisely the deviations involved in contemplative retreat that the pandemic did seem, at times – to risk allying myself with the two-thirds of American Christians who believed that the virus was God urging humanity to change – like a Divine intervention, an imposition of vows, the conversion of the world into the vast monastery St Francis of Assisi believed it to be.

The dishabituation. The timelessness, or rather, the strangely dual sensation, familiar from my five days at Solesmes, of time simultaneously slowing down and speeding up to the extent that it blurred, that you had to concentrate to notice it passing. The collapse of the temporal order: with no end to lockdown in sight the days both yawned and melted into one another, a strangely propulsive stasis you could imagine swallowing your life before you'd had the time to live it. (Dom Erik: 'Time does pass extraordinarily quickly in a monastery.')

The silence. Pre-lockdown, our road was a miniature Monza of sociopaths in aspirated supercars taking advantage of the weirdly long gap between speed cameras. And then they were gone, the road all but deserted, the buses passing with no passengers in them, all the more desolate after dark, when the little cameos in the lit windows were only apertures on absence, silent, sliding reminders of nobody there.

What to make of this? Stay at home, save lives. The perversity of pulling together by pulling apart, of doing your bit for society by shunning it? And, vice versa, of expressing your indifference or contempt for the common good by hanging out with your friends in the park? Had there been a more ironic or unexpected reversal than that wrought on the place of screens in our lives? About five seconds ago they had been our chief agents of loneliness and societal breakdown, ruinous enablers of the wrong sort of retreat, a mindless, egocentric opting-out. Now they were the only way we could see our friends. Joining my first virtual drinks party a couple of weeks into lockdown, I was struck first of all by how it favoured the unabashed room-dominator, the kind of guest that launched into an anecdote within seconds of taking off his coat, the slow accretion of side-conversations until everyone was drunk enough to take and cede the floor rendered all but impossible by the mechanics of teleconferencing. It wasn't teleconferencing: it was telepontificating. Toggling from Active Speaker to Gallery View the main impression was of a support group for extreme introverts gatecrashed by an egomaniac. There had been reports of a growing fashion for 'virtual monastic retreats', 'silent Zooms', where people logged on, waved a quick hello, and then sat there for hours in companionable silence. I could see how these might really catch on: a Zoom grid of more and more thumbnail displays, until each was no bigger than a pixel, the whole world in its separate cells, not saying anything, together and apart like the Carthusians.

The other suspicion was that we were being lured into an ever deeper and less reversible reliance on a technology that would go back to being plain old brain-addling and corrosive of social relations when and if the pandemic ever ended. I began to wonder if the better idea might be to embrace the opportunity for withdrawal offered by the virus, to sod the Zoom parties and e-drinks and go full domestic-hermit. I was on the way there anyway. Lockdown was a measure of how deep in retreat you already were: the milder the shock, the greater the reclusiveness you might not, pre-lockdown, have fully been acknowledging in yourself. It was like the incidental diagnosis of a disease you didn't know you had, the screening test that comes back positive.

When my father received his letter advising him that as a clinically vulnerable person he should shield for twelve weeks, I was put in mind of the period immediately following my mother's death, when I assumed that life as a widower would not be so different from the years he'd spent alone after Mum moved into the nursing home. That he was trained in bereavement. Likewise with lockdown. Dad had been shielding for close to ten years. What difference would another three months make? The main adjustment that the shielding seemed to involve was that Dad's isolation was no longer occasioned by an imaginary danger, but a real one, a mortal one, with all the dread that came with it – a dread that, even so, faded as the weeks went by, when life in imposed isolation turned out much the same as the chosen isolation of life before it, a crawl with no news to report.

Similarly, I was finding the gap between life pre- and post-lockdown perhaps concerningly easy to bridge. This was, of course, in large part a result of my privileged position. I hadn't, as yet, fallen ill, knew no one that had, or had seriously, and lived in a comfortable flat with some outside space and no-one liable to subject me to domestic abuse. As with retreat, the viability of life during the pandemic divided sharply along racial and economic lines; being white and middle class my chances of avoiding both getting infected and the worst effects of isolation were correlated with the likelihood, in normal circumstances, that I'd have the time, cash and cultural capital to spend on three weeks of meditation in Nepal.

Still, it did seem as if the smoothness of the transition might owe something to the similarity of the conditions imposed by lockdown and the kinds of elective retreat I had spent the previous eighteen months studying, and whose principles had sunk deeper into my bones than I had perhaps realised. In the weeks leading up to full social distancing, when we were, as a species, gradually if uncertainly backing away from one another, it was striking to see people abandon the handshake or hug in favour of the Namaste, the *anjali mudra*, a development my more conservative friends saw as the final capitulation to raw-food woo but which did, in its way, presage the contemplative element of lockdown to an uncanny degree.

The word 'quarantine' derives from *quarantena*, the Venetian dialect term for 'forty days'. The idea dates to the height of the Black Death, 1347–51, when forty-day restrictions on movement were imposed not because they were known to confer any epidemiological benefit but because of the significance of the number: Moses' three forty-day spells on Mount Sinai; the forty days of Lent, marking the forty days and nights that Jesus spent in the Judaean desert. Requiring people to stay put to slow or halt the spread of disease has its roots in spiritual retreat. Under Covid-19, for the secular majority, life had been hijacked by the invisible, a force that was everywhere and impossible to place, and which I for one was trying to appease with acts of propitiation not too far removed from the signs of the cross I'd seen the Romanian prison guards make on Mount Athos.

The hand-washing. Wiping down each and every item in our online shopping delivery with an anti-bacterial floor wipe. The chances of catching coronavirus from a cauliflower were, I felt, on the low side, but still, I'd wipe it down, taking care to work the wipe into the fissures between each floret, where, it was conceivable, a worker at the cauliflower distribution centre might have brushed his virus-riddled finger. By granting the sufferer a 'beautiful' death, writes Susan Sontag, TB 'spiritualizes' life. Covid-19 *monasticises* it, requires us to isolate ourselves in the name of a higher power whose unknowability we can make tolerable through ritual gesture. The virus was a vanitas, a reminder of life's brevity, and not only because of the death toll: because it was ageist. It took your risk of dying this year and doubled it. A friend in her seventies told me that she'd never felt old before. Now it was unignorable. (Imagine a coronavirus outbreak at the Modern Elder Academy). As in a monastery, the withdrawal from humanity necessitated by the virus was done in humanity's interests. The monk was not alone, said Father Michael at Solesmes. 'He's a member of the human race. He's bringing up society with him.' And the monk's task, to sweep aside all impediments and look eternity in the eye, was now an obligation imposed on us all, try as we might to ignore it, by the regular toll on our news feeds.

As the weeks went by and the new normal lost its novelty I began to think of my self-isolation, the immaculacy of it, as somewhere between a superstitious ritual and an obsessive compulsion. Satsumas were where the process of disinfecting the groceries tipped either into madness or a mindful-cleaning exercise. Could I get away with wiping down all eight of them in their plastic mesh? Probably not. So I'd tear the net open, wash my hands again, then wipe down each satsuma in turn, noting my anger, both at the inconvenience of wiping down eight individual satsumas, and at my own OCD in thinking it necessary, then, as the anger passed, noting the little rockpools in the peel, and how the anti-bacterial liquid frothed on contact and left a few bubbles in each pool. Week nine of this and I still hadn't been further than the bin enclosure in our front garden.

One Saturday the bell went and I opened the door to see our old friends Jules and David, and their two teenage boys, waiting at the far end of the front garden, like kids a few seconds too slow at Knock Down Ginger. It was a beautiful afternoon, and as our place lay on their cycle route into central London, they had stopped off to see how we were. I told them I hadn't left the flat in two months.

'Why?' said Jules. 'Are you scared?'

It was a good question. Was I? I didn't think so, or no more than I should have been. But in my failure to articulate a response – I may have muttered something along the lines of, well, you know, in for a penny – I sensed the return of an old awkwardness, the loss of social instincts I'd felt returning to the city after long periods looking after my mother. *That* was my answer. I wasn't scared. I just preferred it indoors, felt the undertow of retreat, the feedback loop of desocialisation. My wife was going out running, queuing at the butcher's, joining the socially distanced crowd in a nearby street, where, every Thursday evening at six, a young guy in a second-floor flat sat in his open window and played acoustic Bowie covers I could make out, just, if I opened *my* window, like the faint chattering noise I thought I could hear when my concentration improved in Salford. The one time I did venture further than the bins, for a walk in or around week eleven, I was so taken aback by the new etiquette of the pavement, walkers and runners swerving or stepping into the road to maintain distance, that I cut the walk short and went home. It had been like a rather heavy-handed allegorical ballet satirising modern urban alienation. That half the people I passed had been conspicuously half-disguising their efforts to give me the swerve – as I, probably, had been half-disguising mine – had only made it sadder and more surreal. It was hard to believe that this wasn't a permanent change, a change that had been coming anyway.

It had been a while since I'd heard from Oscar. I knew that he'd bought a place in Italy, that it was a wreck, that he had typically Oscar-like plans to turn it into a one-stop silk-printing workshop to rival the great textile houses of Venice. It was only when I saw the photos that I realised what he'd taken on. Oscar's 'place' was a palace, an eighteenth-century villa built as a retreat for a noble family that had once supplied Venice with a doge. It had been abandoned for decades before a fire in 2012 caused the roof to fall through the four storeys below it.

Not the sort of minor drawback to deter Oscar. The villa sat in three thousand square metres of once artfully wild gardens, now overgrown for real, with its own chapel, a large lake hidden in reeds and a mile-long avenue of cypresses leading to the road into the village, a further two miles away. Venice was thirty-five miles by road to the south-west. About twenty-five miles to the north, the Dolomites erupted like thunder on a cloudless day, the intervening landscape notable chiefly for its featurelessness, a vast and intensively farmed plain that might have detracted from the palazzo were it not for its enclosure of trees. On Google Maps the house looked desolate, stranded. From inside the grounds you might have been deep in the woods. It was a strange sort of sanctuary, insisting on its interiority amid the openness of the plain, like a hermit's hut in the desert. 'The house at the end of the world—' Oscar called it, in the letter he enclosed with the photos. 'Before the East—The silent world of Titian—'.

He liked his em dashes, Oscar—like Emily Dickinson did, the indeterminacy in them, the acknowledgement that words weren't quite enough—they were gangplanks over the ocean of unsayability. The local authorities had been so keen to get the villa off their hands that Oscar had picked it up for a song. Which was as well, as he didn't have any money. And so he set about renovating his Venetian palazzo when earnings and a succession of small conservation grants allowed it: a wall rebuilt here, the garden drained there. A modest inheritance from his mother furnished him with a roof and four storeys of floor joists. One of the photos he sent me had been taken lying in bed, his size-twelve feet and the cuffs of his stripy pyjama bottoms visible, in a grand second-floor room overlooking the cypresses, the doge's bedchamber, with no glass in the window frames and islands of exposed stone in the lagoonish grey plaster. There was no glass in *any* of the window frames.

It was going to take him the rest of his life. On one level this seemed okay, as Oscar was the sort of person who would live to a hundred and twelve: you could imagine him in his nineties, in a brocaded cape, a goose on his lap, admiring the cornices now they were three-quarters done. He hadn't been to Crete in six years. Sometimes he wondered if the cave hadn't been enough, that he needed a more permanent hideaway, somewhere that demanded such an investment of time, money and love that he'd have no choice but to live out his days there. In the last fourteen months, Rowena had been on three visits lasting three or four days each. Oscar had spent the rest of the time alone, setting up the printworks, clearing the grounds with an axe after his chainsaw broke, sleeping in the chapel when the main house got too cold.

But the isolation could be crushing. Before lockdown Oscar had been too busy to think about being miserable. Now he *really* had no choice, now the virus had made his isolation mandatory, he wasn't sure he wanted it any more. The original family had escaped to the villa during outbreaks of plague. And then they returned, to the commerce of the city, its stink and noise and intrigue. From his earliest days there, one of the things Oscar most liked about the villa was the length of the drive, how it held the world at arm's length, the early-warning system it represented. You could see Paolo the scaffolder jouncing along in his flat-bed truck ten minutes before he arrived. Now no one ever came down it, and Oscar would often sit in the doge's room, focusing on the vanishing point of the cypresses, wondering if he was vanishing himself, if the renovation and the gesture at solidity he'd thought it represented was in reality an act of self-abnegation, if he wasn't the doge but the hermit, slowly merging with the landscape.

Or I was up a hill above Dharamshala, having left Tenzin Palmo and joined Phil at his apartment in McLeod Ganj, across the street from the Tibetan government-in-exile. At this elevation the world *did* seem like a monastery, the range of snow-veined peaks framed by the valley we had just climbed so silent and in-humanly vast it squeezed the ego out of you like the bells before Compline. The storm that had broken over the nunnery had moved on, but it remained overcast, cool for the time of year, with a pall of grey mist hanging in the valley. We lay for a while on the grassy plateau overlooking the mountains. Normally, Phil explained, the hiking trails would be busy by this time of day, but since the first Covid cases in Delhi the usual stream of backpackers and dharma tourists had slowed to a trickle. Save for a couple of Indian guys heading up towards the snow-line and the Lahesh Caves beyond, we had the Himalayas to ourselves.

'You worried?' I said.

'Not so much by the virus.' Phil had picked a blade of grass and was rolling it between his thumb and forefinger. 'Not yet, anyway. It's more the reaction to it that worries me.'

'What do you mean?'

'There's an idea that if you're a Westerner you're responsible for it. I've been coming here for twenty years and have always felt safe. Now I have to watch my back. Seriously. It's bad.'

Trump, Bolsonaro, Modi: it was only just dawning that a crisis whose one consolation was its universality might be used to stoke nationalist tensions, further disengagement, retreat. I had worries of my own, albeit on a more personal scale. The next day I was due to fly to Gorakhpur then make the five-hour bus journey to the meditation centre run by Dhammasoti. But there were rumours that people were being turned back at the Nepalese border. I was beginning to wish I'd stayed at home.

'You can always come back here,' said Phil. 'There's a res-taurant with rooms across the street from my place. We could do a proper three-day hike.'

'Sounds like a plan.'

'Then if you wanted to do your retreat we could see if any of the monasteries around here would rent you a cabin.' Phil got to his feet and gestured up towards the snowline. 'Alternatively, there's no shortage of caves.'

He was only half-kidding. Phil held out a hand. I grasped it and pulled myself up. McLeod Ganj lay three hours below us. The mist was rising; we'd need to get a move on before it engulfed the entire mountainside.

The heat almost had me on day one. Dhammasoti had mentioned in an email that the area was prone to power cuts. To the extent that I'd taken in the information at all it was as encouraging evidence of remoteness, simplicity, authenticity, etc. Now I understood his email as fair warning. With no working fan my little hermitage on the edge of the compound was, if anything, even hotter than the dharma hall. The only reason I had, for now, decided to put up with it was that the presence of the other meditators, all of them, it seemed, superhumanly focused and impervious to the pools of sweat leaking from their meditation cushions, threatened to tip a merely excruciating experience into one that might genuinely send me out of my mind. Life was *dukkha*.

So I sat in my hut with the door open, with my mosquito net wrapped around my shoulders as if the massive, hairy, red-fanged spider in the babul tree outside had cocooned me in its silk and was poised to inject me with its digestive juices. Focusing on the breath presented an extra level of challenge in an environment so humid there didn't actually appear to be any air. The moment I managed to still my mind to the extent of noting an in-breath, thoughts related to breath and its absence rushed in like bargain seekers on Black Friday – the terror of sucking at the air and finding nothing good in it, nothing breathable; the cool breeze on the mountain with Phil, just two days ago; the hypoxic Covid patients and the hiss and snap of their C-PAP machines; the absolute necessity of getting the hell out of this temple to unnecessary suffering and catching the next flight home.

It had been easier than expected getting in. The rumours of the border closing had turned out to be unfounded. I had disembarked from the bus, handed my thirty dollars to the border official, and after a wait of about an hour, while the driver argued with a passenger trying to board with a crate of live chickens, we were back on the road and on our way into Nepal. I had arrived at the meditation centre in the late afternoon. Beyond the gaudy white and gold arch at the entrance, the centre consisted of a cluster of low, unremarkable brick buildings arranged around a planted courtyard, and a dozen or so modern brick *kuttis*, or meditation huts, that looked like the sort of graffiti-prone electricity substations you find in suburban woodland. Along the tiled walkway that cut through the dusty, tree-shaded gardens, meditators in sweat-soaked, scoop-neck T-shirts moved with the same exacting slowness as at the Saraniya Centre, eyes fixed on the ground, intent on nothing but the sensation of movement itself.

The precepts were just as they had been under Bhante Tarraka – no talking, stealing, sex, drugs, booze or mobile phones – except enforced with a rigour that bordered on the totalitarian. On my first morning, walking from breakfast to my *kutti*, I was intercepted by a nun, and told in no uncertain terms to slow down. To stop looking around. And so I walked on, eyes on the tiles. Later that day, walking back from my *kutti* for lunch, I passed a young, curly-haired man in patterned Aladdin pants. Despite trying my best to keep my eyes down, I had a strong sense of him trying to communicate. I dared a glance up.

'Hey,' he mouthed.

Here we go, I thought. Another non-joiner. Seconds later, Dhammasoti, the Sayadaw, rounded the corner of the meditation hall, and I dropped my gaze for fear of another tongue-lashing. Dhammasoti was, admittedly, an improvement on the nun, if not actively warm then at least free of the sense that you, as his pupil, represented a condensed form of samsara in all its mundanity and deludedness. Shaven-headed, lithe in his red-brown robes, he spoke in the softest counter-tenor, as if he was trying not to aggravate a sore throat. At my first interview, on day two, I admitted I was finding the heat hard to bear.

'Use this difficulty,' he said. 'Use it as a focus for your attention. Concentrate very hard on it. What is it like? Notice the details. If you think that you are noticing them, you are not. Notice harder.'

On the morning of day five the young curly-haired man stopped me as I emerged from my *kutti*. I made an apologetic face and mimed zipping my lips. But the young man persisted.

'Sorry,' he said. His accent was American-sounding without quite being American. Israeli, perhaps. 'But this is important.'

The Indian government had suspended all tourist visas, effective immediately. Quite how my curly-haired friend had found this out he didn't say, although, what with his rebel attempts at small talk on the footpath, I wouldn't have put it past him to be hiding a satellite phone in his *kutti*. I returned to mine. Obedient yogi that I was, until this point I had kept my mobile switched off and buried in my suitcase. Realising, however, that if I couldn't get back into India, I'd be unable to catch my flight home, I felt justified in a little precept-breaking. I switched my phone on. No reception. Not a flicker. There was, in truth, no immediate reason to panic – I had plenty of time to re-route my flight via Kathmandu. It was only that I didn't want the distraction of worrying about it. Despite my initial difficulties with the heat, it seemed that the last few months of regular practice had begun to pay off – by my fourth eighteen-hour day of meditation my mind had returned to the level of biddability it had reached in Salford. Surpassed it, in fact – I found I could sit for three-and-a-half or four hours without so much as shifting on my cushion. Random thoughts arose and dematerialised with an ease that quickly became self-fulfilling. What had seemed hard, bleak, inhospitable, now felt like love, like liquid embrace. Like swimming in a warm sea. It was precisely because the meditation was going so well that I wanted to get my travel sorted as soon as possible, whatever Dhammasoti might say about using my stress as an attentional focus. At least for a rookie like me, some things were just too stressful, and as the curly-haired man was now nowhere to be seen, I dropped round to the main building to ask if I could use the office phone.

'No phone,' said the nun.

'Yes, I realise that. I just thought in the circumstances ...'

'No phone.'

'Okay. Would it be possible to use the computer, then? Just for ten minutes.'

'Not possible. No phone. No computer.'

'It's quite urgent, you see.'

No answer. Remember, said the Buddha. You are the first victim of your own anger. Breathe. Let it pass. *None of this is actually happening.* In the end we came to a compromise. I could leave the compound for an hour after breakfast. The nun thought I might get mobile reception beyond the monastic zone. A minute longer than an hour, and I wouldn't be let back in. By seven the next morning it was already pushing thirty degrees. Take a right out of the compound and within five minutes' walk you were at the Mayadevi Temple, supposed birthplace of the Buddha. From the outside it looked like a 1930s lido in a depressed English seaside resort, grubby white and castellated with red and yellow flags hanging limply at each corner.

I checked my phone. Still no signal. I had forty-seven minutes. Heading back past the turning to the meditation centre I pressed on, past the temples funded by wealthy Sri Lankans, Thais, Koreans, French, a sort of permanent Buddhist World's Fair that looked more like Las Vegas, or Las Vegas ten years into the pandemic, many of the buildings half built or beginning to fall down, exposed rebar weeping blood-brown rust down their poured-concrete bases. Outside the Vietnamese Temple my phone picked up a signal, a single bar, which had gone by the time I tried to dial the airline. Three long beeps. No Service. And so I walked on, drenched in sweat, out of the International Monastic Zone into the town proper, past the backpackers' hostels and shops selling flip-flops and SIM cards – no signal there either, naturally – until my phone sprang into life on a dirt track bordered on both sides by a swamp that stretched to the horizon. Four bars: a religious moment.

I stood, rooted to the spot, for fear of losing the signal, listening to 'Bittersweet Symphony' by the Verve, interrupted at two-minute intervals by a cheery voice assuring me someone would be with me shortly, as I squinted into the distance, trying to make out if the dark blur hovering above the vaguely vegetal sludge was in fact the swarm of mosquitos it appeared to be. Oops. An actual voice saying hello. Did I put repellent on my toes? Sorry. No available flights from Kathmandu. I could try back in a week.

There were two kinds of retreat, I had learned, and it was up to you which kind your retreat turned out to be. There was the open kind, and the closed kind, the movement towards and the movement away, the urge to enlightenment or to deeper shadow. Secluded places suited both, but either kind of retreat could happen anywhere, in a monastery or shopping mall, a cave or a crowd. Retreat was a mental state, not a place. And if one thing was clear, it was this: to stand a chance of happiness, a chance of fulfilment, you had to conceive of retreat in positive terms. As the movement towards, the retreat to life, not away from it. Do this – by which I mean, step back and breathe – and the rewards were not only considerable but amounted, collectively, to a precondition for continued existence: staying awake. Increased mental focus; decreased mind-wandering and the stress, anxiety and depression it could bring about; a decreased tendency to react to that stress, or to suffer unnecessarily from pain by overreacting to it; an increased ability to solve novel problems, when in normal circumstances that ability declined with age; a shoring-up, for that matter, against more general age-related cognitive decline and dementia. All were local instances of something larger, the great and potentially life-saving enhancement retreat put within our reach: the slowing or reversal of our otherwise inexorable closing-down, our inclination to shut our eyes and ears, to become stale, set in our ways, to concede to our internal models. And the longer these models remained unrefreshed by reality, the less accurate they became, the more wrong we became about the world. Open retreat wasn't only the opposite of the closed kind, it was our best means of preventing it.

There were a few points worth noting, for all that. First, that with a bit of effort you could begin to notice some differences surprisingly quickly, but that to induce long-term effects, to rewire yourself neurally, took a good deal of hard work. Second, that the hardest part of the hard work was trying not to work too hard – that you couldn't force yourself to concentrate, that you had to remain calm, give in to the tedium, until something shifted and the effort became effortless, and you occupied the paradoxical state of 'active relaxation' Giuseppe Pagnoni had described. (Worth noting, too, that there were traditions of 'effortless meditation' that held receptive awareness to be available instantaneously – but that to let go of effort, of the instinct to try, was itself a formidable challenge.)

It had also to be said that achieving a level of concentration could feel good, even rapturous, but that the Tenth Army of Mara was pride; that the oceanic feeling, or bliss, or God, or whatever you wanted to call it, was incommunicable; that there was pleasure but also danger in spending time with your tribe; that while progress was being made, retreat was still often reserved for the privileged; that while the extraction of mindfulness from its devotional context had brought its benefits to a vastly wider audience, this had, in combination with the chaotic post-Christian hunger for something, anything to believe in, left it vulnerable to exploitation by all manner of grifters and narcissists and well-meaning bullshit-artists eager to put a doctrine of selflessness at the service of self-development;

that you had to be careful, all in all, that your retreat wasn't a closed one in open clothing.

And to find the closed kind of retreat you didn't have to look far. It was the modern condition. There was retreat on the Caltrain to San Jose, in my manspreading neighbour's noise-cancelling headphones – and in his manspreading, for that matter, although it looked like encroachment. There was retreat in pseudo-public spaces, the quiet appropriation of our parks and squares and thoroughfares, free to use until they weren't, until you said the wrong thing or took the wrong photo, and were required to leave by a private security guard. There was retreat in the logic of late capitalism, in its hatred of anything shared. There was retreat in political polarisation, in the abandonment of the centre, in the occupation of positions armour-plated by the very quality that made them ridiculous, their rejection of consensus. There was retreat in the belief that vaccines caused autism, that 5G weakened our immune systems, that a cabal of Satan-worshipping paedophiles ran the world. There was retreat in cancel culture, in the fingers campus liberals had stuck in their ears. Democracy was in retreat. Reason was in retreat, and with it the chance that the retreats that might do for us all, of the ice sheets, and of the populations displaced by heat or rising sea levels, might be slowed. What was most in retreat was the future, forcing us all, depending on which side of the ideological barricades we fell, either to occupy a present moment we might rather ignore, or to ignore it, to fall back on our priors, to trust in the comforting illusion of business as usual.

It might be argued, in this light, that this was not the time to absent yourself – unless, as I saw now, you could make yourself more present by stepping back for a while, engage by temporarily disengaging. You had, of course, to bear in mind that introspection was not for everybody, that depending on the strength of your internal models, even the temporary loss of your sense of self could be terrifying as well as exhilarating. That you needed enormous mental strength to go it alone and not go mad. All that said, what remained was the realisation that you could be unconvinced of the existence of God, or an afterlife, or reincarnation, but find yourself opening – perhaps more and more as you aged, and the world turned in on itself in more and more calamitous ways – to some sense of a beyond.

Back in the *kutti* I was sweating so much my glasses kept slipping off my nose. Notice harder, Dhammasoti had said. And what I had noticed was that there was more than one kind of noticing. *Thinking thinking*. All the physical descriptions in my notebook, for example. 'Like a less comical Cheshire cat.' 'A laugh like an outboard motor.' Was that really noticing? Or cocooning someone in words? Like me in this mosquito net? Back to the abdomen. *Rising, falling*.

Rising, falling. Rising, falling. A rare and blessed breeze through the open door of the *kutti*. Hang on: the spider's not there. Does that mean it's in the *kutti*? *Worrying worrying*. Back to the breath. Breathe each breath as if it were your last, said the Buddha. At high enough concentrations spider venom can cause paralysis and eventual asphyxiation. The Covid wards. How could you focus on your breath if you were struggling for the next one? *Thinking thinking*.

A little cooler today. But the pain in my right hip is outrageous. *Focus on it*, says my internalised Dhammasoti. Stop calling it outrageous. And he's right, of course. The pain begins to collapse, crumble into seven or eight different sensations, none of which feel like pain. One of them feels a bit like arousal. Everything is close to unbearably clear, like putting on glasses when you're already wearing contact lenses. I am down-regulating my internal models, de-potentiating my priors. Of neurobiological accounts of meditation Tenzin Palmo said, 'They're exploring. And well done. As long as they don't think they have the answers.'

All international flights are now suspended. Idea for a novel/ screenplay: a Buddhist reworking of *A Handful of Dust*. A rich Westerner is stuck for eternity in a Nepalese meditation centre and forced to read the sutras to his deranged Belgian Sayadaw. 'We will not 'ave any *Abhidhamma Pitaka* today ... but to-morrow, and ze day after zat, and ze day after zat ...'

I'm not breathing my breath, it's being breathed.

I am not here.

I'm at home, behind my closed door, writing this, on day eighty-seven of lockdown. It's a warm June afternoon, so I've got the window open a crack, and if I stop and refocus my attention, I can hear the young guy in the neighbouring street singing 'Life on Mars'. A branch of the plane tree in our front garden is tapping lightly on the window pane. The veined undersides of its leaves are a pale lustreless green so delicate I can feel it in my bronchioles. The kids are in the garden, taking turns to spray each other with the hose. A shriek and a spray of spritz bubble-wraps the window. From somewhere further off I can hear the collared dove cooing. Coo-*cooo*-coo. Above me, in the kitchen, I hear the scrape of a chair pulled back from the table, then the creak of the boards, my wife's footsteps, my primary object. Then silence.

Acknowledgements

'Forgive me, father, for I have made thee break thy rule.' Setting out to research this book, I was acutely conscious of the potential for contradiction, or even resentment, in poking my nose into the lives of those who had chosen to shield themselves from view. I worried that I'd be the idiot mountaineer, reaching the summit with a cheery hello just as the ragged hermit was about to count his millionth in-breath. Oh, *cheers*, mate: back to the start. My worries were misplaced. It's perhaps less of a paradox than it seems that researching a book about stepping back from society should have turned out to be such a social experience. If there was anything that linked many of the monks, meditators, artists and contemplatives I met along the way, it was their kindness, the love for humanity that came of gaining some perspective on it. I owe my biggest debt of gratitude to all the people who appear in this book, and who made working on it such an unprecedented joy – and one it's poignant to look back on, near the end of a year-long period when social contact has become the rarest of resources.

As a rule of thumb, all my expert and academic sources, as well as major interviewees like Sara Maitland, Randi Skaug and Tenzin Palmo, appear under their own names. With all but a few exceptions, in the interests of protecting their privacy, I've anonymised the people I met on retreat. However they appear, massive thanks are due to all of them. I'm especially grateful to all those who checked the manuscript for any errors I'd made in their areas of expertise: Professor Giuseppe Pagnoni on the neuroscience of meditation; Professor Christopher Eccleston on the psychology of pain; Professor Mark Edwards on functional neurological disorders and the risks of introspection; Professor Sat Bir Singh Khalsa on the physiological and neurological effects of yoga; Fr Erik Varden on the Trappist order and monastic vocations more broadly; Fr Michael Bozell on Solesmes and the Benedictines; Fr Cyprian Consiglio on the Camaldolese and life at the New Camaldoli Hermitage; Dr Max Sternberg on Cistercian architecture and the history of Western monasticism; Jake Osborne on R.D. Laing and the Philadelphia Association.

There are also the sources not named in the text who, nonetheless, provided invaluable guidance in a number of notoriously complex areas. Dr Jim Mallinson at SOAS could not have been more enlightening on the history, metaphysics and scriptural basis of yoga. I owe many thanks to Dr John McManus at the British Institute at Ankara for pointing me towards Victor Turner's theories of structure and liminality. In my potted history of the self in Western thought, I have leaned heavily on Professors John Barresi and Raymond Martin's excellent overview of the subject, 'History as Prologue: Western Theories of the Self'. I am also very grateful to Professor John Marenbon of Trinity College, Cambridge for his views on the matter. The brilliant father-and-son team of Drs Patrick and Niall Campbell were my tutors in the gate-control theory of pain and hyperstimulation analgesia; Max Bryant and Elise Dennis effortlessly filled the gaps in my knowledge of gaming and VR technologies; Robin Baird-Smith took time out of a busy schedule to share his thoughts on the various Catholic monastic orders. I am also indebted to Alfred Osborne for checking over the passages on the Orthodox Church, and to David Macy, who, quite apart from being the most welcoming host in the Western hemisphere, set me straight on a few misunderstandings about MacDowell and artists' colonies in general.

For their help, advice, hospitality and good company on my travels, I'd also like to thank Dudi Appleton, Polly Astor, Dom Jean Babeau of the Parkminster Charterhouse, Taz Bashir, Catherine Bavin-Currie, Julia Bindman, Lydia Blaisdell and everyone at the Marble House Project, David Bodanis, Ilana and David Bryant, MyAnna Buring, Natalie Chen, Caroline Chubb Calderon, Grisha Coleman, Dimitri Collingridge, Robert Collins, Oliver Craske, Carl D'Alvia, Lisa Dubost, Andrea Elliott, Danielle Epstein, Gill Ereaut, John Evans, Hope Gangloff, Rory Golden, Jess Grieve, Jen Harnetty, Geoff Harrison, Dana Hawkes, Jerilyn Hesse, Amanda Huebsch, Paula Huston, Daniela Intieri, Harriet Jarman, Ash Jones, Nasreen Munni Kabir, Catherine Kelley, Hanne Kristensen, Monique Ledesma, Mark Levy, Lisa Littlebird, Eden McNutt, Gill Meller, Rev. Kevin Murdoch, Rosie Peppin Vaughan, Fr Rufus Pound at Mount St Bernard Abbey, Lori Putnam, Simon Quarterman, Antonia Quirke, Shaparak Rahimi, the late and much-missed Jackie Saccoccio, Becca Salvidant, Dina Schapiro, Yasmine Seale, Seymour, Amy and Hudson Segnit, Rupert Shortt, Brooke Singer, Dr Paulina Sliwa, Paul Smith, Hans Syvertsen, Fr Isaiah Teichert and all the monks at the New Camaldoli Hermitage, Reuben Thomas, Jina Valentine, Liz Vater, Willem Voorvaart, Karen Watson, Christy Williams and Sr Margaret Yam at the Carmelite Monastery in Quidenham.

Parts of this book first appeared in *1843* magazine and as an essay for BBC Radio 3. Many thanks to Rosie Blau, my editor at *1843*, to Duncan Minshull, who commissioned the radio piece, and to Ciaran Bermingham, who produced it.

Special thanks are due to Clare Reihill, who has been so supportive of this project from the outset, and to the brains trust of friends who read and responded to early drafts with such candour and insight: Julia Bueno, Andy Mitchell, Pedro Ramos Pinto, and, as ever, James Lever, who has no need of meditation to penetrate the true nature of phenomena. He sees things no one else can see.

None of this, of course, would have been possible without my agent, Will Francis, who combines a forensic intelligence with strategic nous and the kindest, most supportive disposition. Thanks also to Ren Balcombe, Kirsty Gordon and everyone else at Janklow & Nesbit. My brilliant editor at The Bodley Head, Stuart Williams, has guided this book from its hesitant beginnings with the surest, clearest-minded judgement and a calmness of purpose the Zen masters would envy. I couldn't have been in better hands. I'm also indebted to Aidan O'Neill, who did such an ingenious job of publicising the book, to Fiona Brown, who copy-edited the manuscript with such skill and sensitivity, and to Will Hammond, Lauren Howard and the rest of the team at Vintage.

Finally, my deepest thanks to my late parents, Jack and Clare, for a lifetime of love and support. And to my wife, Niki, who not only read and commented on every draft of this book, but acted as my sounding board from the moment it first emerged as an idea, and, while I was away researching it, juggled childcare with the demands of her own new book. Niki, Edie and Raff are both the refuge I retreat to and the joy without which life, I get the feeling, would amount to the kind of retreat I'm not prepared to make.

Select Bibliography/ Further Reading

Artists' colonies and the artist

Berger, Ted et al., 'From Surviving to Thriving: Sustaining Artist Residencies' (Alliance of Artists Communities, 2012)

Carey, John, *The Intellectuals and the Masses* (Faber, 1992)

Greenblatt, Stephen, *The Swerve: How the Renaissance Began* (Bodley Head, 2011)

McGee, Micki (ed.), *Yaddo: Making American Culture* (Columbia, 2008)

Wiseman, Carter (ed.), *A Place for the Arts: The MacDowell Colony, 1907–2007* (MacDowell Colony, 2007)

Buddhism

Buddhist meditation and philosophy

Coleman, Graham (ed.), *The Tibetan Book of the Dead: First Complete Translation* (Penguin, 2006)

The Dalai Lama, *Dzogchen: Heart Essence of the Great Perfection* (Shambhala, 2020)

Goldstein, Joseph, *Mindfulness: A Practical Guide to Awakening* (Sounds True, 2013)

Kornfield, Jack, *Bringing Home the Dharma: Awakening Right Where You Are* (Shambhala, 2011)

Mackenzie, Vicki, *Cave in the Snow* (Bloomsbury, 1998)

Pagnoni, Giuseppe and Guareschi, Fausto Taiten, 'Remembrance of things to come: a conversation between Zen and neuroscience on the predictive nature of the mind', *Mindfulness*, vol. 6, no. 4 (2015)

Palmo, Jetsunma Tenzin, *Into the Heart of Life* (Snow Lion, 2011)

Pandita, Sayadaw U, *In This Very Life: The Liberation Teachings of the Buddha* (Wisdom 1992)

Thurman, Robert A., *Essential Tibetan Buddhism* (Bravo, 1997)

Watts, Alan, *The Way of Zen* (Pantheon, 1957)

Buddhist-influenced mindfulness and meditation

Brewer, Judson A., *The Craving Mind: From Cigarettes to Smartphones to Love – Why We Get Hooked and How We Can Break Bad Habits* (Yale, 2017)

Harris, Sam, *Waking Up: Searching for Spirituality Without Religion* (Bantam, 2014)

Kabat-Zinn, Jon, *Mindfulness Meditation for Everyday Life* (Piatkus, 1994)

Puddicombe, Andy, *The Headspace Guide to Meditation and Mindfulness* (Hodder, 2011)

Christianity

Catholic monasticism

Barnhart, Bruno, *Second Simplicity: The Inner Shape of Christianity* (Paulist Press, 1999)

Consiglio, Cyprian, *Prayer in the Cave of the Heart: The Universal Call to Contemplation* (Liturgical Press, 2010)

Coomans, Thomas, *Life Inside the Cloister: Understanding Monastic Architecture: Tradition, Reformation, Adaptive Reuse* (Leuven, 2018)

Corrigan, Felicitas, *Benedictine Tapestry* (Darton, Longman and Todd, 1991)

Griffiths, Bede, *The Golden String: An Autobiography* (Templegate, 1954)

Leigh Fermor, Patrick, *A Time to Keep Silence* (John Murray, 1957)

Merton, Thomas, *The Seven Storey Mountain* (Harcourt, Brace, 1948)

Merton, Thomas, *The Journals of Thomas Merton*, vols. 1–7 (HarperSanFrancisco, 1995)

St Teresa of Ávila, *The Life of Saint Teresa of Ávila by Herself*, transl. Cohen, J. (Penguin Classics, 2004)

St Thérèse of Lisieux, *Story of a Soul: The Autobiography of Saint Thérèse of Lisieux*, transl. Clarke, John (ICS, 1996)

Thurston, Bonnie Bowman, *Merton & Buddhism: Wisdom, Emptiness and Everyday Mind* (Fons Vitae, 2007)

Christianity and the history of monasticism

St Augustine, *Confessions*, transl. Pine-Coffin, R.S. (Penguin, 1961)

Benedict of Nursia, *The Rule of Benedict*, transl. White, Caroline (Penguin Classics, 2016)

Brown, Peter, *The Making of Late Antiquity* (Harvard, 1978)

Brown, Peter, 'The Rise and Function of the Holy Man in Late Antiquity', *Journal of Roman Studies*, vol. 61, 80–101 (1971)

Henry, Patrick (ed.), *Benedict's Dharma: Buddhists Reflect on the Rule of Saint Benedict* (Riverhead, 2001)

MacCulloch, Diarmaid, *A History of Christianity* (Allen Lane, 2009)

Saulnier, Dom Daniel, *Gregorian Chant: A Guide to the History and Liturgy*, transl. Berry, Dr Mary (Paraclete, 2009)

Varden, Erik, *The Shattering of Loneliness: On Christian Remembrance* (Bloomsbury, 2018)

Ward, Benedicta (transl.), *The Sayings of the Desert Fathers* (Cistercian, 1975)
Williams, Rowan, *The Way of St Benedict* (Bloomsbury Continuum, 2020)
Wroe, Ann, *Francis: A Life in Songs* (Cape, 2018)

Orthodox Christianity and monasticism

Leigh Fermor, Patrick, *The Broken Road: From the Iron Gates to Mount Athos* (John Murray, 2013)
McGuckin, John Anthony, *The Orthodox Church: An Introduction to its History, Doctrine, and Spiritual Culture* (Wiley-Blackwell, 2008)
Norwich, John Julius and Sitwell, Reresby, *Mount Athos* (Hutchinson, 1966)
Ware, Timothy, *The Orthodox Church: An Introduction to Eastern Christianity* (Penguin, 2015)

Hinduism

Yoga and Hindu philosophy

Anonymous, *The Bhagavad Gita*, transl. Mascaró, Juan (Penguin, 1962)
Cahn, B. Rael et al., 'Yoga, Meditation and Mind-Body Health: Increased BDNF, Cortisol Awakening Response, and Altered Inflammatory Marker Expression after a 3-Month Yoga and Meditation Retreat', *Frontiers in Human Neuroscience*, vol. 11, article 315 (2017)
Dalrymple, William, *Nine Lives: In Search of the Sacred in Modern India* (Bloomsbury, 2009)
Mallinson, James and Singleton, Mark (eds.), *Roots of Yoga* (Penguin Classics, 2017)
Remete, Shandor, *Shadow Yoga, Chaya Yoga: The Principles of Hatha Yoga* (North Atlantic, 2009)
Sadhguru and Subramaniam, Arundhathi, *Adiyogi: The Source of Yoga* (Harper Element, 2017)
Singleton, Mark, *Yoga Body: The Origins of Modern Posture Practice* (OUP, 2010)
Wu, Yin et al., 'Yoga as Antihypertensive Lifestyle Therapy: A Systematic Review and Meta-analysis', *Mayo Clinic Proceedings*, 94(3), 432–46 (2019)
Yogananda, Paramahansa, *The Autobiography of a Yogi* (Self-Realization Fellowship, 1948)

The Neuroscience of Meditation and Belief

Gard, Tim, Lazar, Sara et al., 'Fluid Intelligence and Brain Functional Organization in Aging Yoga and Meditation Practitioners', *Frontiers in Aging Neuroscience* 6 (2014)
Dahl, Cortland J., Lutz, Antoine and Davidson, Richard J., 'Reconstructing and deconstructing the self: cognitive mechanisms in meditation practice', *Trends in Cognitive Sciences* xx 1–9 (2015)
Goleman, Daniel and Davidson, Richard J., *The Science of Meditation: How to Change Your Brain, Mind and Body* (Penguin Life, 2017)

Lazar, Sara et al., 'Meditation experience is associated with increased cortical thickness', *Neuroreport,* 16(17), 1893–7 (2005)

Marchant, Jo, *Cure: A Journey into the Science of Mind Over Body* (Canongate, 2016)

Newberg, Andrew and D'Aquili, Eugene, *Why God Won't Go Away: Brain Science and the Biology of Belief* (Ballantine, 2008)

Pagnoni, Giuseppe and Cekic, Milos, 'Age effects on gray matter volume and attentional performance in Zen meditation', *Neurobiology of Aging,* 28, 1623–7 (2007)

Pagnoni, Giuseppe, Cekic, Milos and Guo, Ying, '"Thinking About Not Thinking": Neural Correlates of Conceptual Processing during Zen meditation', *PLoS ONE,* 3(9) (2008)

Sanatoriums, mental illness and pain

Ariès, Philippe, *The Hour of Our Death* (Allen Lane, 1981)

Britton, Willoughby B., 'Can mindfulness be too much of a good thing? The value of a middle way', *Current Opinion in Psychology,* 28, 159–65 (2019)

Bryer, Jackson R. and Barks, Cathy W. (eds.), *Dear Scott, Dearest Zelda: The Love Letters of F. Scott and Zelda Fitzgerald* (Scribner, 2019)

Clay Large, David, *The Grand Spas of Central Europe* (Rowman & Littlefield, 2015)

Cooper, R., 'Seeking Asylum: R.D. Laing and the Therapeutic Community', in Rachid, Salman (ed.) *R.D. Laing: Contemporary Perspectives* (Free Association, 2005)

Eccleston, Christopher, *Embodied: The Psychology of Physical Sensation* (OUP, 2016)

Kabat-Zinn, Jon, *Full Catastrophe Living: How to cope with stress, pain and illness using mindfulness meditation* (Piatkus, 2013)

Laing, R.D., *The Divided Self* (Tavistock, 1960)

Melzack, Ronald and Wall, Patrick, *The Challenge of Pain* (Penguin, 1982)

Menezes Jr, Adair and Moreira-Almeida, Alexander, 'Religion, Spirituality, and Psychosis', *Current Psychiatry Reports,* 12, 174–9 (2010)

Palmer, Richard, '"In This Our Lightye and Learned Tyme": Italian Baths in the Era of the Renaissance', *Medical History,* Supplement No. 10, 14–22 (1990)

Parks, Tim, *Teach Us to Sit Still* (Harvill Secker, 2010)

Sass, Louis, Pienkos, Elizabeth and Nelson, Barnaby, 'Introspection and schizophrenia: A comparative investigation of anomalous self experiences', *Consciousness and Cognition* 22, 853–67 (2013)

Sontag, Susan, *Illness as Metaphor* (Farrar, Straus and Giroux, 1978)

The Self

Barresi, John and Martin, Raymond, 'History as Prologue: Western Theories of the Self', *The Oxford Handbook of the Self* (OUP, 2011)

Lindahl, Jared R. and Britton, Willoughby B., '"I Have This Feeling of Not Really Being Here": Buddhist Meditation and Changes in Sense of Self', *Journal of Consciousness Studies,* 26, No. 7–8, 157–83 (2019)

Marenbon, John, 'The Self', in Cameron, Margaret (ed.), *Philosophy of Mind in the Early and High Middle Ages* (Routledge, 2019)

Nietzsche, Friedrich, *On the Genealogy of Morality,* transl. Diethe, Carol (Cambridge, 2006)

Wilber, Ken, Engler, Jack and Brown, Daniel P., *Transformations of Consciousness: Conventional and Contemplative Perspectives on Development* (Shambhala, 1991)

Solitude, silence, hermits and hermitages

Ballard, J.G., *Concrete Island* (Cape, 1974)

Cain, Susan, *Quiet: The Power of Introverts in a World That Can't Stop Talking* (Viking, 2012)

Campbell, Gordon, *The Hermit in the Garden* (OUP, 2013)

Dickinson, Emily, *The Complete Poems* (Faber, 2016)

Kafka, Franz, *The Burrow*, transl. Hofmann, Michael (Penguin Classics, 2017)

Laing, Olivia, *The Lonely City: Adventures in the Art of Being Alone* (Canongate, 2016)

MacCulloch, Diarmaid, *Silence* (Allen Lane, 2013)

Maitland, Sara, *A Book of Silence* (Granta, 2008)

Montaigne, Michel de, *On Solitude*, transl. Screech, M.A. (Penguin Classics, 1991)

Parks, Tim, *Cleaver* (Harvill Secker, 2006)

Schama, Simon, *Landscape and Memory* (Knopf, 1995)

Stoppard, Tom, *Arcadia* (Faber Drama, 1993)

Storr, Anthony, *Solitude* (Flamingo, 1989)

Thoreau, Henry David, *Walden* (Penguin Classics, 2016)

Updike, John, 'The Hermit', *The Music School* (Knopf, 1966)

Winnicott, Donald, 'The Capacity to Be Alone', *The International Journal of Psychoanalysis,* 39, 416–20 (1958)

Technology and the virtual

Gaming, internet addiction and virtual reality

Alter, Adam, *Irresistible: Why We Can't Stop Checking, Scrolling, Clicking and Watching* (Bodley Head, 2017)

Lanier, Jaron, *Dawn of the New Everything: A Journey Through Virtual Reality* (Bodley Head, 2017)

Silicon Valley and Californian Counterculture

Barbrook, Richard and Cameron, Andy, 'The Californian Ideology', *Science as Culture* vol. 6 (1996)

Kripal, Jeffrey J., *Esalen: America and the Religion of No Religion* (Chicago, 2007)

Markoff, John, *What the Dormouse Said: How the Sixties Counterculture Shaped the Personal Computer Industry* (Viking Penguin, 2005)

Purser, Ronald, *McMindfulness: How Mindfulness Became the New Capitalist Spirituality* (Repeater, 2019)

Schmidt, Eric and Rosenberg, Jonathan, *How Google Works* (John Murray, 2014)

Turner, Fred, *From Counterculture to Cyberculture: Stewart Brand, the Whole Earth Network, and the Rise of Digital Utopianism* (Chicago, 2006)
Wolfe, Tom, *The Electric Kool-Aid Acid Test* (Bantam, 1971)

Miscellaneous

Fadiman, James and Frager, Robert (eds.), *Essential Sufism* (HarperOne, 1997)
Pollan, Michael, *How to Change Your Mind: The New Science of Psychedelics* (Allen Lane, 2018)
Seymour, John and Sally, *Self-Sufficiency* (Faber, 1973)
Turner, Victor, *The Ritual Process* (Routledge & Kegan Paul, 1969)

Index

penguin.co.uk/vintage